"What a wonderful and truly beneficial gift that Anthony Biglan has given us! Thought-provoking and inspirational, Biglan shares with us his wisdom and provides a compelling call to individuals, families, schools, communities, organizations, corporations, and policymakers to be part of creating nurturing environments. *The Nurture Effect* is a science-based prescription for creating a more health-enhancing society. Biglan concisely summarizes his hard-earned wisdom from a remarkable career as a clinician and scientist, his knowledge of diverse scientific fields, as well as his rich life experiences, including as husband, father, and grandfather. Transformative and practical, it provides a guide for the foundation of a more caring and health-promoting society."

> —**Kelli A. Komro, PhD**, professor of health outcomes and policy at the College of Medicine, associate director of the Institute for Child Health Policy, and Research Foundation Professor at the University of Florida

"Anthony Biglan's vast intelligence and scientific experience are brought together in *The Nurture Effect* to provide a vision, a road map, and a sense of optimism about solving the very real social problems facing our country. Evidence-based behavioral programs and policies provide the basis for Anthony's argument that greater attention to nurturing, as opposed to coercion—at home, in schools, with peer groups, within communities, and even as public policy—will lead to healthier and better-adjusted youth and adults. The book is critically important as we consider how we are raising the current and next generations, and can serve to guide discussions on next steps in science, policy, and practice."

> —**Cheryl L. Perry, PhD**, professor and regional dean at The University of Texas School of Public Health, Austin Regional Campus

"In *The Nurture Effect*, Anthony Biglan offers a challenge and a road map for making our society more effective and successful. His message is at once simple and overwhelming. There is a science of human behavior, and we need to use it."

> —**Rob Horner, PhD**, endowed professor of special education at the University of Oregon

"Anthony Biglan's latest book *The Nurture Effect* is a powerful reminder of the transformational impact a nurturing environment has on individuals' well-being throughout their lives. In documenting many carefully selected examples of evidence-based interventions from early childhood and through subsequent stages of development, it makes an outstanding contribution to the field of prevention science. Biglan makes a compelling case for widely implementing scientifically supported interventions that create nurturing environments in our homes, schools and communities. When individuals develop the social and emotional competencies they need to do well, their lives are permanently transformed. This book challenges policy makers, professionals, and the community at large to think well beyond individual benefit, and consider that behavioral science knowledge can apply to entire populations. I unreservedly endorse this excellent and timely contribution."

—**Matthew R. Sanders, PhD**, professor of clinical
psychology and director of the Parenting and Family
Support Centre at the University of Queensland, as well
as founder of the Triple P – Positive Parenting Program

"Read this book, please read this book! ... The nurture effect impacts us daily in our health, intelligence, behavior, emotions, work, and relationships. The daily nurture effect even codes our gene expression—something my scientific colleagues and I only began to suspect one or two decades ago, but have proof of now. This book maps how we can intentionally nurture ourselves, our loved ones, our communities, and even our nations. All of this is based on rigorous practical science. If you want to improve the now and better the future, read this book and apply the nurture effect at home, at work or at school, and in your community."

—**Dennis D. Embry, PhD**, president and senior scientist
at PAXIS Institute

"*The Nurture Effect* is a remarkably ambitious book that draws the blueprints for creating prosocial communities aiming to help people live healthier, value-directed, and enjoyable lives. Biglan explains how people can work together to reduce suffering and improve quality of living for each other, and supports these plans with reliable behavioral research. The science of this book is captivating because Biglan expresses the ideas in an understandable and practical manner. In other words, he simplifies the science of human behavior so you can use it to improve your own community. *The Nurture Effect* hits the ground running with clear, concise, well-stated facts about creating a social context for people to experience a life well-lived. Throughout the book, Biglan expands these ideas into the different branches of community, such as family, schools, work, peer-relations, and discusses how—when approached appropriately—they can make lasting positive contributions to individuals. The perspectives you gain from this book will not only assist you in helping your community to become stronger and healthier, but will also help you as an individual to experience those same positive outcomes."

> —**D.J. Moran, PhD**, founder of Pickslyde Consulting and
> the MidAmerican Psychological Institute

"*The Nurture Effect* is exciting because it is grounded in science but leads us well beyond the fragmented slivers in which scientific findings are often delivered. Anthony Biglan persuades us that rather than focusing on preventing individual problems of family dysfunction, drug addiction, academic failure, child abuse, and even crime, we need to cut to the chase and attend to what all of these have in common. Biglan shows that poverty consistently makes it harder to help, and that nurture is so frequently missing. By integrating findings from the past fifty years in psychology, epidemiology, education, and neuroscience, he pulls out the common threads to show that it is possible to make families, schools, and the larger social context more nurturing, and ultimately to create the nurturing environments so vital to well-being and to preventing widespread harm."

> —**Lisbeth B. Schorr**, senior fellow at the Center for the
> Study of Social Policy, and coauthor of *Within Our Reach*

"This marvelous book integrates the most compelling scientific knowledge about how we can improve the lives of citizens of this country with a bold call to action. Fundamentally, Anthony Biglan—a gifted and experienced behavioral scientist—challenges us to ask, 'What kind of society do we want? How can we use what we know to create such a society?' His central thesis is that widely implementing what we have learned over decades in developing programs that nurture children, adolescents, parents and adults in families, in schools, and in the larger society—which he calls a *revolution in behavioral science*—will make a huge difference.

The book contains highly practical, specific recommendations for families, practitioners, and policy makers. Biglan rightly recognizes that to significantly change society for the better, we must address larger social forces—for example, the negative effects of poverty and economic inequality, or of marketing tobacco and alcohol to youth. Eminently readable, this book comprehensively reviews evidence based on a lifetime of experience as a social scientist, and knits it together with a compelling agenda, that if enacted, could lead to a significant, positive transformation of our country."

> —**William R. Beardslee, MD**, director of the Baer
> Prevention Initiatives at Boston Children's Hospital,
> and Gardner-Monks Professor of child psychiatry at
> Harvard Medical School

"This work is Anthony Biglan's magnum opus. He has pulled together many ideas from multiple disciplinary domains. It is required reading for anyone who is serious about fixing the problems in our education system and alleviating poverty. Anyone who liked David Brooks' *The Social Animal* will also like this. Although Biglan is a self-identified and proud behaviorist, this work shows his openness to other perspectives. I was especially happy to see his new nuanced view of the role of reinforcement in human behavior (pages 28-29). Intrinsic motivation is more powerful in the long term than extrinsic motivation."

> —**Brian R. Flay, DPhil**, professor of social and
> behavioral health sciences at Oregon State University,
> Corvallis, OR, and emeritus distinguished professor
> of public health and psychology at University of Illinois
> at Chicago, Chicago, IL

"The author's engaging writing style enables readers to appreciate the elegance of applying knowledge based on rigorous research to develop and apply evidence-based interventions that prevent problems and promote well-being on a societal scale."

—**Marion S. Forgatch, PhD**, senior scientist emerita at the Oregon Social Learning Center (OSLC), where she developed and tested programs for families with children at risk or referred for child adjustment problems and substance abuse

"*The Nurture Effect* is one of those rare books that draws from a lifetime of careful scientific study to provide clear prescriptions—in language non-scientists can understand—about how to make our world a better place. Pushing back against contemporary fatalism, Anthony Biglan shows us that we know more than ever about how to promote human flourishing. The problem is that we're not applying this knowledge as we should. *The Nurture Effect* explains how we could change that, and, even more important, how *you* can help make the change happen."

—**Jacob S. Hacker, PhD**, Stanley B. Resor Professor of political science, director at the Institution for Social and Policy Studies, and coauthor of *Winner-Take-All Politics*

"Tony Biglan's book puts forth a bold and thought-provoking plan to help every community ensure that our young people grow into caring and productive adults. It's well worth reading."

—**Senator Merkley**

"Biglan [has crafted] an easy-to-read book about an integrated perspective on raising healthy children and what we need to change in our policies to achieve this goal. He asserts that it is in our collective best interests to reduce conflict and increase cooperation in our society. ... Biglan [takes] a total environmental view, which incorporates diet, education, health care resources, and natural conditions. ... He [establishes] a bulkhead for the need to create a society-wide goal of increasing the ability of families to nurture children... Kudos to Biglan for daring to write this book, and let's hope for all of our sakes that policy makers adopt some of the principles."

—**Roberta E. Winter**, *New York Journal of Books*

The
Nurture
Effect

How *the* Science *of* Human Behavior *Can* Improve Our Lives *&* Our World

ANTHONY BIGLAN, PHD

New Harbinger Publications, Inc.

Publisher's Note

This publication is designed to provide accurate and authoritative information in regard to the subject matter covered. It is sold with the understanding that the publisher is not engaged in rendering psychological, financial, legal, or other professional services. If expert assistance or counseling is needed, the services of a competent professional should be sought.

Distributed in Canada by Raincoast Books

Copyright © 2015 by Anthony Biglan
New Harbinger Publications, Inc.
5674 Shattuck Avenue
Oakland, CA 94609
www.newharbinger.com

Cover design by Amy Shoup
Acquired by Catharine Meyers
Edited by Jasmine Star

The Library of Congress has cataloged the hard cover edition as:

Biglan, Anthony.
  The nurture effect : how the science of human behavior can improve our lives and our world / Anthony Biglan, Ph.D.
    pages cm
  Includes bibliographical references.
  ISBN 978-1-60882-955-2 (hardback) -- ISBN 978-1-60882-956-9 (pdf e-book) -- ISBN 978-1-60882-957-6 (epub) 1. Nurturing behavior. 2. Social psychology. 3. Human behavior. I. Title.
  BF723.N84B54 2015
  302--dc23
                                            2014039184

Printed in the United States of America

20   19   18

10   9   8   7   6   5   4   3   2

To Georgia. She has restrained my most selfish excesses, put up with my many foibles, and nurtured me and everyone around her.

Contents

PART 4
Evolving the Nurturing Society

Foreword

The Hope of Science and the Science of Hope

Think of this book as a beacon of hope.

The dire statistics and horrific stories that litter our newscasts present the modern world as aimless, chaotic, and lost, going backward in almost every area of social importance. There is an element of truth to that characterization, but there is also a force for good in the modern world that has the potential to reverse all of these trends. What it is and what it says is what this book is about.

We can have a large impact on the prevention and amelioration of abuse, drug problems, violence, mental health problems, and dysfunction in families. As this book shows, we know how to do it, we know what it would cost, and we know how long it would take. We even know the core principles that underlie these successful approaches, so we can narrow our focus to what really matters. We know all these things because modern behavioral and evolutionary science has proven answers that work. The careful, controlled research has been done. The answers are in our hands.

Unfortunately these answers and the foundations they stand on are often invisible to policy makers and to the public at large. Some of this invisibility is unintentional—it is sometimes difficult to separate the wheat from the chaff in scientific knowledge. Some of this invisibility comes because vested interests are threatened. Tobacco companies, for example, thrived on the ignorance and confusion that they themselves fostered.

Beacons are needed in exactly such situations. They cast light so that what was unseen can be seen. They give direction so that instead of wandering aimlessly, we can stay on course during long and difficult journeys. And they allow us to mark and measure whether we are making progress, providing reassurance that every step we take is bringing us closer to our destination.

Tony Biglan brings four decades of experience on the front lines of behavioral science to this far-reaching, carefully argued, and compelling book. A major prevention scientist, Tony knows many of the people who have tested these methods; he himself was involved in key studies, policy innovations, and legal struggles. He tells the stories of knowledge developers and of the people whose lives have been affected, showing in case after case that these methods are powerful tools in the creation of deliberate social change.

Tony is not content merely to list these solutions; he organizes them and shows the core principles by which they operate: increasing nurturance, cooperation, and psychological flexibility, and decreasing coercion and aversive control. He distinguishes empirically between the psychological and social features that are engines of change, and the psychological or social features that come along for the ride. And he nests this knowledge in an examination of what might need to change for us to make better use of it.

Over and over again, the same small set of features have been shown to have profound and lasting effects. Spend a dollar on the Good Behavior Game with children in first or second grade, and save eighty-four dollars in special education, victim, health care, and criminal justice costs over the next few decades. Aggressive boys randomly assigned to play this simple game at age six or seven had two-thirds fewer drug problems as adults!

There initially may be a "too good to be true" reaction to results like this, but Tony takes the time to walk the readers through the research, and its quality and replication. As common themes emerge, unnecessary skepticism gradually washes away and we begin as readers to wake up to an incredible reality. Because of our belief in science and the hope it provides, we as a society have spent billions on research to learn what works in addressing our social and psychological problems. Today we have a mountain of answers that could enormously impact our lives.

Tony provides the means for parents and others to take advantage of what we know right now. At the end of every chapter he provides sections on action implications for particular audiences, and summarizes what has been shown into a manageable set of bulleted takeaway points. He opens the door that policy makers and the public might walk through by listing the policy implications of what we know for the ability to better our children and our society.

As the book progresses, you realize that our failure to work together to ensure that research matters in the creation of a more nurturing society is itself produced by features of our current system. Children are nested within families, who are nested within communities. Communities are nested within political and economic structures. All of this is evolving—but not always positively. Sometimes social evolution is crafted by organized forces linked to economic visions that are producing rapidly increasing economic and health disparities. This wonderful book casts light and provides direction even here. Regular people can play the social evolutionary game too. We can develop our systems toward a purpose if we have the knowledge and foresight needed to do so. This book provides a healthy serving of exactly that knowledge and foresight.

In the end readers will know that together we can create a more nurturing and effective society, step by step. We have the knowledge to do better—much, much better. And ultimately we *will* follow such steps—knowledge of this level of importance does not remain forever unused. But why wait? Why not act now? By bringing together the fruits of behavioral and evolutionary science, the modern world can begin a grand journey, buoyed up not just by the hope of science in the abstract but by the substantive scientific knowledge we already have in hand. We will learn more as we go, but because of the hope that science represents, we as a human community have already funded the knowledge developers who have created this body of work. It is time to use what we have together created. It is time to apply the science of hope.

—Steven C. Hayes
    Foundation Professor and Director of Clinical Training
    University of Nevada
    Author of *Get Out of Your Mind and Into Your Life*

Acknowledgments

If it takes a village to raise a child, it also takes a village to nurture the development and productivity of behavioral scientists. I have been extremely fortunate in that respect. Bob Kohlenberg got me to read B. F. Skinner's work and put me on a path that has guided my entire career. David Kass mentored my budding behaviorism during my internship at the University of Wisconsin.

Then there is the behavioral science community of Eugene, Oregon. Peter Lewinsohn showed me how to develop a research project and get it funded. Jerry Patterson, Tom Dishion, John Reid, Marion Forgatch, and Hill Walker have made such important contributions to science and have continued to inspire me. I thank Kevin Moore, my good friend, whose admiration for my work meant more to me than he realizes.

My many colleagues at Oregon Research Institute (ORI) have nurtured me for thirty-five years. Ed Lichtenstein and Herb Severson collaborated with me on our first project at ORI. Hy Hops, my good friend and amiable colleague, showed me how to have fun and do science at the same time. Then there is Christine Cody. Her skill as an editor has made this a better book, and without her, I would have published many fewer things over the past fifteen years. Sylvia Gillings has taken care of so many aspects of my work, just as she has nurtured everyone else at ORI.

Steve Hayes has had a profound impact. His work has transformed my research and my life, and his friendship has supported and inspired me.

I thank Dennis Embry, my most enthusiastic ally, who leads the way in making the fruits of behavioral science available to everyone.

David Sloan Wilson is leading a worldwide movement to organize the human sciences within an evolutionary framework. He has promoted prevention science and provided critical mentoring for me in writing this book.

My career would not have happened had it not been for funding from the National Institutes of Health, and I thank both the institutes and the people in them who have been so supportive over the years: the National Cancer Institute (especially Cathy Backinger, Bob Vollinger, and Tom Glynn), the National Institute on Drug Abuse (especially Liz Robertson, Zili Sloboda, and Wilson Compton), the National Institute of Mental Health, and the National Institute of Child Health and Human Development.

This book is about creating nurturing environments. I am blessed by a nurturing family. Georgia, my wife of forty years, and I have grown so much closer as we learned to apply the insights that her work and mine have taught us about human behavior. My son Sean has a keen eye for the flaws in an argument, which has sharpened my thinking. Some of the most intellectually stimulating conversations I had as I wrote this book have been with him. I have watched my son Mike and my daughter-in-law Jen nurture their children, Ashlyn and Grayson, as I have written this book. Without them, I would be bereft of examples! I also thank my sisters, Hekate and Kathie. Hekate read so many versions of so many chapters, provided many insights, and always cheered me on. And Kathie has nurtured the ties of family that have kept us connected across many miles and many years.

When I began working with New Harbinger on the editing of this book, I was wary of where they seemed to be trying to take me. No more! This is a far better book thanks to the clear, direct, patient, and richly reinforcing feedback from Jess Beebe, Melissa Valentine, and Nicola Skidmore.

Lastly, humans are not the only species that has nurtured me. As I write this, my cat, Charlie, is sitting in my lap with his head and paws draped over my left arm, purring. Thanks, Charlie!

Introduction:
The Way Forward

After forty years of working on prevention of a wide range of common and costly psychological and behavioral problems, I am convinced we have the knowledge to achieve a healthier, happier, and more prosperous society than has ever been seen in human history.

I have been doing behavioral science research for over four decades. For the past thirty-five, I have been a scientist at Oregon Research Institute, conducting research funded almost entirely by the National Institutes of Health. My research has involved efforts to prevent the psychological and behavioral problems of young people that account for most of society's social and health problems. Perhaps because I have studied so many different problems, I was fortunate to be elected president of the Society for Prevention Research in 2005. That led to a 2007 request from the Institute of Medicine (IOM) to serve on a committee reviewing the progress the United States had made in preventing these problems.

The IOM is part of the National Academy of Sciences, which President Lincoln created to articulate the state of scientific knowledge in every area. As our committee reviewed the huge body of evidence accumulated since the 1994 prevention report, we realized that a far more nurturing society is within reach. As our report stated, "The scientific foundation has been created for the nation to begin to create a society in which young people arrive at adulthood with the skills, interests, assets, and health habits needed to live healthy, happy, and productive lives in caring relationships with others" (IOM and NRC 2009, 387).

As ambitious as this sounds, I believe we can achieve it. While working on the IOM committee, I began to see common threads that ran through all successful prevention programs, policies, and practices. If you look into these programs, you find that all of them make people's environments more nurturing. They encourage families to abandon conflict. Step-by-step, they teach people to support each other's well-being and development. They convince families and schools to abundantly reinforce young people for helping each other and contributing to their schools and communities. They limit opportunities and influences to engage in problem behavior. They encourage us to persevere in pursuing our most cherished values, even while facing significant obstacles, including thoughts and feelings that discourage us from trying. Nurturing environments are key to creating a healthier, happier society.

We can make our environments more nurturing by widely implementing the preventive interventions that research is identifying. But contextually focused behavioral science is also identifying how the larger social context for families and schools must change to fully realize nurturing environments in society. We have evolved a worldwide system of corporate capitalism that has brought us great prosperity and unimagined technological innovations. But it also increases poverty and economic inequality in developed countries and promotes materialistic values and practices that undermine nurturance in families, schools, neighborhoods, and communities. Although the behavioral sciences have not made as much progress on how to reform this larger social system as they have on making families and schools more nurturing, the outline of what is needed is becoming clear.

The tobacco control movement provides a good model for how to achieve massive societal changes. In 1965, over 50 percent of men and 34 percent of women smoked. By 2010, only 23.5 percent of men and 17.9 percent of women were smoking (CDC 2011). These numbers represent one of the twentieth century's most important public health achievements. When public health officials, epidemiologists, and victims of the cigarette industry united to mobilize opposition to the unfettered marketing of a product that was killing four hundred thousand Americans each year, they moved a mountain. They formed a network of government agencies and advocacy organizations that showed the public how harmful cigarettes are. That created a growing movement that convinced most Americans that the cigarette industry had been lying to them. It also mobilized support for policies that encouraged people to quit—or not start—and educated them about the problem. Think of the last few meetings or social events you attended. Was anyone smoking? Forty years ago, such events probably would have taken place in smoke-filled rooms. We have evolved a largely smoke-free society, despite powerful opposition.

Just as we have created a society in which it would be unthinkable to light up a cigarette in the Kennedy Center lobby, we can create a society where it is unthinkable that a child suffers abuse, fails in school, becomes delinquent, or faces teasing and bullying. We could have a society in which diverse people and organizations work together to ensure that families, schools, workplaces, and neighborhoods are nurturing and that our capitalistic system functions to benefit everyone.

Addressing all the problems we confront might seem daunting. Would we need a similar movement for each problem? Largely, we have that now: Mothers Against Drunk Driving combats alcohol problems; the Community Anti-Drug Coalitions of America battle drug abuse; the criminal justice system fights crime; schools foster academic success. However, a broad, science-guided social movement that works to ensure that all facets of society support nurturance is possible.

This book is about how we can create such a movement. Nearly all problems of human behavior stem from our failure to ensure that people live in environments that nurture their well-being. I am confident that, if we marshal the evidence for nurturing environments and use the advocacy techniques that worked so well for the tobacco control movement, we can truly transform society. Not only will we have smoke-free gatherings, we will have communities that see to the well-being of every member. We will have less crime, mental illness, drug abuse, divorce, academic failure, and poverty.

The benefits of this science-based approach to transforming society can extend well beyond prevention of individual psychological and behavioral problems. At this point, we can use a wealth of accumulated knowledge to evolve a society where people cooperate and care for each other. From that fertile soil we can grow a society where businesses, nonprofits, and governments work effectively for the common good. These claims may seem incredible, but that is only because most people—including many behavioral scientists—are unaware of the extraordinary advances of behavioral science.

Evolution takes a long time. Even cultural evolution can go so slowly that it is hard to notice change within a lifetime. This is the case for the behavioral sciences. Fifty years ago, there was not one intervention to treat or prevent a problem of human behavior. But over the ensuing fifty years, behavioral scientists developed numerous programs, policies, and practices to transform families, schools, work organizations, and neighborhoods into nurturing environments that can ensure the successful development of virtually every young person.

Even many people who have made major contributions to this evolution don't realize how comprehensively behavioral science has addressed problems of human behavior. Most scientists work on a fairly narrow range of problems. By concentrating their energies on the myriad details of one specific problem, they advance knowledge by pinpointing its influences or testing refined interventions.

I deeply admire this disciplined approach. I have long felt that I am too undisciplined as a scientist. Those I most admire concentrate on carefully defined and circumscribed problems; I, on the other hand, have worked on a wide variety of problems, and this has limited my contributions in any specific area. Yet my lack of discipline and wide-ranging interests have helped me recognize some basic principles that unite the dramatic advances the behavioral sciences have made in the past fifty years.

In this book, I hope to show you how these principles can guide us toward the kind of society the IOM committee on prevention envisioned. Despite society's countless troubles right now, seeing the tremendous scientific advances we have made in understanding and taking practical steps to nurture human well-being makes me optimistic about our future.

An Overview of the Book

This book has four parts, described below.

A Science Equal to the Challenge of the Human Condition

Part 1 of this book consists solely of chapter 1, which provides an overview of the scientific principles that guide our progress. I don't claim that this is the one true account of behavioral science. Indeed, one of the things emerging from research on human behavior is the recognition that what we say about the world is better thought of as talk that may be useful for some purpose, rather than truth with a capital T. So I ask you to consider this take on the status of the behavioral sciences in terms of its usefulness for advancing the human condition.

Nurturing Well-Being Through Prevention and Treatment

In part 2 of the book, I describe interventions that have been developed to provide treatment or prevention to individuals or families. Chapters 2 through 4 focus on prevention. Prevention science integrates findings from the past fifty years in psychology, epidemiology, education, and neuroscience into a public health approach to ensuring everyone's positive development. Although the field of prevention science has only been around for about twenty years, it has produced a large number of programs, policies, and practices with proven benefit.

Figure 1 is from the Institute of Medicine's report on prevention (IOM and NRC 2009). Each entry refers to one or more programs shown to prevent development of psychological, behavioral, or health problems. Most of the interventions focus on families or schools, since these are the major environments affecting young people's development. Most interventions address multiple problems. For example, the Nurse-Family Partnership (Olds et al. 2003), which provides support to poor single mothers during pregnancy and the first two years of the baby's life, not only prevents child abuse but also improves children's academic performance.

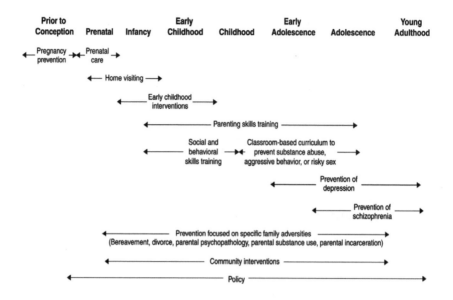

Figure 1. Interventions by developmental phase. (Reprinted with permission from *Preventing Mental, Emotional, and Behavioral Disorders Among Young People: Progress and Possibilities* [2009] by the National Academy of Sciences. Courtesy of the National Academies Press, Washington, DC.)

As you can see, there are effective interventions for every phase of development. In addition, many of these programs produce benefits long after the program's implementation. For example, the Nurse-Family Partnership reduced the number of children arrested for delinquency as adolescents by more than 50 percent (Olds 2007). Finally, most preventive interventions save more money than they cost. For example, the Good Behavior Game, which helps elementary school children develop self-regulation and cooperation skills, saves about eighty-four dollars for every dollar invested in it. It does this because it prevents problems ranging from crime, smoking, and alcohol abuse to anxiety and suicide attempts (Kellam et al. 2008).

The two most important environments for building a highly prosocial society are families and schools. Virtually every problem we seek to prevent emerges because of families and schools that fail to nurture prosocial development. In chapter 2, I describe numerous effective family interventions. In chapter 3, I describe what we have learned about how schools can nurture the social and academic skills of children from preschool through high school. The third major influence on young people's development is their peer group. Chapter 4 describes how peer groups can influence young people in harmful ways and how to prevent this.

However even in a world in which families and schools nurture development, there will be many people who arrive at adulthood with significant problems. Chapter 5 describes the tremendous progress in the treatment of psychological and behavioral problems of adults over the past four decades.

Addressing Well-Being in the Larger Social Context

Truly transforming societies so they ensure nearly everyone's well-being requires a perspective beyond attention to individuals, families, schools, and peer groups. We have to translate this knowledge into benefits for entire populations. Behavioral scientists have now begun to figure out how effective programs can be made more widely available.

Families, schools, and peer groups exist within a larger social environment that affects them in many ways. The larger context for individuals, families, and schools includes corporations, government agencies, and nonprofit organizations, whose practices have enormous impacts on well-being. We need a scientific understanding of these impacts. And we need scientific advances to help us understand how we can evolve organizational practices that are more supportive of well-being.

For this reason, part 3 provides an analysis of the larger social context affecting human well-being. In chapter 6, I present the public health framework, which can guide this analysis. Public health practices evolved out of efforts to deal with physical illness. They are now being applied to behavioral influences on well-being and the factors that affect these behaviors. The public health framework looks at well-being in terms of the incidence and prevalence of behaviors and the actions of groups and organizations. In chapter 6, I use the example of the tobacco control movement to show how a public health approach can advance the goal of making societies more nurturing.

In chapter 7, I describe corporate marketing practices that harm people. These include the marketing of tobacco, alcohol, and unhealthful food. I propose standards for determining when the need to regulate marketing in the interest of public health outweighs the need to limit government interference in marketing.

Chapter 8 addresses the problems of poverty and economic inequality. The United States has the largest proportion of young people being raised in poverty of any economically developed nation. We also have the highest level of economic inequality. These conditions stress millions of families and limit the effectiveness of even the best-designed family interventions. Despite much public discussion to the contrary, poverty and economic inequality are far from inevitable. In chapter 8, I describe how the recent evolution of public policy has contributed to these problems.

Chapter 9 examines the recent evolution of corporate capitalism. Over the past forty years, public policy affecting economic well-being has shifted dramatically away from ensuring that every member of society has at least a basic modicum of material well-being. This is the direct result of well-organized and well-funded advocacy conducted on behalf of some of the wealthiest people and largest corporations in the United States. I analyze this evolution in terms of the economic consequences that have selected corporate lobbying practices and the resulting implications for how we can evolve corporate practices that are more likely to contribute to the evolution of a nurturing society.

Evolving a Nurturing Society

If we can bring to bear everything that the behavioral sciences have taught us over the past fifty years, I believe we can evolve societies that nurture unprecedented levels of well-being. Part 4 of this book consists of two chapters outlining concrete steps we can take to make this a reality. Because caring relationships among people are so important, in chapter 10 I describe the psychological and interpersonal processes that are needed to help people cultivate caring relationships with everyone around them. Building on this, in chapter 11, the final chapter, I envision a social movement that could influence the evolution of society such that our families, schools, neighborhoods, corporations, and governments all become more nurturing.

PART 1

Science Equal to the Challenge of the Human Condition

In this section I provide an overview of the scientific principles that have led to so much progress over the past fifty years. Biological and behavioral sciences are converging on a view of what human beings need to thrive and what leads many people to develop psychological, behavioral, and health problems. Thanks to an explosion of experimental evaluations, we have identified programs, policies, and practices with proven benefit in preventing multiple problems and nurturing successful development.

CHAPTER 1

A Pragmatic Science of Human Behavior

In the past 150 years, science has dramatically transformed a world that was largely unchanged for centuries. In 1850, it took two and a half months to get from New York to San Francisco. Today you can fly there in five and a half hours. It took a month to get a letter from Utah to California in 1850; today you can talk to *and see* almost anyone in the world instantly. In 1854, London was the world's largest and most prosperous city. Its Soho neighborhood suffered a cholera outbreak that killed over six hundred people. Today, we would be shocked to hear that anyone died of cholera in London.

Could the scientific study of human behavior produce similarly remarkable transformations? They are well within reach. Yet because the conflict, abuse, and neglect occurring in so many families have been with us for millennia, they sometimes seem inevitable. In this book, I will describe numerous tested and effective programs that reduce family conflict and abuse and ensure children's successful development. The same is true for schools. Throughout history, a sizable proportion of young people failed to gain the social skills and knowledge necessary to succeed in life. Thanks to careful research on the impact of school environments, we have developed effective approaches to teaching and to nurturing social skills and values that help young people become cooperative and caring people. If these facts conflict with your impression of the state of schools and families, it is because these science-based strategies are not yet widespread enough to produce massive change. But that will happen.

Then there are the so-called mental illnesses. When I began to study psychology in the 1960s, not one treatment procedure reliably alleviated psychological disorders. In chapter 5, I will tell you about dramatic advances in treating all of the most common and costly psychological and behavioral problems.

Historic transformation of societies requires change not only in individuals, families, and schools. Businesses, governments, and nonprofit organizations must be transformed if we are to reduce the stresses these systems now place on so many people. Science has not made as much progress in creating change in the latter systems. But I will show you how the same pragmatic and evolutionary principles that informed the development of effective family, school, and clinical interventions can show us the flaws in our current system and what we can do to make it more conducive to human well-being.

In sum, I hope to show you how we can evolve societies where most people live productive lives in caring relationships with others. Science has altered the physical world beyond anything our great-grandparents could have imagined. Yet those changes generally have not made people happier or better at living together; in many cases, they have produced massive threats to human well-being. But the scientific advances in our practical understanding of human behavior put us in a position to create a world where we have not only previously unimaginable creature comforts, but also the psychological flexibility and loving interpersonal relations that can enable us to evolve societies that nurture human well-being and the ecosystems on which we depend.

Evolution and Pragmatism

In my view, the key feature of the science that has brought all this progress is evolutionary theory (D. S. Wilson et al. 2014). Until Darwin, the primary framework for thinking about causation in science was mechanical. Scientists made tremendous progress in understanding the relations among physical objects by studying the ways those objects influenced each other. Thinking about these relations as one would think about a machine, the focus was on the parts of the world, their relations, and the forces that influence those relations. Our understanding of the physical world has come largely from building and testing models of these mechanical relations—whether the influence of gravity on the motion of planets, or the relations of time and space (Isaacson 2007). The emphasis was on the antecedent conditions that influenced the phenomenon of interest.

Darwin introduced a new model of causation: selection by consequences. He wasn't the first to recognize that species evolved (Menand 2001), but he was the first to see that it was the consequences of the characteristics of species that determined whether a species would survive—and with it, its characteristics. This was a profound development in scientific thinking. Humans readily discern antecedent causes. Indeed, the tendency to see this kind of causation probably evolved out of the fact that antecedent causation is so common and seeing it is vital to surviving. (In fact, we are so inclined to look for antecedent causes of events that there is a Latin phrase for the tendency to misattribute causation due to antecedents: *post hoc, ergo propter hoc*, or "after this, therefore because of this.")

Although the genetic mechanism that underlies species selection was not known in Darwin's time, most thinking about evolution in biology has centered on genetic selection. However, the principle of selection by consequences is also relevant to understanding the development of behavior—the epigenetic process that has only recently been recognized as playing an important role in both biological and behavioral selection, the symbolic process involved in human language, and even the evolution of groups and organizations, such as those involved in capitalism (Jablonka and Lamb 2014; D. S. Wilson et al. 2014). Throughout this book, I will point out how our understanding of human behavior and development is influenced by consequences and how this understanding contributes to our ability to evolve a more nurturing society.

Evolutionary thinking also contributed to the development of the philosophy of pragmatism, which is the other defining feature of the science I want to describe. Unlike mechanical analyses of causation, evolutionary thinking starts with the unique event and its context. Evolutionary biologist David Sloan Wilson (1998) describes how features of the bluegill sunfish differ within a single lake depending on whether they inhabit open-water or shoreline areas. An evolutionary analysis starts by studying the phenomenon of interest and its context and seeks to explain the phenomenon as a function of its context. This is true for behavioral explanations as much as it is for the study of species and genes.

In his Pulitzer Prize–winning book *The Metaphysical Club* (2001), Louis Menand describes how the philosophy of pragmatism grew out of evolutionary thinking and the tragedy of the American Civil War. The death of 600,000 shattered Americans' certainty about their beliefs. A number of prominent thinkers, such as Charles Pierce, Oliver Wendell Holmes, William James, and John Dewey, began to evaluate their ideas not in terms of their correspondence to the world they were said to describe, but in terms of their value in achieving a goal. They focused on the consequences of their ideas in the same way that evolutionary thinking focused on the success of species characteristics in a given environment. In both cases, the question was not whether success would hold in every environment, but whether it worked in the particular environment in question.

Once you start to evaluate your ideas in terms of their workability, you must specify your goals. A variety of pragmatic systems have been developed (Hayes et al. 1993); they differ in terms of the goals they specify. One version of pragmatism is what Steven Hayes (1993) has called *functional contextualism*, in which the goal is to "predict-and-influence" behavior or other phenomena. The phrase is hyphenated to emphasize a focus on scientific analyses pinpointing variables that predict and influence behavior or other phenomena of interest.

This approach to the human sciences guides my thinking. I don't claim that this is the one true way to do science. Indeed, it is not yet the dominant way of thinking about science even in the behavioral sciences, and I can offer no criterion to prove it is better than the mechanistic tradition. Mechanism and functional contextualism are simply different ways of doing science.

I would argue, however, that if you choose to pursue predicting *and influencing* individual behavior or organizational practices, you will be more likely to identify malleable contextual conditions you can use to influence whatever you are studying. And if you are studying a problem like drug abuse, antisocial behavior, depression, or anxiety, your work may contribute to finding more effective ways to prevent or ameliorate that problem.

In sum, I believe that the progress in understanding how to improve the human condition that I report in this book stems largely from pragmatic evolutionary analysis, which has pinpointed critical environmental conditions that select useful or problematic functioning, and has led to increasingly effective interventions as a result.

Humans: The Cooperative Species

This is an exciting time for the human sciences. Biobehavioral sciences are converging on a pragmatic, evolutionary account of the development of individuals and the evolution of societies (D. S. Wilson et al. 2014). We have an increasingly clear understanding of what humans need to thrive and which conditions hamper development. This science has made enormous practical progress on how we can create conditions that nurture human thriving and prevent a gamut of psychological, behavioral, and health problems.

The Evolution of Cooperation

A key insight organizing current thinking is that, among vertebrate organisms, humans are uniquely cooperative. David Sloan Wilson (2007) points out that multicellular organisms arose when they had a survival advantage over individual cells in certain environments. When the environment is favorable to the success of coordinated action among multiple units—be they genes, cells, people, or groups of people—those coordinated entities are likely to survive and reproduce. Conversely, when the environment favors individual units, those units will be selected even at the group's expense.

This view has sweeping implications for life and well-being, whether concerning cancerous cells that reproduce to their benefit while harming the organism; individuals who engage in antisocial behavior to the benefit of the individual and the harm of the group; or corporations that maximize their profits to the disadvantage of the larger society. The challenge for our well-being is to ensure that cells, people, and organizations contribute to the group. Whether that happens is a function of the environment's favorability to the coordinated action of members of the group. Thus, at every level, success and survival require an environment that selects that coordinated action.

Helpful Babies

Humans have evolved levels of cooperation that are unprecedented among primate species. You can see it even in babies. Say you are playing with a baby and begin to put the toys in a box. If you point to one of the toys, the baby is likely to put it in the box (Liebal et al. 2009). If a baby sees one person cooperate with another while a second person does not, the baby will reward the first person but not the second (Hamlin et al. 2011). Human babies are more likely than other primates to follow another's pointing or gaze. Thus, even before adults have socialized them, babies show tendencies to be in sync with the social behavior of others, to infer others' intentions to cooperate, and to prefer cooperation in others.

Prosociality

These wired-in tendencies are foundational for developing prosociality. *Prosociality* refers to a constellation of values, attitudes, and behaviors that benefit individuals and those around them (D. S. Wilson 2007; D. S. Wilson and Csikszentmihalyi 2008). Examples of prosocial behavior include cooperating with others, working for their well-being, sacrificing for them, and fostering self-development. These behaviors are not only "nice"; they are the essential components of the success of groups. Prosocial individuals contribute to others' well-being through kindnesses, productive work, improving their community, and supporting family, friends, and coworkers, as well as creative acts of all kinds, from solving technological problems to composing music or making an entertaining movie.

From an evolutionary perspective this makes great sense. All of these behaviors and values contribute to group survival. Groups full of prosocial, cooperative people can outcompete groups with selfish individuals. Doesn't this capture the problem our societies face? How can we suppress or control the selfish actions of individuals in the interest of the group? Examples abound: An employee steals from the company and the company goes bankrupt. A father demands that family life revolve around his needs to the detriment of his children's development. Isn't this the problem we confront as a nation when, for example, a corporation acts in the interest of its profits but harms others in the process?

Wilson's evolutionary analysis lines up nicely with evidence about the benefits of prosocial behaviors and values for the individual. Prosocial people have more and better friends (K. E. Clark and Ladd 2000) and fewer behavioral problems (Caprara et al. 2000; Kasser and Ryan 1993; Sheldon and Kasser 2008; D. S. Wilson and Csikszentmihalyi 2008). They excel in school (Caprara et al. 2000; Walker and Henderson 2012) and are healthier (Biglan and Hinds 2009; D. S. Wilson 2007; D. S. Wilson and Csikszentmihalyi 2008; D. S. Wilson, O'Brien, and Sesma 2009).

We have been accustomed to thinking that highly skilled people who place great value on supporting those around them are some kind of fortuitous gift to the community. But behavioral science is teaching us how to create environments that foster these qualities. In an effort to promote these qualities, my colleagues and I, working together within the Promise Neighborhoods Research Consortium, have created an overview of the social, emotional, behavioral, cognitive, and health milestones for children at each developmental phase (Komro et al. 2011). These are "marching orders" for any effort to increase the number of young people who develop successfully.

Antisocial Behavior and Related Problems

If prosociality is good for the individual and for the group, why is there so much antisocial behavior and human conflict? One way to understand this is to consider the details about how human groups evolved. Yes, human groups that were good at cooperation were more likely to survive. But one thing they needed to do to survive was defend themselves from competing groups. So we are selected for in-group cooperation and for being quick to aggress against those in other groups.

Additionally, during the evolution of our species, humans have had to cope with periods of great deprivation and threat. During those times, cooperation might not have worked. Survival required being on high alert for danger, perhaps at every moment, and being quick to aggress against those who might be a threat. In addition, reproduction required having babies as early and often as possible. In those times of danger, becoming depressed may have also had advantages, because it reduces the tendency of others to attack or dominate (Biglan 1991).

While humans have the propensity to develop a suite of prosocial behaviors, they are also capable of developing antisocial behavior, engaging in substance abuse, experiencing depression, and bearing children at an early age. These behaviors are detrimental to the people engaging in them and to those around them. Young people who develop aggressive behavior tendencies are likely to develop problems with tobacco, alcohol, and other drug use; to fail academically; to have children at an early age; and to raise children likely to have the same problems (Biglan et al. 2004). Academic failure contributes to poverty and poor health and undermines workforce productivity in ways that harm the entire society.

All of these problems affect people's health. Academic failure, depression, and use of tobacco, alcohol, and other drugs are risk factors for our most common and costly illnesses: cancer and cardiovascular disease (Rozanski, Blumenthal, and Kaplan 1999; Smith and Hart 2002).

I led a review of research on adolescent "problem behavior" during a year at the Center for Advanced Study in the Behavioral Sciences, which is now part of Stanford University. Ted Miller, an economist at the Pacific Institute for Research and Evaluation, analyzed the costs of many of these problems (T. Miller 2004). His estimate of the annual cost of antisocial behavior, substance use, risky sexual behavior, school dropout, and suicide is $608 billion in 2012 dollars. Note this analysis was just for youth problem behavior. Although most of these problems begin when people are adolescents, many continue into adulthood. Indeed, many are lifelong.

In talking about these problematic behaviors, I do not intend to blame those of us who have them. One of my major goals in writing this book is to convince you that these problems stem from our environments. Blaming or stigmatizing struggling people for the problem is neither consistent with the evidence nor likely to prevent or mitigate the problems.

In short, we have ample reason to prevent these problems and promote prosociality. Behavioral science has fortunately pinpointed the kind of environment needed to ensure the development of prosociality and prevent virtually the entire range of common and costly societal problems.

Nurturing Environments

We can boil down what we have learned in the last fifty years to a simple principle: we need to ensure that everyone lives in a nurturing environment. Such a simple statement may seem to fly in the face of the enormous heterogeneity of behavior, genes, and environments. But all evidence points to the fact that people become prosocial members of society when they live in environments that nurture their prosocial skills, interests, and values. Conversely, they develop various patterns of harmful behavior when their environments fail to nurture them in specific ways.

Imagine how this simple summary could organize efforts to improve human well-being. If it is scientifically accurate to say that people thrive and are prosocial amid nurturing environments, then we have a simple, readily understandable, and easily communicated message that could organize us from the level of our individual efforts to make our way in the world to the priorities of nation-states. At every level and in every interaction, we must ask ourselves whether we are contributing to the safety and supportiveness of our environment, both for us and for those around us. Nurturance becomes a standard and a value for our interpersonal interactions and by which to judge our public policies. Do they contribute to safety, comfort, and positive development, or do they stress and threaten people? Imagine what such a standard might imply for policies about incarcerating youth, cutting unemployment insurance, or decreasing subsidies for low-cost housing.

As noted in the introduction, the tobacco control movement is probably the most significant science-driven behavioral change our culture has ever seen. It helped that cigarette smoking is a discrete, easily measurable, and highly harmful behavior. The goal of the tobacco control movement could therefore be stated very simply: "We have to get everyone to stop smoking." Whatever people working on this problem did, they could evaluate it in terms of one simple question: Did the activity reduce smoking?

When it comes to other problems—from crime to drug abuse to depression—it may seem that we need a unique campaign for each problem. For the most part, research and practice have proceeded as if problems like depression and crime have nothing in common and require completely different solutions.

But suppose that the same nonnurturing environment contributes to both of these problems and many others? Suppose that following the simple dictum "Make our environments more nurturing" could guide us in preventing almost every problem we face? If that is true, we can create a unified movement that consolidates everything we have learned about the prevention of each of these problems in a way that unites the forces and resources of all the disparate efforts to alleviate human suffering into one broad, powerful movement. This movement would be clear and simple enough to inspire a dad to find gentler ways of guiding his son, but scientifically sound enough to organize research and public health efforts.

My analysis of the details of tested and effective preventive interventions has convinced me that creating nurturing environments is fundamental to preventing most problems of human behavior and producing the kind of caring and productive people every society values. All successful interventions make environments more nurturing in at least three of four ways:

- Promoting and reinforcing prosocial behavior

- Minimizing socially and biologically toxic conditions

- Monitoring and setting limits on influences and opportunities to engage in problem behavior

- Promoting the mindful, flexible, and pragmatic pursuit of prosocial values

Teach, Promote, and Richly Reinforce Prosociality

If we want a world in which most people are prosocial, we need to create environments where prosociality is taught, promoted, and, most importantly, reinforced. We need parents to help their young children develop the ability to restrain impulsive behavior and cooperate with others. We need schools to teach students how to be respectful and responsible, give them opportunities to be good school citizens, and recognize and reward their contributions to the school. We need communities to recognize citizens' contributions to their communities and hold them up as community models, thus promoting prosociality in others.

Families, schools, and communities can promote prosocial behavior and values through stories, models, and recognition of those who act in prosocial ways. However, we could flood a community with stories and models designed to promote prosociality and yet get very little increase in such behaviors if we don't also richly reinforce those behaviors. What do I mean by "richly" reinforce? I mean that we should be less stingy with praise, appreciation, public recognition, attention, interest, approval, smiling, touching, love, and tangible rewards such as pay. Reinforcement is critical to nurturing human well-being, so I want to emphasize it here.

In my view, the fact that human behavior is selected by its consequences is the most important scientific discovery of the twentieth century. The most prominent advocate of the theory that human behavior is a function of its consequences was B. F. Skinner. In 1953, he published *Science and Human Behavior*, which claimed that human behavior was shaped and maintained by its consequences, just as consequences were known to affect rat and pigeon behavior. Not surprisingly, given our conceit that humans differ from all other animals, this assertion caused quite a stir. At the time, there was not a shred of evidence for the effects of consequences on human behavior. But by the 1960s, psychologists were beginning to publish empirical studies that supported Skinner's assertions. The *Journal of Applied Behavior Analysis* began publication in 1968. Every issue presented evidence that human behavior was affected by its consequences. Alone, such evidence could hardly shake the beliefs of someone who assumed that human behavior involved autonomous individual choice. But within the context of Skinner's fundamental assumption that behavior was selected by its consequences, each new finding cried out for further exploration of this assumption.

Initially, I ardently opposed behaviorism. As a civil libertarian, I saw it as antithetical to allowing people to choose their behavior freely. But just after I got my PhD, Bob Kohlenberg, a colleague at the University of Washington, persuaded me to read Skinner's work. When I read *Science and Human Behavior*, I began to see that Skinner was simply extending evolutionary thinking to behavior. Organisms evolve features that contribute to their survival, and one of those features is the ability to learn new behaviors when they achieve consequences that aid in survival.

I also found inspiration in Skinner's vision of a society in which most people would fully develop their potential and work for the good of others (Skinner 1953). Mining the assumption that all human behavior is selected by its consequences opened up the possibility of achieving that vision. The question of untoward control over people's behavior—such as Huxley depicted in the dystopian *Brave New World* (1932), written as an attack on behaviorism—was really a matter of controlling who would control the reinforcers. As Skinner pointed out in a later book, *Beyond Freedom and Dignity* (1972), most movements to preserve human freedom involve trying to eliminate the use of coercive and punitive means of controlling behavior. These efforts helped evolve more just and beneficial societies. However, an exclusive focus on eliminating coercive control overlooked the fact that many positive reinforcement systems, such as gambling, prostitution, and the marketing of cigarettes, exploit humans.

Ubiquitous Reinforcement

A common misconception about reinforcement is that it is involved in human behavior only when we provide tangible rewards like food or stickers. However, consequences constantly guide our behavior. My friend and colleague Dennis Embry provided one of the best demonstrations of how ubiquitous reinforcement is for human behavior. In 1974, he started graduate school at the University of Kansas Department of Human Development. A number of Skinner's disciples had settled there and were seriously exploring the power of reinforcement. Dennis was working in the laboratory of Frances Horowitz, who was one of the first people in the world to show that newborn infants learned through social reinforcement.

It isn't easy to show scientifically that newborns respond to social reinforcement. Tiny babies have almost no ability to control their movements—except their gaze. The researchers rigged up a special screen on which they could project slides in front of the newborn. Dennis and another grad student were stationed behind a divider panel, observing the baby's eyes. One of them sat on the right of the baby and the other on the left. The baby was propped up in a way that made it easy to look at or away from the screen. There was also an audio speaker underneath the screen. The observers could tell if the baby was looking at the screen from its reflection in the baby's eyes. When the baby's pupils reflected the screen image, the observers pressed a button that turned sounds on or off or changed the screen image. This allowed them to study which consequences reinforced the baby's behavior of looking at the screen. If a baby looked at the screen, the observers changed the image or sound to see whether the change made the baby look at or away from the screen. Dennis says they learned some astounding things. This is how he described it to me:

> Day-old babies quickly learned to look at a target on the screen in order to keep the sound of their mother's voice on the speaker. That is, listening to the sound of Mom's voice was reinforcing compared to any mixture of other women's voices. These day-old babies would look away to switch the sound to their mother's voice, and then look

back at the screen image (same picture) to "turn on" Mom's voice. They kept looking much longer at the image if they could hear Mom's voice; it was number one on the hit parade. As a guy, I was distressed to discover newborns had no preference for Dad's voice.

Little babies did not like to look at frowning faces, angry faces, or disgusted faces; they liked to look at smiling faces. If a sad or mad face came on the screen, the babies quickly learned that they could look away and change the face on the screen to a smiling face. Clearly pleasant faces and Mom's voice were reinforcing what babies looked at.

Over the last fifty years, thousands of researchers have explored the scope and depth of Skinner's assumption that human behavior is selected by its consequences. Behaviorists have studied the effects of all kinds of consequences. One of the most powerful reinforcers is simply human attention. Why? Because it precedes virtually any other reinforcement you might get from another person. From the day we are born to the day we die, virtually anything we get from someone else—food, drink, hugs, touch, help, advice, approval—starts with that person simply giving us attention. We have also learned that many experiences are intrinsically reinforcing. Engaging in physical activity, mastering a skill, playing, and learning something new are all reinforcing.

Although there proved to be fundamental flaws in Skinner's approach to key features of human behavior, the relentless study of environmental influences on behavior has produced a science that has proven its ability to improve human well-being immensely (Biglan 2003). In families, schools, workplaces, recreational facilities, and institutions, we have learned to richly reinforce prosocial behavior.

Resistance to the Use of Reinforcement

Despite overwhelming scientific evidence of the power and importance of reinforcement, people continue to resist its use. For most of my career, this resistance has troubled me. One reason is that I am aware of many programs that use the principle of reinforcement to treat or prevent the problems of childhood and adolescence. Given what I know, rejecting reinforcement-based programs seems as harmful to children as refusing to have them vaccinated.

My belief in the importance of reinforcement is also motivated by the overwhelming evidence that the behavior of all species, including humans, is a function of its consequences. Reinforcement processes are an evolved capacity of organisms, which operate according to the same principles of variation and selection that underpin genetic evolution. Therefore, I find it implausible that reinforcement could be a fundamental influence on all other species but not humans. That strikes me as just another prideful human conceit, like rejecting Copernicus's heliocentricity or Darwin's theory of evolution.

The archenemy of reinforcement is Alfie Kohn. In his book *Punished by Rewards* (1993), he argues that rewards are no different than punishments—that both are means of control that produce only temporary obedience. He claims that rewards are essentially bribes and actually undermine people's motivation.

This argument distresses me for at least two reasons. First, it overlooks overwhelming evidence of the benefits of reinforcement in helping children develop important skills. Second, it discourages parents from getting the help they need. Before behaviorists started using reinforcement techniques to help children develop key skills, most children with developmental disabilities lived short and brutish lives in institutions. Children with aggressive behavior problems—that might improve after five or ten sessions with a psychologist—would develop lifelong patterns of criminal behavior.

Nonetheless, I have recently found myself forming a more nuanced view of the role of reinforcement in human behavior. There are circumstances in which the use of rewards is problematic. Researchers at the University of Rochester (Deci, Koestner, and Ryan 1999) have delineated situations in which rewards for behavior are either ineffective or counterproductive. They found that when rewards influence people to feel they aren't competent or that another person is trying to control them, they may actually undermine motivation.

It took me a long time to get this, but my son Sean taught me a lesson about it. Sean was born six years after his brother Michael. Having an older brother can be a challenge, especially in a family that gets excited about kids learning a lot. If you are five and your brother is eleven, who knows more? Who can shoot baskets better?

Sean was an exceedingly perceptive kid. At an early age, he understood that his dad was a behaviorist who believed that behavior could be shaped by praise and rewards. It took me much longer to understand that when I praised Sean, such as for shooting baskets well, it meant to him that he was not yet sufficiently competent. I fear my theory of reinforcement blinded me to the irritation he felt when I communicated, through attempts to praise him, that he was not yet fully competent.

Similarly, I sometimes see instances in preschool settings, especially for children with developmental disabilities, when the teacher's use of praise in attempts to teach a skill may actually be unpleasant for the child. When praise and other rewards are delivered in a situation where children feel they are being pushed into doing something they don't want to do, words like "Good job!" may be no more reinforcing than statements like "Do what I say!"

Psychologists are slowly converging on a view of child development that integrates the emphasis on children's need for autonomy with the importance of reinforcement. Early childhood educators stress the importance of following the child's lead, and behaviorally oriented psychologists have shown that a parent's or preschool teacher's attention to a child in situations in which the child leads an activity reinforces what the child does (Webster-Stratton 1992).

In sum, I ask you to remain open to the possibility that we could improve human well-being by greatly increasing positive reinforcement for all the prosocial things people do—not simply through extrinsic rewards, which may often be needed, but through all the ways in which we show interest, support, love, and appreciation for what others do. In the process, we will build a society of highly skilled people who are adept at making their way in the world and are strongly motivated to contribute to the well-being of others.

Minimizing Coercion, the Fundamental Process in Human Conflict

Reinforcement works as Skinner said it would. Initial studies on helping families with behavior problems showed that getting parents to reinforce children's appropriate behavior reduced aggressive behavior (for example, Zielberger, Sampen, and Sloane Jr. 1968). But what made children aggressive in the first place? The pursuit of this question led to work that was unprecedented in human history. The direct observation and analysis of the moment-to-moment interactions of family members revealed that coercion is at the root of human conflict. Coercion involves using aversive behavior to influence another's behavior. When you realize how pervasive this process is, you begin to see that reducing coercion is essential to creating a nurturing society.

Jerry Patterson was one of the first psychologists to show that reinforcement affects children's behavior. I describe his seminal contributions to behavioral parenting skills training in chapter 2. But I think his work on coercion was even more important (Patterson 1982). He and his team of researchers were the first to go into homes to observe interactions between aggressive children and their parents and siblings. Observers coded the talk of each person in terms of whether it seemed pleasant or unpleasant and the immediate reaction of others. For the first time, scientists studied in real time the consequences that each person provided to other family members' behavior and the effects of those consequences.

At the time, no one believed that such mundane interactions between parents and children could produce career criminals. But Patterson and his colleagues showed that these seemingly trivial events are the crucible that molds lifelong patterns of aggressive, intimidating, and cruel behavior.

You might think that families would shut down when strangers were sitting in their living rooms, but they didn't. Early in this line of inquiry, researchers discovered that families with aggressive children couldn't fake good behavior—even when instructed to do so. For families with a great deal of conflict, negative reactions to each other are so ingrained that they seem to happen automatically.

Patterson found that families with aggressive children—usually boys—had more conflict and handled conflict differently from other families. One person might tease, criticize, or needle another person. The other person might deal with that by teasing back. Because neither person liked what the other was doing, eventually one of them would escalate, getting angry, shouting, or hitting. That got the other person to back off.

Patterson looked at this in terms of *negative reinforcement*. Rather than a positive event, such as praise or attention reinforcing the behavior, removing an unpleasant or aversive event functioned as the reinforcer. For example, say Timmy teases his older brother Dustin, and Dustin gets mad. He says something like "Fuck you!" Timmy laughs at him and calls him a baby. Dustin hits Timmy, and Timmy runs to his room.

What just happened? Timmy's teasing was aversive to Dustin. An *aversive event* is one a person is motivated to terminate. For example, if you were wired up to a machine that gave you a shock, you would work like hell to get it to stop. If you had a lever that stopped it, you would press it frequently and vigorously. Dustin got irritated because that is how people respond to aversive stimuli. He said, "Fuck you!" because sometimes that had worked to get people to stop teasing. He was pressing a lever that worked for him in the past.

Not this time. Timmy keeps teasing. So Dustin escalates and hits Timmy. This works. Timmy leaves him alone. Dustin is reinforced for hitting because it ends Timmy's teasing. And Timmy is reinforced for running away because it allows him to escape further assault from Dustin. However, each is left feeling angry at the other, which makes another occurrence in this ongoing and increasingly destructive cycle more likely.

Patterson's careful analysis of hundreds of hours of these types of interactions revealed that highly aggressive children live in families where bouts of coercion are common and the only thing that works to terminate them is one person escalating. On average, a deviant child is aversive once every three minutes at home and on the playground. A bout of such conflict occurs about once every sixteen minutes. People in these families have a hair trigger. Each person is skilled in using taunts, threats, anger, and physical aggression to get others to back off. No one is happy, but anger and aggression are what work to get people to stop being aversive.

This pattern has clear evolutionary roots. Organisms under attack are more likely to survive if they fight back. If they are reinforced by signs that their attacker is harmed or by the attack ending, they are more likely to be effective fighters. Followers of Skinner (Azrin, Hutchinson, and McLaughlin 1972) demonstrated this process. They found that monkeys who were shocked would press a lever repeatedly if it gave them an opportunity to attack other monkeys. The monkeys assumed that the shock was due to the other monkeys. After all, monkeys didn't evolve around psychologists, they evolved around other monkeys.

Thanks to our genetically determined tendencies to counteraggress and our propensity to be reinforced when counteraggression harms the attacker or buys even a brief respite from others' aggressive behavior, humans readily fall into patterns of coercive interactions. Patterson and his colleagues followed a sample of aggressive and nonaggressive children into adulthood (Capaldi, Pears, and Kerr 2012). Early on, they found that, thanks to repeated bouts of coercion in their families, aggressive children had a finely honed repertoire of aggressive behavior by the age of five. Unfortunately, they had not learned "nicer" skills like taking turns, obeying adults, inhibiting their first impulse, or using humor to soften family interactions—skills found in the families of nonaggressive children.

The results were disastrous at school. The aggressive children were uncooperative with teachers and therefore did not learn as much. They were irritating to other children, who then avoided them. So they learned fewer of the social graces that emerge in the normal course of interactions with others.

When the aggressive kids in Patterson's study reached middle school, they were falling behind in academics and had few friends. Due to conflict at home, their parents had given up trying to monitor what they did or set limits on their activities, so they were free to roam the neighborhood with other aggressive, rejected kids.

Since Patterson began this work, an enormous body of evidence has accumulated showing that families with high levels of conflict and coercion contribute to all of the common and costly problems of human behavior. Children raised in coercive families are more likely to act aggressively, fail academically, begin smoking, develop drug and alcohol problems, and become delinquent. As adults, they are more likely to battle with their partners, get divorced, and raise children with the same problems (Biglan et al. 2004). These children are also likely to have depression. And due to the stress these young people experience—in their homes and in their often conflictual relations with others—they are more likely to develop cardiovascular disease later in life (Wegman and Stetler 2009).

The work on coercion is an example of an important but subtle shift in how we think about behavior. It is easy to see a child's aggressive behavior. Because it is troubling, we may pay a great deal of attention to it, discuss it, complain about it, punish it, worry about it, and so on. But it is much harder to see the consequences of behavior, let alone to see how consequences select behavior. Until the twentieth century, no one realized that behavior could be selected by its consequences. Getting people to see consequences is itself an important step in the evolution of our culture. Indeed, getting people to see the consequences that influence behavior and to work toward having consequences that shape and maintain the kind of behavior that benefits them and those around them could be one of the most important developments in cultural evolution.

Coercion in Marriage

Patterson's work on coercion pinpointed for the first time the major mechanism of human conflict. Although most of his empirical work focused on aggressive children and their families, he also found coercion at the root of marital discord. A book chapter he wrote with Hyman Hops (Patterson and Hops 1972) proposed that the coercion process underlying parent-child conflict could explain why married couples fight. A host of other researchers have since shown this to be true (for example, Weiss and Perry 2002). Couples who aren't getting along act in angry or quarrelsome ways because this is intermittently successful in getting the other person to stop being aversive.

Troubled couples I have counseled typically have several complaints about each other. He gets angry and irritated when she doesn't discipline their child. She complains that he doesn't help around the house. Both think that if the other would just do what they say, things would improve. But each resists being "pushed around"; and neither is willing to praise, thank, or acknowledge the good things the other does because they think, *I shouldn't have to*, or fear that doing so will excuse their partner's transgressions. So over months and years, couples become locked into using anger—or silence—to get the other person to back off or to punish the other. No one has fun, but each is sometimes reinforced by the brief respites from conflict anger produces. Although anger gets the other person to back off, it never contributes to finding more peaceful and caring ways to interact. Often the process ends in divorce.

Coercion and Depression

You can see how aggressive behavior like teasing, hitting, or getting angry can cause someone else to back off. But you might be surprised to learn that even the behavior involved in depression can get others to stop being aversive. In 1980, I began working with Hyman Hops at the Oregon Research Institute on a study of whether coercive processes were involved in depression. I had been studying depression in work I did with Peter Lewinsohn at the University of Oregon, and I had read Patterson's papers on coercion. I thought coercive processes might be involved in depression, and Hy had the expertise to develop a system for coding the behavioral interactions of couples. We proposed to observe family interactions to study how depressed women and their families interact. We were fortunate to get project funding from the National Institute of Mental Health.

Our study (Biglan, Hops, and Sherman 1988) showed that depressed women's sad and self-critical behavior is reinforced because it gets other family members to reduce their aggressiveness. For example, we did a moment-to-moment analysis of husbands and wives discussing a problem. It showed that when a depressed woman's husband criticized her or complained, he would typically stop if she cried, acted sad, or complained about her inadequacies. No one is having fun, but being sad brings a brief respite from criticism, teasing, or angry behavior.

Nick Allen, an Australian psychologist, has since argued that depression has evolutionary roots (Allen and Badcock 2006). When others are threatening, acting sad may decrease the risk of attack. Moreover, groups that tended to those who were hurt or incapacitated might have had a survival advantage compared with groups that left the weak by the side of the trail.

I hope you can see how important the problem of coercion is. If there is one thing that we can do to significantly reduce the burden to society of all of the common and costly problems of human behavior, it is to help families, schools, workplaces, and communities become less coercive and more nurturing of children's positive social behavior.

As the importance of coercion has become clear, family therapists have focused on helping families replace coercive practices with gentler, more effective means of reducing children's aggressive and uncooperative behavior and worked with parents to increase positively reinforcing interactions with their children. Similarly, couples therapists help couples abandon angry and argumentative ways of trying to get what they want from their partner. They help couples listen to and paraphrase each other, and they aid both partners in letting go of the feeling that they must defend themselves. The agenda shifts to finding mutually satisfying ways to be together. A multitude of studies show that these interventions significantly reduce strife and often reignite the love that couples once had (Shadish and Baldwin 2005). Couples counseling can also reduce depression. When conflict declines, women no longer need to be depressed to survive a day with their spouse (Beach et al. 2009).

Monitor and Limit Influences on Problem Behavior

Another colleague of mine, Ed Fisher, researches health behavior. In conversation, he once observed that people working to help people lose weight sometimes mistakenly believe that successful treatment should get people to the point where they can be in a room full of cream pies and ask for an apple. That ain't gonna happen. In a world full of abundance and enormous freedom, we face constant exposure to temptation. It is unrealistic to think that we can make people resistant to temptations that hundreds of thousands of years of evolution have created. Instead, we need to create environments that minimize these influences.

One of the most important arenas in which we need to do that involves adolescents. In one study (Richardson et al. 1993), researchers looked at what happens when ninth-grade students have no supervision after school. They found that, compared to peers who had a parent at home or attended adult-supervised after-school activities, those who were at home unsupervised were significantly more likely to experiment with drugs, be depressed, and get poor grades. They had even greater problems if they were hanging out with other teens after school. In chapters 2 through 4, I will tell you about programs that help parents, schools, and communities monitor and set limits on what teens are doing while also gradually allowing them to manage their own free time in safe, fun, and productive ways.

Teens also develop problems when they have access to tobacco and alcohol. I bought my first pack of cigarettes when I was fifteen and remained addicted to cigarettes until I was twenty-six. Even though it was illegal to sell cigarettes to those under eighteen, no one gave it a thought. As recently as the 1990s, when colleagues and I were conducting a smoking prevention study in Oregon, we were unable to get police to enforce the laws against selling tobacco to teens—despite research showing that easy access to cigarettes was one of the reasons that so many youth were getting addicted (Biglan 1995). Such sales have greatly diminished thanks to stepped-up enforcement and programs to reward clerks for not selling tobacco to minors.

Youth access to alcohol also poses problems. Laws prohibiting sales of alcohol to minors are seldom enforced. Many adults supply alcohol to young people, calling it a rite of passage. Sadly, more than five thousand people under age twenty-one die each year in alcohol-related car crashes or due to alcohol-fueled violence (National Institute on Alcohol Abuse and Alcoholism 2013).

Then there is marketing. Young people witness a large volume of very effective marketing for tobacco, alcohol, and unhealthful foods (Grube 1995; National Cancer Institute 2008; Nestle 2002). Limiting these influences would reduce youth consumption of these products.

Promote Psychological Flexibility

So far, I have emphasized how our understanding of reinforcement has enormous power in helping create environments that nurture well-being. We can richly reinforce all of the cooperative, prosocial behaviors that benefit individuals and those around them while also making sure that problems don't develop because people are living in environments that are coercive or that entice them to develop costly behaviors. But this is far from the whole story. We also must ensure that people develop a pragmatic and resilient approach to living in a way consistent with their values and unhampered by the rigid influence of language.

Language and the Blessing of Symbolic Processes

Humans have a capacity that separates us from other species: we talk. We use our words to analyze our world and solve problems that other organisms can't solve. We can relate a blueprint to the dimensions of the actual building and transform a vacant lot into a fine house. We can think about how compressing a gas changes its temperature and use that information to invent a heat pump. Our ability to talk about the world and relate our language to things in the world has given us the power to become the planet's dominant species—for better and for worse.

Behavioral scientists have struggled with how to effectively analyze human language capacities. Behaviorists with a Skinnerian orientation insist it can be understood as simply verbal behavior that is shaped by reinforcing consequences, just as any other behavior is. That view led to considerable success in helping children with developmental disabilities learn how to talk. But it fell short of the goal of a comprehensive understanding of human language. Cognitive psychologists insisted that human language and cognitive processes could not be understood in terms of reinforcement processes. In fact, some argued that the influence of cognition on human behavior proved that the laws of learning that had been worked out with animals were irrelevant in accounting for human behavior (Seligman 1970).

Quite recently, however, a convergence has emerged that yields an integrated and powerful understanding of cognitive or language processes. Evidence from both behavioral and cognitive traditions shows that the fundamental feature of human language involves the capacity to arbitrarily relate stimuli and to apply those relational responses, or "frames," to the world in ways that enable effective manipulation of our environments. These relational or symbolic abilities have been shown to arise from the same reinforcement processes involved in learning simpler behaviors, such as walking or imitating others (Törneke 2010). And once a broad repertoire of symbolic processing has been established, it constitutes a distinct process that in numerous situations overrides the immediate effects of the reinforcing contingencies affecting other organisms.

Here is an example: Thanks to thousands of occasions where children get reinforced for following others' requests, instructions, and advice, humans develop a repertoire of rule following that serves them very well. Consider what we teach our children about cleanliness. When my grandkids, Ashlyn and Grayson, were each about two, they enjoyed a book called *Yummy Yucky* (Patricelli 2012). Each page has a picture and a little story about something that is yummy or yucky. "Spaghetti is yummy. Worms are yucky." Thanks to that book, they learned that worms, blue crayons, and many other things don't go in our mouths, while things like blueberries and spaghetti do. The book helped my son Mike and his wife Jen teach their kids how to interact with a whole lot of things—without Ashlyn and Grayson having to eat something that harmed them or having to be punished for doing so. Once they learned the concepts yummy and yucky, they could easily learn about hundreds of additional things if Mike and Jen simply labeled them as "yummy" or "yucky." "Yucky" can even be used to override the naturally reinforcing effects of unhealthful foods. For example, if Jen and Mike told Ashlyn and Grayson that Big Macs were yucky, it could influence them to not want Big Macs.

This kind of symbolic processing has allowed humans to pass a vast body of knowledge from generation to generation without having to expose children directly to all of the things our language symbolizes. For example, you don't have to gain weight and have a heart attack in order to learn that obesity can cause heart attacks.

Thus, human symbolic processing enables us to transcend the limits of having to learn solely through exposure to the direct consequences of our behavior. It enables us to persist even when immediate consequences would not support our behavior. For example, one of the primary motivations for our pursuit of learning comes from our ability to imagine the reinforcement we will achieve if our education leads to a good job or prestigious profession. In short, our symbolic processes have been the force that has enabled us to transform the world.

Mindfulness and the Curse of Literality

There is a dark side to the power of language, however. We have so much experience and success with treating our talk about things as though the words were the things that we often don't notice that the word is not the thing. This is the problem of literality. The same symbolic abilities that enable us to surround ourselves with creature comforts in a warm, well-lit home can make us want to kill ourselves.

Like other organisms, we make avoiding danger our highest priority. It is a simple evolutionary story: organisms that didn't do so simply didn't survive. Kelly Wilson, a friend and colleague who has helped therapists around the world use the principles of symbolic processes in their work, likes to say that it is better to miss lunch than to be lunch. He talks about a bunny rabbit out in a meadow. If that bunny finds some really good veggies and becomes so engrossed in them that she doesn't keep looking around, she is liable to be eaten by a cougar. Only bunnies that learned to eat while keeping a constant eye out for predators remain to inhabit this earth.

But unlike bunnies, we humans can describe the past and possible futures. I can think about how my father died of carotid artery blockage and worry that the same thing might happen to me. You can think about your child at school and worry that he is being picked on by other kids. Although our thoughts about the future can make us thrilled in anticipation of good things to come, we are also prone to crippling visions of bad things that might happen to us, thanks to our evolutionary bias to avoid danger. Then, thanks to our verbal, relational abilities, we can inhabit a terrifying world while sitting in a perfectly safe, quiet room.

In Robert Sapolsky's delightful book *Why Zebra's Don't Get Ulcers* (1994), he talks about what happens when humans think about the dangers they can so readily imagine. A lion chasing a zebra instigates a cascade of hormones that puts the zebra's body into high gear. If the zebra has the good fortune to have an older, slower zebra nearby, it escapes the lion and the process is reversed. Hormones return to normal levels, heart rate slows, blood pressure returns to normal.

But thanks to our minds, humans can be in the presence of threatening stimuli all the time. Did you ever have a conflict with someone and find yourself lying in bed thinking about it? That person isn't in your bed—the person might even be dead—but there you are, still stressing about him.

Sapolsky's book is a compendium of the harm that chronic stress causes: insomnia, colds, irritable bowel syndrome, ulcers, miscarriages, memory impairment, major depression, hypertension, cardiovascular disease, adult-onset diabetes, osteoporosis, immune suppression, and drug addiction. Stress can even stunt children's growth.

Stress also affects our behavior. Stressed people don't make good companions, parents, siblings, doctors, lawyers, or friends. They are more irritable, angry, argumentative, anxious, depressed, and disinterested in others.

Think about how literality can affect whether families and schools richly reinforce cooperation and prosociality or, conversely, descend into conflict and violence. For example, say the mother of a young child has trouble getting him to cooperate. Her own mother often talked about willful children and how kids are born that way. Viewing her son's behavior through this lens, she readily becomes irritated with him. She also overlooks and fails to reinforce times when he is cooperative. Over time, she becomes increasingly punitive. The research I describe in chapter 2 reveals that the boy's behavior can easily be changed by increasing reinforcement for his cooperation, and a good family therapist can help the mother learn this. But it will be hard to do as long as she continues to view her son as willful and incorrigible.

Until very recently, at least in the Western world, the most common answer to the problem of literality has been to try to control or get rid of all the verbal lion attacks. In chapter 5, I describe how research by clinical psychologists is helping people escape the curse of literality. Rather than seeing the world through our thoughts, we can learn to step back, notice that they are thoughts, verbally construct what we want in our lives, and take whatever steps seem likely to move us in valued directions.

This orientation is what many psychologists call *psychological flexibility*. It consists of acting based on chosen values while being in contact with what is happening within us and around us, and not trying to judge, change, or control our present-moment experience. The mother who keeps having the thought that her son is willful can think about what she wants for him and what she wants for her relationship with him. In this context, she can notice her thoughts and her irritation and yet choose to listen to him, notice when he is cooperative, and be attentive to him at those times. In many instances, she may find that when she pays attention to what he is feeling and how he is acting, she can help him become better able to experience strong feelings and, rather than throw a tantrum or act impulsively, do something that is more likely to get reinforced, such as tell his sister that he wants his toy back.

Social environments can undermine psychological flexibility in several ways. Teaching children they shouldn't feel certain ways, such as angry or anxious, can encourage a lifelong pattern of avoidance of such feelings. And in order to successfully avoid such feelings, people need to avoid the situations that bring on those emotions. This might work well in some cases. For example, if you decide that your frequent arguments with your spouse aren't good for you because they often leave you feeling angry, it might contribute to a more loving relationship with your spouse. On the other hand, if you avoid other people because you feel anxious when you are around them, that might prevent you from learning important things or making valuable friends.

Our culture teaches us that it isn't good to have "negative" thoughts and feelings. This is often done in seemingly caring ways, as when someone tries to get you to not feel so bad. But it is also often done quite punitively, with statements like "I'll give you something to cry about." Both approaches reflect avoidance on the part of the other person. People often don't want to feel what they feel when you tell them what you feel, so the message is "Shut up about it."

Thus, one key in promoting psychological flexibility is accepting others' emotions and thoughts so that we don't purposely or inadvertently motivate them to try to control, resist, or deny their experience. A second thing that promotes psychological flexibility is using a detached and even playful way of talking about thoughts (Hayes, Strosahl, and Wilson 1999). Try putting the phrase "I'm having the thought that…" before every thought you state. For example, I might say, "I'm having the thought that I will never finish this book." It puts a little space between me and the thought. It is a thought, not reality. I don't have to act on the thought. It can just be there.

The third thing our environments can do to build psychological flexibility is encourage us to be clear about and keep thinking about what we want in our lives—what we most value—and what we can do that will further our values.

Building a Nurturing Society

In this chapter I have provided an overview of how a science of human behavior and society is helping us to understand what people need to thrive. I don't claim that it is the one true take on this science. Keep in mind that, for a pragmatist, words are not seen as definitive descriptions of the way the world *is*, but as ideas that may be useful. In the remainder of this book, I will describe how this way of thinking about science and humanity could guide us to a more nurturing society.

PART 2

A Wealth of Knowledge About How to Help People Thrive

In this part of the book, I will describe how the scientific principles I described in chapter 1 have helped in the development of interventions that assist families, schools, and peer groups to become environments that nurture human development and well-being. I will also tell you about recent advances in clinical psychology that have made it possible to ameliorate most psychological and behavioral problems—not in every case, certainly, but with a much greater success rate than ever before.

CHAPTER 2

Nurturing Families

Thanks to research over the last fifty years, we now have programs that can help families reduce coercive interactions and become much more successful in reinforcing and guiding young people's development. If we implement these programs widely, we can decrease the number of young people who develop problems like antisocial behavior and drug abuse, reducing incidence to much lower levels. In this chapter, I will describe programs created to help families nurture children's development from the prenatal period through adolescence.

It all started in the 1960s with research on behavioral parenting skills training. Many people contributed to this work, but Jerry Patterson was the first to write a book for parents explaining the principles of reinforcement in ways that could help parents make good use of them. The book, written with Elizabeth Gullion, was *Living with Children* (1968). It described specific things parents could do to teach young children to cooperate with requests, not be aggressive, and follow common routines, such as going to bed at a certain hour.

In 1972, when I was living in Seattle and had just started learning about behavioral approaches, my sister Kathie and her daughter Robyn visited on their way from Los Angeles to Rochester, New York. Kathie had split up with her husband in Southern California two years before and had moved back home to Rochester. Robyn had just spent her kindergarten year living in California with her father and his second wife. Robyn's father had decided that she should return to live in Rochester with Kathie because his new wife and Robyn weren't getting along. Newly freed from an unhappy situation, Robyn was testing all her limits and showing some talent at pressing Kathie's buttons, particularly with bedtime. Kathie and Robyn needed some help.

I knew what a handful Robyn could be. Two years earlier, I had been visiting Kathie at Christmastime in Anaheim. Robyn kept getting out of bed, and nothing could get her back. At one point, she was sitting on the sofa next to me, with a glass of milk in her hand, and I said something snide about her behavior. She calmly looked me straight in the eye and poured the milk on my lap.

During their visit, I gave Kathie a copy of *Living with Children*. In a way I'm sure could have been more considerate of her feelings, I told her the book could help her with Robyn. Desperate for some useful guidance, she devoured the book and told me later that she kept it at her bedside for times when she needed a refresher. Kathie started using rewards for cooperative behavior, including things like going to bed and helping around the house. She also began to use time-outs rather than yelling for misbehavior.

It all worked for Kathie. Robyn became much more cooperative and much less defiant. She became more fun to be around. And contrary to the common criticism of behaviorism at the time, she did not become meek and submissive. The negative behavior she was using to get what she wanted morphed into a charming style of assertiveness and confidence that served her well.

These days, just about every kid who has been in a preschool knows what a time-out is. But in the 1960s, it was a new development. Instead of hitting, yelling, or severely punishing a child, parents would have them sit quietly for several minutes before returning to whatever they had been doing. Millions of people have been able to replace harsh or abusive parenting with this calm, nonviolent approach. It has prevented much child abuse and probably saved some lives.

In his work on using reinforcement with children, Jerry Patterson planted a tree that has grown many branches. The Institute of Medicine report that I helped write (IOM and NRC 2009) sets forth numerous tested and effective family interventions, many with roots in Patterson's work, that provide critical help to families from the prenatal period through adolescence. I am convinced that these programs are the single most important building block for the society we want to create.

Nurturing Development During Pregnancy and the First Two Years of Life

On the night of October 6, 1998, Russell Henderson and Aaron McKinney took Matthew Shepard to a remote area outside Laramie, Wyoming, pistol-whipped him, robbed him, and left him tied to a fence. A cyclist found him eighteen hours later. He died five days afterward, having never regained consciousness.

The nation was shocked. Shepard was gay, and the crime was apparently due to Henderson's and McKinney's hatred of gays. But there was more that didn't make the headlines. Both Henderson and McKinney were addicted to methamphetamine. At the time of the murder, they were drunk and tweaking (coming down from meth), which is when aggressive and impulsive behavior is at its worst.

Hatred of gays and meth addiction may have been the immediate causes of this tragic event, but Henderson and McKinney had been put on the road to this horrific act by their toxic families. As young children, both had endured mistreatment from parents and other adults. One suffered from the effects of fetal alcohol syndrome, the other from disturbed experiences with his mother. One of the killers had been sexually victimized as a seven-year-old and locked in a basement each day as a young child because his mother worked at a low-paying job and couldn't afford child care; the other had been physically abused by his mother's boyfriends and was subsequently removed from the home.

Prenatal alcohol and drug exposure and poor maternal nutrition produce infants whose brain functioning is impaired (Soby 2006). It makes them more irritable and difficult to soothe as infants. For parents who are stressed and unskilled, such infants become aggressive and uncooperative, which leads to poor performance in school and social rejection. Abuse and neglect put infants into a state of constant high arousal that alters normal functioning of stress hormones in ways that keep children hyperaroused and ready to fight or flee (G. E. Miller et al. 2009). They feel as though there is constant danger.

Help for Poor, Single, Teenage Mothers

Suppose we could intervene to help parents who have the kind of problems that Henderson's and McKinney's mothers had. How much trouble could we prevent?

Consider Claire, a sixteen-year-old girl who became pregnant. This isn't an unusual occurrence in the United States, which has the highest rate of teenage pregnancy of any developed country. Like 80 percent of pregnant teenage girls, Claire didn't want a baby. However, she chose not to have an abortion, unlike nearly one-third of pregnant teens (Henshaw 1998).

Claire and her baby face very significant challenges. Her boyfriend became angry when she told him and accused her of trying to get pregnant. They broke up, and although Claire wants him to provide support, she doesn't want to marry him. Her parents are furious, blaming and criticizing her, and in their worry and distress, they are oblivious to the fact that Claire needs caring and support.

Claire is poor and hasn't been doing well in school. She is unlikely to graduate. With Claire unmarried and uneducated, she and her baby will probably face a life of poverty. The Institute of Medicine report I coauthored (IOM and NRC 2009) documents how such poverty makes it much more likely that Claire's baby will be unhealthy and develop costly problems, and will not develop the social and verbal skills needed to succeed in school. In one study of poor teenage mothers, about 35 percent of their children were arrested by age fifteen. Now, with nearly eighty out of every one thousand teenage girls getting pregnant each year (CDC, n.d.), the United States has a bumper crop of children headed for problems that will cost them, their families, and their communities for many years to come.

What Claire needs is someone to help her through the coming months and years. Could a warm supportive person really make a difference? The answer is emphatically yes.

The most comprehensive and well-researched program for women in Claire's situation is called the Nurse-Family Partnership (Olds 2007), created by developmental psychologist David Olds when he was at the University of Rochester. Its benefits are so well established that it inspired the Obama administration to propose putting billions of dollars into implementing it, along with several other carefully researched family support programs.

If Claire had the good fortune to have the Nurse-Family Partnership in her community, a nurse would contact her during her pregnancy. That nurse would befriend her, listen to her concerns, clarify her hopes for herself and her baby, and help her begin to move in a direction she desires. Her newfound mentor would advise her about ways to resolve conflict with her family and boyfriend and begin to get the support she needs from them, or from others if her boyfriend and parents are unwilling to provide it. The nurse would make sure Claire gets the prenatal care necessary to ensure a successful pregnancy. Together, they would develop plans for Claire to get her education. As Claire takes steps on all these fronts, she would find that she has a wise and supportive friend to help her through difficulties and cheer her progress.

Fast-forward a bit, to when Claire has a healthy baby boy. She names him Ethan. Having a first baby is a huge challenge for any family, especially for a single teenager. Fortunately, Claire's nurse would be there when Ethan is born and during his first two years of life. She could reassure Claire about the worries that naturally arise, such as when a baby cries and is difficult to console. In such a situation, it is natural to be frustrated and distressed, especially when you aren't sure you are doing the right thing. Claire's nurse would reassure her that a crying baby is normal and would help her provide the patient, soothing care that is vital to bonding between Claire and her baby. Through patience, practice, and support, Ethan can learn to let Claire comfort him—the first step in his development of emotion regulation.

The benefits of the Nurse-Family Partnership have been documented in three separate randomized trials over the past twenty years. Compared with high-risk mothers who didn't get the program, mothers who did had children who were better adjusted; they also waited longer to have a second child, made more money, and were less likely to abuse their children or be on welfare (Olds, Sadler, and Kitzman 2007).

In David Olds's first study, about 35 percent of the children of high-risk first-time mothers who did not participate in the Nurse-Family Partnership program were arrested by age fifteen (Olds et al. 2003). The children whose mothers participated in the program were arrested less than half as much. That is a lot of crime prevented.

Finally, the Washington State Institute for Public Policy analyzed the costs and benefits of the Nurse-Family Partnership program (Lee et al.

2012). They concluded that for every dollar spent on the program, $3.23 was saved, a 223 percent return on investment.

Nurturing in the First Two Years of Life

The principles guiding the Nurse-Family Partnership are vital for every family during pregnancy and the first two years of life. During pregnancy mothers must provide a nontoxic environment for their baby by eating a diet rich in nutrients (WebMD 2013). And, of course, they shouldn't smoke, drink alcohol, or take drugs. Smoking causes premature birth, miscarriages, low birth weight, increased risk of asthma, impaired cognitive function, and sudden infant death syndrome (Van Meurs 1999). *Any* alcohol consumption increases the risk of facial deformities, retarded development, brain and neurological problems, low tolerance for frustration, and impaired development of academic skills (American Academy of Child and Adolescent Psychiatry 2011).

It is also important to minimize stress during pregnancy. Stressful events increase a mother's production of cortisol, which can not only influence fetal development but even result in impairment in children's cognitive development as late as age eight (Douglas Mental Health University Institute 2014). In Claire's story, I described above some of the most common stressors—namely, aversive behavior of other people. This is another example of how important it is to create environments that minimize coercion and conflict.

Minimizing coercion continues to be important for both parents and infants during the first two years of a baby's life. Parents can be stressed by the uncertainties of how to care for a newborn and by conflict with and criticism by those around them. As for infants, those who do not receive warm, patient, soothing interactions from their caretakers will fail to develop the healthy attachment they need to gain the capacity to be soothed.

Rather than a harsh and punitive environment, what all family members need is an environment where they are richly reinforced. Parents benefit from having people around who patiently and approvingly help them navigate the first two years of the baby's life. Babies benefit from patient, soothing interactions with lots of stimulation, such as eye contact, talking and cooing, smiling, and cuddling. These interactions reinforce the infant for interacting, smiling, and laughing, and they increase hand-eye coordination, fine and gross motor skills, and emotion regulation skills.

The Critical Role of Emotion Regulation

I want to highlight emotion regulation, because this is a critical skill that everyone needs to develop beginning in infancy. Let's start with crying babies. Evolution has engineered babies to cry because it motivates parents to take care of them and develops their parenting behaviors. Dramatic evidence of this comes from a study of colicky babies done by M. M. de Vries in Africa (1987). Colic involves a pattern of uncontrollable crying that affects from 5 to 25 percent of babies (Roberts, Ostapchuk, and O'Brien 2004). We still don't know exactly why it happens. De Vries rated a large sample of babies on how much they cried uncontrollably. By coincidence, a famine occurred soon after the ratings were completed. When de Vries went back months later, he found that more of the colicky babies had survived. It turns out that there is a strong evolutionary reason why babies cry: in difficult circumstances, those who cry more are more likely to be fed.

So from the very start, infants cry and parents are highly motivated to calm them. In some families, the result can be tragic, as in the case of shaken baby syndrome, which involves brain damage due to shaking an infant. Parents may use this approach because, initially, shaking reinforces the parent by silencing the child. However, it typically results in severe brain damage and often the death of the infant.

Fortunately, in most families parents learn how to calm their infant through patiently soothing, rocking, and talking. A key part of the process involves nurturing infant behavior that is an alternative to crying. This process is fundamental to child development. It creates a bond between parents and children. It also helps children develop the ability to calm themselves and fosters rudimentary behaviors that are alternatives to crying.

Nurturing Young Children

Even if infants are well cared for during the first two years of life, their further development will be hampered if they don't get the nurturance they need. What happens from age two until about age five, when they enter kindergarten, can make the difference between eventually becoming a college-educated professional or a dropout. During these early years, parents can use the hundreds of opportunities that arise each day to help children develop the cognitive, language, and emotion regulation skills that are vital to success as they mature.

The Power of Attuned, Attentive Interactions

You can see the fine-grained details of what young children need by watching how a skilled adult interacts with a young child. Take our granddaughter, Ashlyn, and her interactions with "Grandma Georgie." From the time Ashlyn was a baby, Georgia has been talking to her—nonstop. I sometimes joked that Ashlyn's first full sentence would be "Will someone let five minutes go by without labeling things?" But she hasn't said that yet because Georgia's talk is always in sync with what Ashlyn is interested in. From the start, she would follow Ashlyn's lead. If Ashlyn looked at a cup, Georgia would describe it: "Oh, that is a cup—a green cup." Then she would encourage Ashlyn to hold it, play with it, and drink from it, extending Ashlyn's skill and knowledge about the world around her, but always in keeping with what Ashlyn was interested in at the moment. She never forced Ashlyn to continue with something she had lost interest in.

Georgia also promotes Ashlyn's knowledge about herself. When Ashlyn is upset, Georgia coaches her about her emotions: "Oh you're upset because you bumped your knee. That must hurt!" In the process, Ashlyn learns words to name both her feelings and the things that cause her emotions. By matching the intensity of her feelings to Ashlyn's, Georgia also conveys empathy and caring. In the process, Ashlyn begins to calm down and Georgia can prompt her to engage in problem solving: "Do you want to come and have me put a Band-Aid on it?" This process is vital to helping Ashlyn learn to regulate her emotions. This is crucial, as children with good emotion self-regulation can have emotions without becoming impulsive or aggressive. They also do better in school and at making friends.

One day when Ashlyn was three years old, she fell from a step stool and hit her face. I braced myself for a long episode of screaming and crying. She started to cry and ran to her mom. Jen comforted her briefly, and in about two minutes Ashlyn was back on the step stool helping prepare a meal. I was stunned at how quickly the episode passed and asked Jen about it. She said that whenever Ashlyn fell, she comforted her and then prompted her to get back to whatever she had been doing. She also made sure that Ashlyn's return to action was richly reinforced, perhaps with extra attention to Ashlyn when she went back to whatever she was doing before she got hurt. At three years old, Ashlyn was learning the essentials of self-regulation, persistence, and resilience!

When I think about the complexity and subtlety of the moment-to-moment interactions involved in building Ashlyn's social, emotional, and cognitive skills, I marvel that so many parents raise successful kids. But once you understand the basic principle that a child's skills are nurtured by parents' ongoing patient attention to the child's developing interest in the world and their support of the child's emotion regulation, you have a grasp of the fundamental features of programs that are helping a constantly growing number of parents succeed.

As infants grow into childhood, they continue to develop new ways to restrain the impulse to cry or get angry. Most parents get good at reinforcing behavior that is incompatible with crying. For example, when our grandson, Grayson, was two years old, he developed an ear-piercing scream that he used whenever his big sister took something he was playing with. Thankfully, my son and daughter-in-law have taught him to instead ask Ashlyn to give back the toy—and also taught Ashlyn to do so.

My point here is that young adults' ability to manage their emotions in ways that allow them to negotiate with others without alienating them is the result of literally thousands of interactions that occur on a daily basis throughout childhood. Helping families develop their ability to nurture emotion regulation is vital not only for children's future well-being, but also for the well-being of society. Children who don't develop the ability to regulate their emotions end up on a life path that often includes aggressive social behavior, substance abuse, poor performance in school, and crime.

Nurturing Children's Prosocial Development

Once you understand that behavior is continuously guided by its consequences, you can begin to appreciate how important parents are in nurturing their children's development. Early childhood educators stress the importance of following the child's lead, and behaviorally oriented psychologists have shown that a parent's attention to the child in these situations reinforces each thing the child does. If you have a young child, you know how important your attention is: "Mommy, look at me!" The reason it is so important is that parental attention is the gateway to every other form of reinforcement parents provide: food, comfort, activities, toys, and so on.

The Incredible Years

One behavioral parenting skills program, the Incredible Years, is particularly attuned to the importance of parents following their child's lead in order to develop mutually reinforcing interactions. It was developed over a twenty-five-year period by Carolyn Webster-Stratton, a professor of nursing at the University of Washington. The Incredible Years helps parents become more skilled in nurturing their children's development (Webster-Stratton, Reid, and Stoolmiller 2008). Although she teaches parents to praise children and reward desired behavior with stickers and other treats, she starts by teaching parents to play with their children. Her first goal is to get parents to let the child take the lead.

Why is taking the lead so important? It ensures that parents are developing a pattern of mutually reinforcing interactions that provide lots of positive attention as children explore their surroundings. In these interactions, parents extend their children's knowledge: "Yes, that's a *red* fire engine."

Think about how these interactions build the cooperation and self-regulation of a child. In ten minutes of playing together, a parent and child might each cooperate with the other a dozen times: "Do you want the yellow block?" "No, give me the green block." Likewise, the parent can repeatedly and gently guide the child to try again when something doesn't happen the way the child wanted it to. These are opportunities to build the child's emotion regulation and persistence.

To teach parents to follow their child's lead, the Incredible Years uses videos that illustrate better and worse ways to handle situations. In one, a mother is asked to play tic-tac-toe with her three-year-old son. They have a big board on which to put three-inch-high X's and O's. The child has never seen the board before and clearly knows nothing about tic-tac-toe. The mother places an X on the board and tells her son to put an O on the board. Instead, he puts it on his ear. She corrects him by telling him, "No, it goes here on the board." Within a few minutes, this cute little boy has completely lost interest in the game. He gets out of his chair, walks over to some cabinets, and tries to open them. His mom's efforts to get him to come back and sit down are fruitless.

Adults are quick to tell children what to do and correct them when they are "wrong." They focus on the situation from their perspective and fail to see it from the child's viewpoint. Often when children don't do what they are asked, parents get angry because they think their child understands what they want and is being willful.

However, parents usually overestimate what children understand and are capable of doing. The Incredible Years gets parents to follow their children's lead so that they are in sync with what the child is interested in and can do. This reduces instances of parents telling their children what to do and prevents children from losing interest in being with Mom or Dad. When a parent connects with what the child cares about, they develop mutually reinforcing interactions. In this program, a mom like the one in the tic-tac-toe video would learn to notice what the child is looking at and doing. She would be encouraged to do things that hold her child's interest. She might put an O on her ear. She might lay the X's and O's on the table and see if her son wants to arrange them. She might tell him the names of these objects and see if he can name them. If he can, she might ask him to give her an O.

By helping parents follow their children's lead, the Incredible Years helps parents create interactions that are much more mutually reinforcing. Too often, parents' interactions with their children include criticism, cajoling, pleading, and anger. By instead following the child's lead, parents can reinforce child behaviors such as talking to the parents, engaging in fine and gross motor activities, cooperating, and persisting in challenging activities. Parental patience, attention, and warmth are reinforced by the child's cooperative behavior—and by all of the cute, warm ways young children behave when they are enjoying an activity.

Think about how these interactions build a relationship of mutual respect and caring. As your child gets older and spends more time out in the world, you are going to need him to tell you what is going on in his life in school and with friends if you are going to prevent problems and encourage good choices. How likely is it that he will tell you what is happening in his life at age ten or fifteen if he doesn't enjoy talking with you at age four?

Carolyn Webster-Stratton's Incredible Years is one of the most carefully researched parenting programs. Over a twenty-year period, she has evaluated it in a series of randomized trials. She and her colleagues did six such evaluations (for example, Webster-Stratton and Herman 2008; Webster-Stratton, Reid, and Stoolmiller 2008), and at least five others have been done (for example, Barrera et al. 2002). Results of those studies consistently show that the program helps parents be more warm and reinforcing and less critical and commanding. They learn techniques for setting limits on problem behavior without resorting to spanking or other harsh methods of discipline. The result is that even children who are aggressive and uncooperative become more loving and cooperative. The program also reduces parental depression.

Communities that want to improve the well-being of their children and families would do well to invest in the Incredible Years. The Washington State Institute for Public Policy analyzed the cost-benefit ratio of the Incredible Years (Aos et al. 2011). The program costs about $2,000 to deliver to a family, but its benefits per family were estimated to be more than $3,000 due to outcomes like reduced health care costs and increased educational attainment. Other benefits included nearly $2,500 in reduced costs to taxpayers (for example, on special education and criminal justice) and about $2,700 in benefits to others. Ultimately, for every dollar spent on the Incredible Years, there was a return of $4.20!

Promoting Young Children's Verbal Development

In helping young children develop prosocial skills, it is highly important to nurture their verbal knowledge about their world and themselves. A child's verbal and cognitive skills are the result of literally thousands of interactions between parents and child. In the 1980s, psychologists Betty Hart and Todd Risley did a study of children's language learning that was a real sleeper. Only in the past ten years have behavioral scientists begun to realize how important their study is. They went into the homes of forty-two families once a month for two and a half years, beginning when the children were seven to twelve months old. They discovered an enormous variability in how much parents talked to their children. Thanks to observing in the home and diligently counting how much was said to each child, they estimated that, in the first three years of the children's lives, parents who were professionals spoke about thirty million words to their child, while working-class parents spoke about twenty million, and parents on welfare spoke only about ten million. The amount and quality of parents' talk with their children during those first three years was strongly related to children's IQ scores at age three and their language skills when in the third grade. It shouldn't be surprising that the families' social class predicted children's language skills in third grade, but this study showed that how much parents talked with their children was an even stronger predictor of children's skill than their parents' social class (Hart and Risley 1995).

More recently, Susan Landry and her colleagues at the University of Texas Health Science Center have created Play and Learning Strategies, a program that helps children develop their cognitive and verbal skills (Landry et al. 2008; Landry et al. 2012). It teaches parents specific skills for interacting with infants and young children to promote child well-being and stimulate early language development.

Thriving in Childhood

If young children don't have the kind of nurturing family I've been describing, they may have significant behavior problems by the time they reach kindergarten. As described in chapter 1, if parents are harsh and inconsistent in how they deal with unwanted behavior, they and their child are likely to develop a growing repertoire of angry, cruel, and even dangerous ways of trying to control each other. Yet even in later childhood it is not too late to help children get on a path toward prosociality. Thanks to research on family interventions over the last thirty years, we can help families replace coercive interactions with warm, patient, and much more effective means of helping children develop the prosocial values, capacity for emotion regulation, and motor, verbal, and social skills they need to thrive.

Achieving Peace in a Family

To give you a feel for how much a family can benefit, here is a description of a case that was provided to me by Kevin Moore, a good friend and a highly experienced behavioral family therapist, who was trained by Jerry Patterson and his colleagues.

Jane was a mother at her wits' end. She had two boys, Mike, age ten, from her first marriage, and Kurt, age six, from her second marriage. Mike had always been a shy and quiet boy who was easy to parent, whereas Kurt was very difficult. He had colic as an infant and was hard to soothe. He yelled so much that he developed nodules on his vocal cords.

Jane said that she was increasingly worried about Kurt and his constant escalation of aggressive behavior. He had started breaking and throwing things when he was upset and saying he hated his parents and brother. He was frequently angry and his anger often escalated into rage.

Jane was also concerned about how often she and her husband were resorting to hitting him. His father was quite stern. When Kurt's behavior became severe, his dad spanked him or slapped his hand. Because Kurt was so unpleasant, Jane found that she was spending less and less time with him and that she seldom had positive interactions with him. But her deepest fear was that she was developing a dislike of him. She was ashamed and scared about such thoughts and feelings. She cried throughout the first two therapy sessions about how this situation was ruining all the relationships in the family.

Kurt's dad refused to come in for family therapy, but he did agree to not use corporal punishment for ten weeks and to not undermine the therapeutic approach Jane was going to try. I began by teaching Jane about the coercive cycle the family was locked into. I explained that corporal punishment wasn't likely to solve the problem because it left Kurt angry at everyone, and because no parent would be willing to use it every time a boy like Kurt misbehaved. As an alternative to hitting Kurt, I taught Jane to use time-outs.

Jane and her husband had tried time-outs, but they hadn't been doing it correctly. They would yell at Kurt while he was in time-out and keep him in it for long periods of time. (Five minutes is plenty of time for a six-year-old.) They often ended the time-out with a long lecture about Kurt's behavior, which simply got him worked up again.

I then showed Jane how to increase positive reinforcement for Kurt when he did what he was asked. Rather than let him watch TV and play video games whenever he liked, Jane made access to these activities contingent on doing what he was asked. I made sure that Jane's requests were clear and unambiguous, for example, "Please come to the table" as opposed to "Dinner is ready."

I also helped Jane set aside a special time with Kurt each day, when she would read stories to him or play a game of his choice for ten minutes no matter how the day had gone. As treatment progressed, Kurt was eventually able to earn ten-minute increments of this special time for specific targeted behaviors, like picking up his toys. This helped Jane get better at defining and reinforcing the specific behaviors that Kurt needed to learn to take care of himself, cooperate, and get along with others.

It worked. By the end of treatment Jane's daily phone reports about Kurt's behavior indicated a big drop in Kurt's problem behaviors, with an incidence similar to that in families with nonaggressive children. Jane also said that Kurt's dad had committed to never using corporal punishment again and that he was now using time-outs appropriately. In addition, she said that her special time together with Kurt was the highlight of her day and that he had softened and was more cooperative. Similarly, his dad was spending more time with Kurt.

Notice how Kevin helped Jane and her family replace coercive methods of trying to control Kurt's behavior with much greater use of positive reinforcement. When Jane had to deal with misbehavior, she used time-outs instead of corporal punishment. In essence, rewards became a prosthetic device to get warm interactions going. Instead of Kurt behaving coercively to get his parents to do what he wanted (which also motivated them to be more punishing), Jane used higher rates of positive reinforcement to foster Kurt's more positive behaviors and get the family out of the coercion trap. Also notice how, contrary to Alfie Kohn's criticism of rewards described in chapter 1, rewards worked very well in establishing positive interactions between Kurt and his mother. Rather than Kurt losing interest in what he did with his mom, they developed a loving, special time that became the high point of each day. The reinforcement provided by Jane's loving interactions with Kurt became a major motivator for him.

Oregon Parent Management Training Goes to Norway

Over the past thirty years, the empirical evidence supporting behavioral parenting skills training programs has mounted. As a result, they are being implemented around the world. For example, the Norwegian government asked Terje Ogden at the University of Oslo to find effective programs for families with aggressive children. His search led him to Parent Management Training–the Oregon Model (PMTO), a version of behavioral parenting skills training developed by Marion Forgatch and Jerry Patterson at Oregon Social Learning Center.

At Ogden's invitation, Forgatch and her colleagues trained family therapists in each of the seven regions of Norway in how to provide PMTO (Patterson, Forgatch, and DeGarmo 2010). They even did a randomized trial to test the effectiveness of the program when done by Norwegians. Their results confirmed its benefit for reducing family coercion, increasing warm and positively reinforcing relationships among family members, and reducing children's aggressive and uncooperative behavior. The program is now in use throughout Norway. More recently, Forgatch has been implementing PMTO programs in the Netherlands, Michigan, Kansas, and New York City.

The benefits of PMTO are clear (Forgatch et al. 2009; Wachlarowicz et al. 2012). A remarkably thorough and careful analysis of its benefits using nine years of data from a randomized controlled trial of the program with divorcing mothers (Patterson, Forgatch, and DeGarmo 2010) showed that it significantly reduced families' use of coercive parenting techniques, such as explosive anger, nagging, and authoritarian discipline. These changes, in turn, led to reductions in delinquency, improvements in the families' standard of living, and even reductions in the chances that the mother would be arrested. PMTO also increased *positive parenting*, which involves reinforcing children's successes and showing affection, respect, empathy, and interest. Improvements in positive parenting during the year in which families participated in the program reduced parents' use of coercive techniques and led to steady improvements in positive parenting over the next three years. These improvements contributed to less delinquency among the children over the next nine years.

PMTO is instrumental in improving all relationships in the family. In one randomized evaluation of PMTO for families in which the mother had just remarried (Bullard et al. 2010), the program not only reduced parents' use of coercive discipline, increased their use of positive practices, and reduced children's behavior problems, but also improved the parents' marital relationships.

Keeping Early Adolescents Out of Trouble

Early adolescence generally refers to ages eleven through fourteen, when most young people go through puberty. Developmental psychologists have shown that this is a time when impulsive, risk-taking behavior increases, which is in keeping with findings that the regions of the brain that control impulsive behavior are not fully developed at this age (Blakemore and Choudhury 2006). In most of the United States, this is when young people transition from elementary to middle school.

All of these changes can make this a difficult period. Adolescents have to cope with newly developed sexual urges and often have to navigate major upheavals in their relations with peers. In research I conducted with colleagues, among a large, representative sample of Oregon adolescents, we found that early adolescents experience higher levels of exposure to bullying and harassment than older adolescents and are more likely to report suicide attempts (Boles, Biglan, and Smolkowski 2006).

In early adolescence, young people begin to experiment with risky behaviors, including delinquency and using tobacco, alcohol, and other drugs. These problems are especially likely among those who are aggressive, who have increasing problems keeping up in school, and who often experience social rejection from peers. These troubled young people tend to join up to form deviant peer groups. One study (Dishion et al. 1996) found that these deviant peer groups are the "training ground" in which most forms of adolescent problem behavior are learned.

Unfortunately, both the physical development of young people at this age and the transition to the less sheltered environment of middle school give many parents the sense that their kids don't need as much guidance as they did when they were younger. And children in coercive families may be particularly skilled in punishing their parents' attempts to guide them, often resulting in these kids being free to roam the neighborhood and hang out with whomever they want.

Thus, nurturance is as important in early adolescence as in earlier stages of a child's development, though the details are a bit different at this stage. Families still need to minimize coercive interactions that involve criticism, yelling, and harsh punishment. Such interactions diminish parents' ability to influence early adolescents, especially in limiting their involvement in risky behavior outside the home. And reinforcement is just as important as it was when the child was younger. Parents' warm involvement with the child maintains their influence, and because it maintains communication, it enables parents to better understand what is going on in parts of the child's life that they can't directly observe. Limiting early adolescents' opportunities to engage in problem behavior becomes particularly important at this time, when such opportunities escalate.

Finally, psychological flexibility is important. Recall that psychological flexibility involves pursuing our values even when our thoughts and feelings seem to function as obstacles to such actions. For the parents of early adolescents, this often means noticing worrisome, negative thoughts they have about their children without succumbing to those thoughts. For example, a father may have the thought that his daughter isn't doing her schoolwork, but rather than nagging her about it and communicating that he doesn't think she is a good student, it may be more useful to redouble his efforts to be positively involved with her. If this seems a bit preachy, I assure you that I wish I'd had this advice when my boys were in early adolescence.

The Family Check-Up

One of the most efficient and effective interventions for families with young teens is the Family Check-Up. It was developed by Tom Dishion, Kate Kavanagh, and Beth Stormshak at Oregon Social Learning Center and, later, at the University of Oregon. They originally created a twelve-session program for groups of parents, which was beneficial in improving parents' effectiveness (Dishion and Andrews 1995). In an independent evaluation of the program, my colleagues and I found that it improved parents' ability to discuss problems with their children, reduced their tendency to overreact punitively or to be lax in their discipline, and improved their feelings toward their children (Irvine et al. 1999). The result was a reduction in antisocial behavior among children whose parents were in the program.

Despite the program's benefits, it proved difficult to get parents to attend twelve sessions. Moreover, the intervention was expensive to provide and reached only a fraction of the parents who might benefit from it. For these reasons, Dishion, Kavanagh, and Stormshak developed a brief, three-session checkup to help individual families. In addition, it was designed to be nonstigmatizing and could be used by any family, regardless of whether they were having problems. Parents didn't have to be incompetent or admit to being incompetent to get assistance. After all, even healthy people get a checkup.

This streamlined version of the Family Check-Up was offered to all parents with children in a series of middle schools in Oregon. A trained parent consultant worked with school administrators to make parents aware of the program. In the first session, the parent consultant befriended the family and began to learn about how parents were handling common problems and what their concerns were. The second session was a home visit during which the consultant made a video of the parents discussing common issues with their middle school student. In the third session, parents got feedback that emphasized the good things they were doing and received suggestions for how they could improve their handling of issues they had expressed concern about. If parents felt the need for additional assistance, they were offered two or three more sessions that focused on how to use reinforcement to promote positive behavior, how to monitor the child's behavior and set limits, and how to improve family communication and problem solving (Dishion et al. 2002).

One of the most common issues for families involves monitoring and setting limits on activities that could cause young teens to get into difficulties. During this stage of development, young adolescents begin to spend more time with peers. In a series of studies, Dishion and his colleagues showed that when parents failed to monitor what their young teen was doing, the youngster was much more likely to get involved in delinquency and substance use (Dishion, Nelson, and Bullock 2004). For this reason, parent consultants encourage parents to monitor where and how their children spent their time after school, and if and when they completed their schoolwork. Parents were encouraged to increase their use of rewards for desired behavior. Often this simply amounted to requiring that their kids do chores and schoolwork before watching TV or playing video games.

Dishion and his colleagues evaluated the program in a randomized trial in three Oregon middle schools and demonstrated its efficacy for a large and ethnically diverse sample of sixth-grade children (Dishion, Nelson, and Bullock 2004). The program significantly increased parents' monitoring and reduced family conflict. When these young people were eighteen, the program—which was delivered only in middle school—helped prevent them from using alcohol, tobacco, or marijuana and made it much less likely they had been arrested (Connell et al. 2007). Another study (Connell and Dishion 2006) found that the program prevented depression in a subgroup of high-risk middle-schoolers. Finally, a study of a subsample of children whose parents were not monitoring their children's activities at the beginning of the study found that the Family Check-Up significantly improved parents' monitoring and that those improvements helped prevent their children from using substances (Dishion, Nelson, and Kavanagh 2003).

Helping Delinquent Adolescents

The family interventions I've been describing show how valuable effective behavioral programs can be in preventing young people from developing common problems. Our society's failure to provide such programs allows a significant number of young people to end up with the kinds of problems that Matthew Shepard's assailants, Russell Henderson and Aaron McKinney, had.

But it is never too late. Using the same principles that underlie all of the programs I've described so far, family researchers have developed interventions that can help families even when an adolescent is already involved in problem behavior. Here too the basic principles of nurturance apply:

- Minimize conflict and coercion

- Teach, promote, and richly reinforce prosocial behavior

- Limit influences and opportunities for problem behavior

- Promote the psychologically flexible pursuit of important values

Two of the best programs for families with troubled adolescents are Multidimensional Treatment Foster Care, which was developed by Patti Chamberlain at Oregon Social Learning Center (Chamberlain 2003; Fisher and Chamberlain 2000), and Multisystemic Therapy (MST; Henggeler et al. 2009), developed by Scott Henggeler at the Family Services Research Center at the Medical University of South Carolina. Both programs have been evaluated in randomized controlled trials, which showed that they significantly reduce further delinquent behavior and do so at considerable savings to taxpayers and crime victims. Indeed for every dollar spent on Multidimensional Treatment Foster Care, more than five dollars is saved in taxpayer, victim, and health care costs (Aos et al. 2011). For Multisystemic Therapy, the benefit is about four dollars for every dollar spent on the program (Aos et al. 2011).

One of the most skilled, passionate, and caring practitioners of Multisystemic Therapy is Philippe Cunningham. I met Philippe when I organized a symposium on family interventions at a meeting of the Association for Behavior Analysis. I'd learned about Multisystemic Therapy a year earlier when I attended a presentation by Scott Henggeler, the developer of the program. Scott couldn't be on my symposium but said Philippe would be great. Scott had emphasized how hard their family therapists worked to establish trust and rapport with families. He told me a story about one of their therapists paying a first visit to a very poor backwoods family whose son had been repeatedly arrested. When the therapist went into the home, the house reeked with an almost unbearable odor. The therapist's first act was to get under the house, where he discovered a dead and rotting possum, which he removed and buried. I told that same story when I introduced Philippe at the symposium. He then told us that he was that therapist.

The work of Philippe and his colleagues illustrates an important general principle: In order to help threatened, angry people, you have to care for them. This is such a contrast to how society in general tends to blame and punish people for their misdeeds and the misdeeds of their children. A public official faced with the horrendous acts of Russell Henderson and Aaron McKinney would think twice about expressing any sympathy for their families. Yet as a practical matter, the most effective way to help such families change is to find ways to befriend them.

Still, doing so can be challenging. In a family where conflict and child abuse are rife, how do you think parents would react to someone knocking on their door and saying he was there to do something about their delinquent child? In Multisystemic Therapy, the therapist's first priority is to get around parents' anger, hostility, and fear and to establish at least a glimmer of trust. In one case, therapists were trying to meet with a family that lived in a rural home at the end of a long gravel driveway. Every time they drove up to the house, the family took off through the back door and fled into the woods. Family members could hear their car coming up the road. Pragmatists that these therapists were, they decided to park out on the highway, walk up the side of the driveway, and knock on the door. When the family answered their knock on the door, the therapists offered them a plate of cookies. Fear transformed into trust, and they started working together.

Philippe, who is African-American, tells the story of a hostile white father in rural South Carolina whose son had been arrested. Philippe told the father that he could help him with his son's behavior. The man said, "No nigger gonna help me with my family." Philippe's immediate reply was "Black folks been helping white folks for hundreds of years."

Both of these programs—Multisystemic Therapy and Multidimensional Treatment Foster Care—work by implementing the four basic principles of nurturance. They greatly increase reinforcement of young people for doing the things they need to do. For example, Multidimensional Treatment Foster Care provides foster parents with training and supervision in implementing a contingency management system where the youth earns rewards for doing chores, attending school, doing homework, and being home on time. Both programs help families replace punitive, angry methods of trying to deal with youth misbehavior with consistent use of more mild consequences, such as the loss of points or assignment of a chore. In addition, they help families do a better job of monitoring what teens are doing to keep them from hanging out with teens who are involved in drug use or delinquency.

Both programs also encourage a flexible, pragmatic approach to parenting. Parents are asked to accept that parenting can be challenging and think about their values for seeing their adolescent develop successfully. Philippe once described a mother he worked with who was addicted to drugs and neglecting her child. He got her to agree to shoot up only after she had put her child to bed. This might not strike you as the ideal situation, but it was an arrangement that improved the child's well-being while also prompting the mother's first step toward becoming more nurturing.

Action Implications

We still have things to learn about how to help families be more nurturing. We need to reduce children's exposure to biological toxins, especially lead (Binns, Campbell, and Brown 2006), and to reduce their consumption of processed foods (Nestle 2002) and foods high in omega-6 fatty acids, which promote obesity, aggression, and depression (Hibbeln et al. 2006). We also need to do more to incorporate principles of psychological flexibility into work with families (Jones, Whittingham, and Coyne, forthcoming).

But we do know enough that if we can make existing programs widely available, we can help millions of families throughout the world. The result will be fewer families breaking up, less child abuse, fewer children who fail in school, and less crime and drug abuse. Many more children will become caring, creative, and productive members of society. Here are specific things that parents, policy makers, and citizens can do to translate all that we have learned into nurturing environments for more young people.

For Parents

- Carolyn Webster-Stratton's book *The Incredible Years* (1992) provides a great deal of helpful guidance about parenting.

- Some of the early behavioral work with children used rather authoritarian language that suggested parents should establish "command compliance." However, research is very clear in showing that it is essential to follow the child's lead, in the way Georgia does with Ashlyn.

  - If your children are young, get down on the floor and play with them. Let them take the lead. These are opportunities to build warm and cooperative relationships. Every interaction is an opportunity to teach them about their world. Give your children many choices so you build their skills at managing their own behavior.

- For older children, notice whether you listen to them or tend to lead the conversation, telling them what you think they should do and believe. Trust that they have the right instincts and, through patient, empathic listening, notice how frequently they arrive at conclusions similar to your own.

- Richly reinforce the development of your child's skills, using reinforcers beyond stickers, treats, and praise. Those can be valuable, especially when children have trouble learning a new behavior. But nearly every interaction between adults and children provides consequences for children's behavior. Your attention, your listening, your interest in them, your time spent playing with them—all are vital to their development. Although some behaviorists suggest providing four positive reactions to children for every negative reaction, that seems stingy to me. If you count simply listening to them or playing with them as positives, shouldn't we do much more than that? Keep in mind that simply telling a child to do something he wasn't already doing (such as "Pick up your toys" or "Time to go to bed") is negative for most children most of the time. How would you feel if your coworkers or friends criticized you or demanded something of you once for every four times they listened to you or praised you?

- Structure, monitor, and set limits. You can prevent much problem behavior by proactively arranging for and richly reinforcing alternative positive behaviors:

  - Give choices wherever possible. It is so much more effective to say, "Would you like to walk to the car or have me carry you to the car?" than "I want you to get in the car."

  - Keep track of what your children are doing and guide them away from risky situations and activities.

  - Use consistent, mild negative consequences when all else fails. Learn how to give simple, brief time-outs rather than getting angry, criticizing, or scolding. You needn't lecture your children about what they did wrong or what they should do next time.

For Policy Makers

- Require the use of evidence-based programs. I hope I have convinced you to explore the tested and effective programs that can significantly reduce the level of psychological and behavioral problems that are so costly to communities, state, and nation. The Institute of Medicine report on prevention, *Preventing Mental, Emotional, and Behavioral Disorders Among Young People: Progress and Possibilities* (IOM and NRC 2009), describes numerous evidence-based programs.

- Investigate the cost-benefit ratio of interventions. Most of these programs save much more money than they cost. *Return on Investment: Evidence-Based Options to Improve Statewide Outcomes* (Aos et al. 2011) carefully analyzes the costs and benefits of many programs and indicates that most offer a significant return on investment.

For Citizens

- Advocate for evidence-based programs. A large constituency isn't yet lobbying for prevention. If you want to see your city have much less crime, drug abuse, teen pregnancy, and academic failure, you can advocate that policy makers learn about the evidence-based family programs that can be made available to those who need them.

CHAPTER 3

Nurturing Schools

.

I still remember the day I took my son Michael to his first day of first grade. I had a feeling of helplessness. If kids picked on him or his teacher disliked him, what could I do? Would I even know about it?

Imagine that you have done a great job in the first years of your child's life and have a healthy, socially skilled, and highly verbal child. But then you must send her to school. Her fate is no longer in your hands alone. If her school is highly punitive, if it allows children to bully one another, or if its teachers are incompetent, this could scar your child for life.

Fortunately, schools are getting better. That might come as a surprise, given repeated reports about children in the United States lagging behind children in other countries in math and science, and considering the amount of bullying and violence we hear about in US schools. But I am convinced that educational researchers' progress in understanding how schools can become more nurturing and how to teach effectively is beginning to spread into schools throughout the country. In this chapter, I will tell you about research-based methods for teaching positive social behavior and academic skills that schools across the country are adopting.

Nurturing Prosocial Behavior

The principles underlying how schools can help children and adolescents develop positive social behavior are the same as those for families. Schools need to minimize coercive and punitive interactions. They must teach, promote, and richly reinforce prosocial behavior. They also need to monitor students' behavior so they can tell what is working to encourage prosocial and academic behavior and modify what isn't.

Minimizing Coercion

When behaviorists began to observe how students and teachers interact in classrooms, they discovered that teachers paid more attention to problem students than to others. It is natural for a teacher to tell a student who gets out of his seat to sit down. The student often complies, so the teacher is reinforced when the student stops his disruptive behavior.

Unfortunately, what also happens is that the teacher's attention reinforces the student's unwanted behavior. As a result, the student gets out of his seat more often. As his misbehavior increases, the teacher gets increasingly frustrated and angry—and so does the student. This is the same kind of coercive process that Jerry Patterson discovered in families (Patterson 1982), as discussed in chapter 2.

Skilled teachers have learned to reinforce desired behavior more than disruptive behavior. They do it by praising, paying attention to, and rewarding cooperative and on-task behavior and ignoring minor disruptions. In the absence of this kind of skilled teaching, high levels of conflict can develop. Humans are quick to learn to punish each other because, as Patterson showed, when you do something aversive to someone who is annoying you, the other person often stops. That immediately reinforces whatever you did to get the person to stop, but in the long run it isn't effective in reducing unwanted behavior. Rather, it evolves into an increasingly punitive environment.

Left unmanaged, schools can become like prisons, where everyone is on guard and angry. An example is the Birmingham, Alabama, school district, which authorized police to use pepper spray in schools. By some reports, more than one hundred students have been pepper-sprayed. In one incident, a girl who was four months pregnant was arguing with a boy who was harassing her. As they were beginning to go their own ways, a police officer handcuffed her and told her to calm down. When she said she was calm, he pepper-sprayed her, causing her to throw up.

Escalating punishment is usually counterproductive. Roy Mayer, a school psychologist at California State University, provided dramatic evidence of this (Mayer 1995). He showed that schools with lots of rules and punishment have *higher* levels of misbehavior and vandalism. As is the case for so many other problems in society, our natural penchant for punishing each other is neither effective nor consistent with humane values.

Promoting Prosocial Behavior

One of the greatest problems educational researchers have faced is how to help teachers move from escalating punishment to using positive reinforcement to nurture prosocial behavior. Over the past five decades, significant progress has taken place. Three good examples of it are the Good Behavior Game, Positive Behavioral Intervention and Support, and the Positive Action program.

The Good Behavior Game

One of the most important developments in using reinforcement to promote cooperation and self-regulation began with Muriel Saunders, a fourth-grade teacher in Kansas in the 1960s, who was at her wits' end due to students' disruptive behavior. Prevention scientist Dennis Embry, who knew Muriel when he was at the University of Kansas, shared her story with me:

> Muriel taught in a small town of less than four thousand souls: Baldwin, Kansas. The other fourth-grade teachers had skimmed off all the "good" kids, leaving her the challenge of a lifetime. Fortunately for her, her students, and the world, she succeeded in creating a strategy that is bringing extraordinary benefits to students throughout the world.
>
> Muriel's story begins in the mid-1960s, when she got a teaching job while her husband was going to graduate school in nearby Lawrence, Kansas, the home of the world-famous Department of Human Development at the University of Kansas. By Thanksgiving, Muriel had become so frustrated with her classroom that she was ready to quit on the spot. But she decided to give it one more go after

talking to her husband's doctoral advisor, Dr. Montrose Wolf. One of Dr. Wolf's other graduate students was Harriet Barrish, who was very interested in studying the impact of behavioral psychology in the classroom, so she joined their cramped but urgent meeting.

Dr. Wolf, always searching for solutions, asked if the class ever behaved better. Muriel initially said no. After a bit of probing, Dr. Wolf asked her if there might be some task or activity in which their behavior was better. "Ah," pondered Muriel, "they do act better and get rather excited when we have a team spelling bee." Dr. Wolf nodded and then said, "Well, perhaps you could make a team contest for being good?"

So they did. They created multiple teams of students. Each team could win a reward for working cooperatively for brief periods of time. Rewards were as simple and inexpensive as an extra five minutes of recess. It was also a soft competition; all teams could win. As teams got better, the length of time the game was played was extended.

In order to evaluate whether the game—now known as the Good Behavior Game—made a difference, Harriet Barrish organized an experiment (Barrish, Saunders, and Wolf 1969). She trained observers to sit in the classroom during math and reading and record all the things that would drive a teacher crazy and disrupt learning, such as students getting out of their seats and talking during lessons.

As you can see from figure 2, prior to their introduction to the game, students were getting out of their seats and talking disruptively most of the time. Then they implemented the Good Behavior Game during the students' math period but not during reading. As you can see, there was a dramatic reduction in the kids' disruptive behavior. When they stopped playing the game in math (indicated by "Rev." in the figure), disruptions skyrocketed. Then they implemented the game during both reading and math, and disruption virtually ended. (You can read a thorough account of the study online; refer to Barrish, Saunders, and Wolf 1969 in the References section for details.)

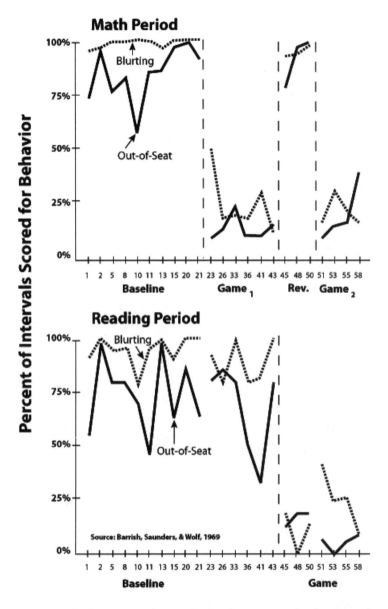

Figure 2. Graph from Muriel Saunders's classroom. The horizontal axis indicates minutes of class time. (Reprinted with permission from H. S. Barrish, M. Saunders, and M. M. Wolf. 1969. "Good Behavior Game: Effects of Individual Contingencies for Group Consequences on Disruptive Behavior in a Classroom. *Journal of Applied Behavior Analysis* 2: 119–124.)

Since the invention of the Good Behavior Game, more than fifty studies around the world have evaluated it (for example, Ialongo et al. 1999; Leflot et al. 2013). These studies showed that, in all kinds of classroom settings, the game motivated children to work together cooperatively and reduced student behaviors that disrupted learning and distressed teachers. But could such a simple game have any lasting benefit?

Shep Kellam, a psychiatrist at Johns Hopkins University, thought it could. He was looking for a way to improve children's social competence and thought it was possible to prevent even fairly serious problems by simply making sure that children develop the ability to cooperate with teachers and get along with their peers. When one of his behavior analyst colleagues brought the Good Behavior Game to his attention, he thought it might be just what he needed. Twenty years later, it is clear that it succeeded beyond his wildest dreams.

Shep Kellam is one of the more interesting characters I've met in my journeys and one of the few psychiatrists in the prevention science community. Thanks to that and the fact that he has been prominent for a long time, he has played a major role in getting prevention science the research support required to show its value. Like Skinnerian behaviorism, the field of prevention science has succeeded because a small number of people were inspired by a vision of what the field could do, long before there was any evidence to confirm that vision.

Kellam's first major contribution was the Woodlawn Study (C. H. Brown, Adams, and Kellam 1981; Kellam et al. 1983), which focused on the Woodlawn neighborhood just south of the University of Chicago. In 1966, he began studying a group of African-American children to see if he could figure out what influenced some children to develop psychological and behavioral problems, such as depression, drug abuse, and criminal activities, and what protected others from the same fate. Studies like this are commonplace now and have revealed an enormous amount about what leads young people to develop these problems. But when the Woodlawn Study began, there was virtually no precedent for the idea that you can learn what influences problem development through a *longitudinal study*—research that assesses people multiple times over the course of years. Kellam and his team of researchers recruited 1,242 African-American families of first-grade students. The families agreed to let them assess these children repeatedly, and Shep Kellam and his wife, Peg Ensminger, ultimately followed these young people to age thirty-two. They found that aggressive children were more likely to use drugs by adulthood, and that low family socioeconomic status and loss of interest in school were associated with substance abuse (Fothergill et al. 2008).

By the time Kellam moved to Johns Hopkins in 1982, he was already famous (well, as famous goes among behavioral scientists). Perhaps for this reason, and because of what he had learned from working with the famed community organizer Saul Alinsky, he was able to get an incredible level of cooperation from the Baltimore school system for testing the impact of the Good Behavior Game on the development of elementary school students. He wanted to see if it could prevent kids from developing academic, social, and behavioral problems; and to do that, he needed to conduct a randomized controlled trial.

Kellam convinced the school district to randomly assign first- and second-grade teachers to classrooms, and then randomly assign classrooms to one of three conditions: using the Good Behavior Game, following a curriculum called mastery learning (an evidence-based teaching strategy), or not receiving a special intervention. This randomization meant that kids who got the Good Behavior Game were pretty much the same as the kids who didn't. Because of randomization, any differences between the groups—whether one, five, or even fifteen years later—was very likely to be due to the Good Behavior Game.

What Kellam and his colleagues found was extraordinary. During the year of the intervention, he had observers go into classrooms and code what they saw. In the Good Behavior Game classrooms, students were on task and cooperative. In the control classrooms (both mastery learning and no special intervention), some skilled teachers had classes that were on task and working well. But most classrooms in the control condition were scenes of chaos. Children were wandering around the room and not paying much attention to the teacher. Very little learning was taking place.

Kellam and his crew followed the kids into sixth grade to see if there were any lasting effects of the game. He found that those who had played the Good Behavior Game in first or second grade were much less likely to face arrest or become smokers (Kellam et al. 1998).

Then, through extraordinary efforts of his research team, they followed these children into adulthood (Kellam et al. 2008). What they discovered may be the single most impressive finding in the annals of prevention science. The kids who had played the game—only for one year, in either the first or second grade—were less likely to be addicted to drugs or suicidal and had committed fewer crimes. An independent analysis of the economic benefit of this intervention indicated that for every dollar spent on the Good Behavior Game, about eighty-four dollars could be saved through reduced special education, victim, health care, and criminal justice costs (Aos et al. 2012; WSIPP 2014).

Think about the lives that this simple game changed. Among the boys who were aggressive in first grade and did not play the Good Behavior Game, 83 percent were addicted to drugs as adults. But among the aggressive boys who played the Good Behavior Game, only 29 percent had drug addiction problems. Given that drug addicts are more likely to die prematurely (Nyhlén et al. 2011), we can safely say that this simple game saved lives.

Positive Behavioral Intervention and Support

Other heroes of prevention science are also working in schools. Education researchers Rob Horner and George Sugai developed a schoolwide system for supporting students' positive behavior, called Positive Behavioral Intervention and Support (PBIS), and it is bringing peace and a nurturing environment to schools around the world. At last count, more than fifteen thousand schools nationwide have implemented the program.

Horner and Sugai both initially worked with severely developmentally delayed young people with serious behavior problems, including very destructive behavior. Their approach usually involved setting up a program to increase reinforcement for desirable behavior and curtail it for problem behavior. But before you can curtail reinforcement for a problem behavior, you have to figure out what the reinforcers are. To do this, they developed a functional behavioral assessment to determine the purposes of specific problem behaviors.

The two most important consequences of problem behavior are escaping from an unpleasant task and getting attention from teachers or other students. If a student becomes angry and disrespectful during a lesson, it may be because she can't do the work; and in the past, angry reactions have typically gotten her sent to the office, allowing her to escape from the task. If the student doesn't have the skills to do the work, it will do little good to increase rewards for doing it. Thus, one of the key ways to prevent the development of behavior problems in schools is make sure instruction is effective.

If attention from teachers or other students seems to reinforce a student's misbehavior, the remedy is to reduce attention for misbehavior and increase attention for desired behavior. That might involve increased attention and praise when the student works appropriately. It could also include a system for providing daily reports to parents about their child's successes so that both parents and teachers can reward these efforts.

Horner and Sugai found that their programs usually worked in the short run. However, it was difficult to maintain the benefits. Moreover, concentrating efforts on the kids who were most out of control didn't prevent other kids, who were getting less attention, from developing problems. They realized they needed a school-wide system.

Influenced by Roy Mayer's (1995) finding that slow escalation of rules and punishment for violations as a response to student misbehavior only further motivated student rebellion, they sought to help schools reduce the number of rules and increase positive reinforcement for following rules. To this end, a team of PBIS teachers developed a small set of simple rules for the school, such as "Be respectful," "Be safe," and "Be responsible." Staff members then taught what these rules meant in every venue in the school. For example, being respectful in a classroom meant listening to what the teacher was saying and treating other students courteously.

The resulting PBIS systems have been evaluated in randomized trials in which some schools engage in PBIS, while others don't. In Maryland, where PBIS is in the process of being implemented in every school, a study by Catherine Bradshaw and her colleagues (2009) found that elementary schools that had already introduced PBIS had fewer suspensions and discipline referrals than those that hadn't. In Illinois, another randomized trial showed that students in elementary schools that implemented PBIS had better academic performance than students in other schools (Horner et al. 2009).

PBIS is an effective system for reducing harassment and bullying. One report (Sugai, Horner, and Algozzine 2011) describes how the system helps create an environment that promotes positive social behavior among students and provides extra positive behavioral support for students who engage in bullying or harassment. In an early evaluation of this system that I was involved in (Metzler et al. 2001), we found that implementing PBIS in a middle school significantly reduced male students' discipline referrals for harassment and increased the proportion of students who said they felt safe in school.

Positive Action

The proliferation of randomized controlled trials of interventions in schools has proved threatening to people who have unevaluated programs. I often hear comments like "I know our program works. We don't have the money to do the research on it, but I'm sure it works." Many researchers, including me, have been skeptical. After all, we are committed to the proposition that science is essential to improving human well-being. The feeling among many researchers is that much of what is being done in the way of school or family interventions hasn't been evaluated, and that some of what has been evaluated has turned out to be useless or even harmful. Meanwhile, over the last thirty years or so researchers have been conducting randomized controlled trials that have identified more effective interventions. Researchers have often seethed at practitioners' resistance to adopting evidence-based interventions, and frequently haven't been very sympathetic or polite toward those who aren't researchers but are sincerely trying to make a difference in people's lives.

One prevention program specialist I know found a unique solution to this problem: she married a researcher. Carol Allred developed a school-wide program called Positive Action in the 1980s and 1990s. She developed curricula for classrooms, materials for parents, a counselor program, and a community program, all designed to help schools and communities replace punitive practices with a culture that promotes positive actions on the part of children and the adults around them. Then, in 1998, she attended the Society for Prevention Research meeting in Park City, Utah, where she met Brian Flay, one of the most prominent methodologists in the behavioral sciences. They fell in love with each other, and Brian fell in love with Carol's program. He was convinced that it was a great program, although it lacked studies to prove it. So he did what any good methodologist would do: he evaluated it.

Brian and his colleagues conducted two randomized trials of Positive Action in elementary and middle school grades; a third trial was done independently of his work. In all three trials, Positive Action had a beneficial effect in reducing the decline in prosocial behavior that is frequently found across the elementary school years (Washburn et al. 2011). PA has also proven beneficial in preventing the development of problems as diverse as substance use, disruptive behavior, bullying, violence, and delinquency (Beets et al. 2009; Lewis et al. 2012; Lewis, Schure et al. 2013), as well as depression (Lewis, DuBois et al. 2013). Additional analyses have shown that Positive Action prevents these problems because it nurtures prosocial norms and behavior (Lewis et al. 2012; Snyder et al. 2013).

Many educators resist implementing programs that are focused on improving social behavior because they feel they must concentrate on enhancing academic achievement. But this is a false choice. Children's interest and ability to learn is enhanced in an environment where they feel safe, have cooperative peers, and receive a lot of positive reinforcement. In the case of Positive Action, evaluations show that schools that implement the program have improved school climate (Snyder et al. 2012) and do better academically. In the randomized trial in Hawaii, Positive Action significantly improved reading and math performance compared with schools that didn't get the program (Snyder et al. 2010). Beneficial effects on reading and math achievement were also found in the randomized trial that was done in Chicago (Bavarian et al. 2013).

Monitoring Behavior

It is easy to see the value of replacing coercive interactions with systems that teach and reinforce prosocial behavior. What may be less obvious is that effective programs include systems for monitoring their impact on students' behavior. For example, in the Good Behavior Game teachers count the number of disruptions and use this information to tell if the game is having its expected effect. Likewise, Positive Behavioral Intervention and Support utilizes a web-based system for recording discipline problems in every venue of the school. This helps staff identify places where extra attention is needed. In order to be sure programs are nurturing desired behavior, they must include a means of measuring their effectiveness.

Creating Schools That Nurture Prosocial Behavior

With their development of the Positive Action program, Allred and Flay provide a particularly striking example of how scientists and practitioners are working together to encourage the nurturance of prosocial behavior. But there are many others. Just as fights among people in different subfields of the behavioral sciences are diminishing, the split between researchers and practitioners is closing as evidence about what young people need becomes more definitive. A growing community of educators, family practitioners, and researchers is coming together to spread positive methods for nurturing students' prosocial behavior. To me, this is one of the most encouraging developments in education in the last fifty years.

The programs I have described are important early steps in the evolution of a more caring and effective culture. Like the family programs I described in chapter 2, they replace coercive and punitive ways of trying to control young people's behavior with more effective, proactive methods of structuring environments to teach and reinforce prosocial behavior and critical academic skills, and they minimize situations that encourage problem behavior. The number of schools that have implemented PBIS (fifteen thousand) is far fewer than the number of schools in the United States (over one hundred thousand), but it is the beginning of a movement that is gaining momentum as evidence for the benefit of these more nurturing strategies accumulates and becomes more widely understood.

Much more publicity goes to dramatic and rare events like school shootings—which, by the way, happen more frequently in states with more punitive schools (Arcus 2002). But slowly and quietly, positive methods like the Good Behavior Game, Positive Action, and Positive Behavioral Intervention and Support are taking hold throughout the country. As they spread and replace punitive practices, we can be confident that more students will learn to cooperate, restrain impulsive behavior, and regulate their emotions. Fewer children will face bullying and harassment. Given the results of the Good Behavior Game in Baltimore, it is likely that as these methods spread, rates of crime, depression, drug abuse, and academic failure will decline dramatically.

Teaching Children Well: The Importance of an Evidence-Based Approach

Even the most socially skilled, prosocial young people will fail to become productive adults if they aren't taught well. Moreover, as noted above, deficits in a student's academic skills can be at the root of behavior problems. If we are going to construct a society in which everyone is both productive and caring, we need schools that make sure that every student learns and loves to learn.

However, year after year, American students do poorly in comparison to students in many other countries. The Trends in International Mathematics and Science Study assesses math and science skills among fourth- and eighth-grade students around the world. In 2007, US eighth-graders did worse in math than students in Taipei, Hong Kong, Japan, Korea, and Singapore (Gonzales et al. 2008). American fourth-graders also did poorly in math compared with students in eight other countries, including the Russian Federation. US eighth-graders did worse in science than those in eight other countries, including Hungary, the Czech Republic, Slovenia, and the Russian Federation.

It isn't that all schools in the United States are doing a poor job. In more affluent communities and neighborhoods, students are doing just as well as the top students in Singapore, the world leader in math and science. Rather, the problem lies in America's failure to ensure high-quality education in high-poverty schools. The US Department of Education reported that nine-year-olds in high-poverty schools are more than three grade levels behind students in low-poverty schools in reading and more than two grade levels behind in math (Perie, Moran, and Lutkus 2005).

These disparities parallel racial and ethnic differences in academic achievement. Black and Hispanic students, on average, do significantly less well than white students (National Center for Education Statistics 2014). Of course, there is a correlation between poverty and ethnicity. I think it is more important to focus on poverty than on race or ethnicity for two reasons. First, focusing on race or ethnicity tends to be stigmatizing and divisive. Second, poverty is something we can change. I will discuss this further in chapter 8. Here, I want to tell you about teaching methods that can overcome the educational disadvantages that face so many children living in poverty.

Conflicting Visions

Although I have done only one study evaluating a curricular intervention (Gunn et al. 2000), I have followed developments in education closely. To me, the progress in education research is another facet of the behavioral revolution that began with Skinner's insistence that human behavior is a function of the environment and that by creating the right kind of environments we can build a better society. However, progress in the improvement of teaching has been slow, owing to the just-mentioned lack of commitment to experimental evaluations and to the dominance of the philosophy of discovery learning.

Discovery Learning

The main idea of discovery learning is highly plausible: children learn best when we let them determine their own pace of learning, deciding when they want to learn new things. Educators who favor this approach argue that children who are systematically taken through a structured curriculum that organizes what is to be learned in the most efficient sequence are being regimented, and that such regimentation will kill their love of learning.

This vision fits with some of the experience that most of us had in school. Weren't there many times when you were bored to tears in school? Wouldn't it have been great if most of your learning had involved the excited pursuit of new knowledge, without being told what to study or when? Indeed, schools such as Sudbury Valley School in Massachusetts allow students to determine what they want to learn and when they want to learn it, and a study of these schools (Gray 2013) documented the considerable success of their (mostly middle-class) students.

But there have also been some significant disasters, such as the whole-language movement. According to the whole-language philosophy, phonics instruction, in which children learn how to sound out words, is unnecessary. Instead, whole-language proponents believe children can learn to read by figuring out the meaning of words from their context. Given that you have gotten this far in my book, you are already a competent reader. But see if you can infer the missing words in the following sentence: "The _____ came running up to the door, _____ all the way."

Absent any empirical evidence of the effectiveness of the whole-language approach, its advocates convinced the state of California to abandon phonics instruction and embrace whole language. The number of children who couldn't read soared. Bonnie Grossen, a friend of mine who is an expert in the direct instruction methods I describe below, spent a couple of years helping the Sacramento school system provide remedial reading instruction in middle schools because so few of the children could read well. More generally, reviews and meta-analyses of the effects of discovery learning do not support its efficacy (Alfieri et al. 2011), particularly for children in need of special education (Fuchs et al. 2008).

Direct Instruction

Unfortunately, as mentioned, many educators are not yet convinced that they should pay attention to empirical research. Therefore, discovery learning advocates have been able to convince them that structured, direct teaching of skills and concepts undermines children's ability to think and that children hate it. That was certainly not our experience when both of our sons learned to read and developed terrific math skills thanks to direct instruction. I would love to take all the credit for this—that it was all the encouragement we provided, or perhaps our "superior genes." But the main reason for their success was the system of direct instruction that my wife, Georgia, had become skilled in.

By the time Michael was four, Georgia had taught him to count and do simple arithmetic. Georgia had received training in direct instruction (DI), a systematic method of developing and delivering curricula. She had a workbook for DI arithmetic at home and introduced Michael to it, and the next thing we knew, he was working through it by himself. We would get up in the morning and find him at the kitchen table doing arithmetic. He loved it!

We were extremely fortunate that the best first-grade teacher in the district, Pat Holland, taught at Parker Elementary School, just down the hill from our house. During teacher introductions at our first parent meeting, a loud whoop went up when Pat was introduced. When Michael started first grade, Pat quickly realized how advanced he was in math and got him into third-grade math. The head start he got in math carried him a long way. He was the mental math champion of Lane County in third grade and the city champion in fifth grade. By the time he finished high school, he had completed two years of college math. He then went to the University of Chicago, where he majored in economics and carried a 3.9 average in this math-heavy field. (Our son Sean showed similar gifts in math and finished a couple of years of college math while still in high school.)

Direct instruction is the brainchild of Siegfried Engelmann, Wesley Becker, and Doug Carnine, initially at the University of Illinois around the time I was a graduate student in psychology there. I can remember seeing Engelmann on the TV news fervently insisting that directly teaching poor preschool children what they needed to know could erase their academic disadvantages.

Engelmann developed his teaching methods by constantly testing everything he did to see if children were learning what was being taught. He discovered that children learned and remembered material best if they had frequent opportunities to give correct answers. A well-designed lesson can be highly reinforcing, not because students are getting rewards, but simply because they are frequently able to demonstrate their knowledge. DI often involves children learning in small groups where the group responds more than ten times per minute. This ensures that the teacher knows whether students are mastering the material so they can go back and work on things the children haven't learned well.

Direct instruction lessons are scripted, giving teachers little leeway in what they teach. This is one reason many teachers have resisted DI, complaining that it is too regimented and that children will be bored or stifled. But that is not the case. When DI is done properly, children enjoy lessons because they experience so much success in learning. And DI is very successful, especially in aiding the success of children who would otherwise fail.

What many teachers don't understand is that the scripting is done to ensure that concepts are taught as efficiently and effectively as possible, not as a way to constrain teachers. If you already understand a concept, you might not see how easily a child who doesn't understand it can be confused by a poorly constructed teaching sequence.

Take the word "under." You can try to teach a child who doesn't understand "under" by showing him a pencil under a table and saying, "The pencil is *under* the table." But without any negative examples— examples of what is not "under"—a child can be quite confused. Maybe "under" means pencils are in some way connected with tables; if you were to put the pencil above the table, the child may say that the pencil is under the table.

A DI sequence includes both negative examples and positive examples. Holding the pencil above the table, you would say, "The pencil is *not under* the table." And to be sure that the child doesn't infer that "under" is about pencils below tables, these irrelevant features of the concept are eliminated in other examples: "The ball is *under* the blanket." "The shoe is *not under* the bed." By carefully sequencing positive and negative examples of concepts, DI ensures efficient instruction.

Research clearly indicates that DI methods are more effective than most other teaching techniques (Adams and Engelmann 1996). Beginning in the 1970s, DI methods were compared to numerous other methods of teaching, and DI outperformed all other approaches—including a discovery learning approach where students selected the tasks they wanted to engage in (Stebbins et al. 1977). DI even improved self-esteem more than a strategy that directly focused on increasing self-esteem. It turns out that children have higher self-esteem when they are experiencing the intrinsic reinforcement of learning new things, whereas trying to raise their self-esteem artificially in the absence of genuine success is useless.

As you might imagine, there have been plenty of examples of the power of evidence-based approaches to instruction. For example, Wesley Elementary School in Houston, Texas, consists almost entirely of poor minority students. Yet by implementing direct instruction, the school has virtually every child reading and doing math at grade level (Carter 2000).

The Emerging Consilience

Biologist E. O. Wilson (1998) has popularized the concept of *consilience*—the idea that evidence from different areas of science can converge in a unified understanding of a phenomenon. I see that happening in education.

For most of my career, the two visions of how children learn described above have been in conflict. I've been frustrated by resistance to the proven teaching methods that have arisen from the behaviorist tradition. I've seen firsthand how powerful these methods are and how our failure to use them has greatly harmed millions of American children. At the same time, I've come to see the wisdom of paying close attention to what children are interested in and following their lead. Too often, behavioral approaches to teaching have focused so much on teaching a skill that they ignore the fact that the child has lost interest in the learning task. Fortunately, it seems that people from each of these two camps are becoming a little less strident and finding ways to work together to improve the effectiveness of teaching methods.

What is emerging is an approach to education that is clear about the core knowledge and skills that children need to learn, that is accountable for achieving good outcomes for all children, and that intensely engages children while allowing them a sense of authenticity. The battles are receding between those who have labeled any highly structured effort to teach children as "drill and kill" and those who have been dismissive of children's need for choice and autonomy. Increasingly, teaching practices have their basis in empirical evidence showing that carefully designed instructional sequences can help at-risk children learn at a level they never could have achieved by waiting until they discovered what they needed to know. That said, there is also a wealth of evidence that children learn best when they have considerable choice and autonomy.

Research in middle schools also demonstrates the importance of engaging students in meaningful learning in contexts that richly reinforce their efforts. When schools are highly competitive, it undermines learning for its own sake. There is considerable evidence that early adolescents need a caring and noncompetitive learning environment that emphasizes mastery of school tasks over academic competition and where they feel highly regarded by teachers. In schools that emphasize competition as opposed to self-development, students are more likely to be depressed and angry, have lower self-esteem, value education less, and have lower grades (Roeser and Eccles 1998).

Achieving Effective Reform in Schools

Fortunately, due to growing consilience concerning educational methods, schools are increasingly becoming places that nurture both the social and the academic development of students through efficient and engaging instructional practices, minimization of punishment and situations that elicit problem behavior, respect for students' autonomy, and lots of reinforcement, both explicit and intrinsic.

Progress on this problem has begun to occur, prompted by a surprising source—the George W. Bush administration. Although the Bush administration ignored scientific evidence in many areas, it did more to bring science into education than any previous administration. Unlike the National Institutes of Health, which had been funding high-quality scientific research in the biological and behavioral sciences for many years, the Department of Education didn't previously have a strong commitment to funding rigorous research or using scientific evidence to guide the choice of teaching practices.

But under the Bush administration, the Department of Education created the Institute of Education Sciences, which funds careful experimental evaluations of teaching methods, as well as studies that shed light on how to get schools to adopt effective methods. The department's What Works Clearinghouse identifies teaching methods that have been proven more effective through randomized controlled trials and promotes the use of these methods. As effective teaching practices become more widely used, we can expect to see many more poor and minority children succeed in school.

One of the most important developments in this regard has been the creation of Common Core State Standards by the Council of Chief State School Officers and the National Governors Association Center for Best Practices. These standards define the key skills and knowledge that students need to have in mathematics, English language arts, history, and social studies. Forty-five states have adopted these standards, and they are collaborating on a set of common assessments that will measure how well students are doing on the skills and knowledge that are vital to their success and the well-being of their communities.

Some educators continue to be concerned that standardized testing will constrain what teachers teach and students learn—that we will "teach to the test." There are certainly reasons to be cautious about testing. In Atlanta, when incentives were placed on teachers to increase student performance, some teachers simply cheated (Copeland 2013).

However, do you doubt that it is a good thing if every child learns to read and do math? I think about the Bethel School District here in Eugene, Oregon, where over the past eight years the district has steadily increased the proportion of students who are performing at grade level and a decreased the disparity between performance of white and Hispanic children. I am confident that, given a choice, the families of at-risk children would choose to have their children be at or above grade level. But if the district had chosen not to measure students' performance, parents wouldn't even know whether their children were progressing.

At the same time, we should not lose sight of the fact that there is much more to human beings than test scores. I hope that, as schools improve, we get better at recognizing the valuable diversity among young people and the fact that they have skills, interests, values, and potential that standardized tests don't capture. Nurturing their development in these areas may prove as important to society as their scores on achievement tests.

Action Implications

I have briefly outlined key research-based teaching strategies that have proven benefit in helping children learn efficiently and develop self-regulation, social skills, and cooperativeness. Science shows that schools can be much more effective at helping our children achieve the social and academic skills they need. The next step is for these beneficial practices to be more widely adopted.

For Parents

- If you have a child who is four or five and interested in learning to read, I recommend using *Teach Your Child to Read in 100 Easy Lessons* (Engelmann, Haddox, and Bruner 1983). Georgia and I taught both of our sons to read with this book and our son Mike did the same with his daughter, Ashlyn.

- Be sure your child's school monitors your child's academic progress, and advocate for adjustments to teaching methods when warranted.

- If phonics-based methods aren't being used to teach reading, advocate for using phonics.

- If your child isn't at grade level in any subject, ask the school how it plans to remedy the situation.

- Make sure your child's school is implementing some form of school-wide positive behavioral support, such as Positive Behavioral Intervention and Support, Positive Action, or the Good Behavior Game. (You can learn more about the Good Behavior Game at http://www.goodbehaviorgame.org.)

- Use the principles outlined in this chapter to support your child's scholastic success:

  - Monitor and guide your child's progress in school.

  - Each day, ask your child about what is happening in school and listen to your child's reply.

  - Make sure your child does all assigned homework. Early on, establish routine times for doing homework. For example, you might require your child to do homework before enjoying "screen time."

  - If your child is having trouble with other students, bring it to the attention of teachers or other school officials and ask them what they will do to remedy the situation.

  - Reinforce your child's academic progress. For children who aren't doing well, it will be helpful to set up a system of rewards. For others, it may be enough to show interest in the child's work and your appreciation and pride in successes along the way.

- Establish a good relationship with your child's teachers.

  - Find, recognize, and express appreciation for the things teachers do for your child.

  - When you have a concern, be sure to raise it with the teacher, but do it with respect, care, and openness to the teacher's input.

- Consult the What Works Clearinghouse at http://www.ies.ed.gov /ncee/wwc for reliable information about effective teaching methods.

For Educators

- Make schools more nurturing by adopting one of the many evidence-based programs that have shown their benefit in enhancing self-regulation, cooperation, and prosociality.

- Use behavioral principles to shape behavior:

    - Reduce the use of punishment.

    - Teach a small number of clear rules and richly reinforce students for following them.

    - Richly reinforce positive behavior through recognition, rewards, and support of students' autonomy.

- Adopt evidence-based teaching methods. These include not only research-based instructional methods, but "response-to-intervention" methods in which frequent monitoring of children's progress guides adjustments in instructional methods in light of their success.

- Ensure that every child is reading at grade level by the end of third grade.

For Citizens

- Ask educators and policy makers whether they are monitoring the use of punishment and the incidence of bullying in schools.

- Advocate that educators and policy makers ensure implementation of evidence-based programs and practices, particularly in reducing punishment and bullying. Consult the What Works Clearinghouse.

- Recognize, praise, approve, and elect those who adopt these practices.

For Policy Makers

- Require that all schools monitor the extent of punishment (including detention, suspension, and expulsion) and bullying to ensure that both remain at a minimum.

- Require the implementation of evidence-based programs and practices shown to minimize punishment and conflict and promote prosocial behavior.

- Require the use of evidence-based teaching methods. Consult the What Works Clearinghouse.

- Require ongoing monitoring of students' academic progress—not just annual assessments, but response-to-intervention techniques that monitor learning progress at least weekly—and adjust teaching methods in response.

CHAPTER 4

Peers and Problems

Nurturing schools are vital to young people's prosocial development. However, as children reach adolescence they are developmentally more inclined to seek reinforcement from peers than from adults. So peer groups are the natural next topic in our exploration of how we can build a society that nurtures prosociality.

Deviancy Training

"So what would you do if your girlfriend got pregnant? Shoot her?"

"No, punch her in the stomach, real hard."

This conversation occurred in an observation room at Oregon Social Learning Center. Tom Dishion and his colleagues were trying to learn more about why some kids become delinquent. He and many other behavioral scientists knew that most adolescents who get in trouble do so with other adolescents. Delinquency is a group enterprise. But Dishion took the research a step further. He wanted to see if he could actually observe the social influence processes that motivate kids to defy adult expectations and engage in criminal acts. So he asked young men who were participating in a longitudinal study of delinquency to bring a friend into the lab and have a series of brief conversations about things like planning an activity or solving a problem with a parent or friend.

What he found was startling. The conversations these young men had about deviant activities provided direct and strong reinforcement of deviant behavior. Even though these thirteen- and fourteen-year-old boys knew their conversations were being observed and recorded, some of them talked quite freely about committing crimes, getting drunk, taking drugs, and victimizing girls. Even more surprising was the fact that the amount of this kind of talk predicted whether individuals engaged in delinquent behavior well into adulthood (Dishion et al. 1996).

You might think this occurred simply because adolescents who are already involved in problem behavior tend to talk more often about deviance. Maybe this topic was a by-product of their delinquent lifestyle and didn't influence their delinquent behavior. But that was not the case. It is true that young people's levels of problem behavior predict their future problem behavior. However, even when Dishion's team controlled statistically for the influence of prior deviant behavior, the level of deviancy talk in these thirty-minute videotaped discussions predicted adult antisocial behavior two years later (Dishion et al. 1996). The conversations escalated their deviant behavior.

Why would deviant talk lead to deviant behavior? And why did some kids talk about deviance while others didn't? The answer Dishion reached is the most interesting thing about his research, and it lines up with the information I've outlined about social interactions in families and schools: if you want to understand why people do things, look for the reinforcers. Dishion and his colleagues (1996) coded not only the deviant talk of these kids, but also the reactions of their friends. He simply coded deviant and nondeviant talk and two possible reactions to each statement: pause or laugh. They found that the more laughs a boy got for what he said, the more he talked about that topic. In pairs where most of the laughs followed deviant talk, there was a great increase in the deviant talk. In statistical terms, 84 percent of the variance in deviant talk related to the rate of laughter for deviant talk. That is huge.

Even more interesting was the fact that the rate of reinforcement for deviant talk strongly predicted later delinquency (Dishion et al. 1996). Boys whose friends approved of their talk of delinquent and violent acts were more likely to engage in these acts. Dishion called interactions like this "deviancy training." In subsequent research he showed that simply letting at-risk kids get together raised the level of their misbehavior (Dishion and Andrews 1995). Those findings led to a series of conferences that alerted policy makers to the harmful effects of bringing at-risk youth together in schools and in the juvenile justice system (Dodge, Dishion, and Lansford 2006).

Think back to what I've said about the lives of aggressive and defiant children. Jerry Patterson's research in families showed that these kids get little reinforcement for cooperative, prosocial behavior (Patterson, Reid, and Dishion 1992). Their families use mostly aversive behavior to control each other. Each family member's aggressive behavior is honed by its effect in getting others to back off, to stop being aversive. These kids don't get much love and approval and don't have much fun.

They don't get much love in school either. Teachers give them attention for their aggressive and uncooperative behavior, but it is mostly negative attention ("Sit down!"). Because these kids haven't developed skills for playing cooperatively with peers, their peers often reject them (Patterson, Reid, and Dishion 1992). And thanks to their inability to do what teachers want, they don't learn as much and eventually fall behind (DeBaryshe, Patterson, and Capaldi 1993).

By sixth or seventh grade, these kids feel isolated and rejected. They are often depressed. They also become increasingly resentful of constant efforts to get them to do the "right" thing. Then they meet other kids with the same background. It's magic! As Dishion's work shows, they finally find friends after enduring years of rejection by other, less aggressive kids. At last they have someone who approves of all the deviant things they want to talk about.

A colleague of Dishion's, Deborah Capaldi, studies violence between men and women. She wondered if the deviancy training that Dishion discovered influenced how boys treat girls. When the boys in Dishion's study were seventeen or eighteen years old, the researchers invited them back to have another conversation with a friend. One thing they asked them to talk about was what they liked and disliked about girls they knew. They coded these conversations in terms of how often they talked in hostile ways about girls. (The example at the beginning of this chapter comes from one of those conversations.) When the young men were twenty to twenty-three years old, Capaldi got data from them and their girlfriends or wives about how often the men were physically violent. Sure enough, those who had talked approvingly about violence toward women years earlier were, in fact, more aggressive toward their partners (Capaldi et al. 2001).

A further analysis of the interactions of these boys when they were sixteen or seventeen (Van Ryzin and Dishion 2013) revealed that the men who were most violent at twenty-two or twenty-three were the ones who not only had received reinforcement for talk of deviant behavior, but also had a friend or friends with whom they had coercive interactions. In addition to assessing the deviancy training I described above, this study coded how much the two friends were coercive toward each other. In this case, coercion was defined as engaging in dominant or dismissive behavior, using profanity, and being abusive to the other person. Even when the researchers controlled statistically for the teens' antisocial behavior as children and the quality of parental discipline, those who talked about deviance the most and were coercive toward their friend were most likely to engage in violence as adults.

This study makes me realize that although it remains very difficult to predict whether a given individual is going to be violent, the violence of many young men is hardly unique or unpredictable. It emerges from highly coercive environments that put young men on a trajectory toward violence in later life. Although we can't predict and prevent every act of violence in society, we can use what we know to make sure that many fewer young men become violent.

The Pathway to Deviance

The accumulated research on families, schools, and peer groups tells a compelling story about how communities produce troubled youth. Young people whose social environments fail to reinforce prosocial behavior go on to commit crimes, mistreat others, fail in school, and become addicted to tobacco, alcohol, and other drugs. They often lead lives marked by poverty, depression, and repeated failure in social relations. Once you understand this process—and all the tools we have available to prevent it—the prescription for a more successful society becomes clear.

Dishion's recent work provides a good example of how children become teens with multiple problems. In one study (Dishion, Ha, and Véronneau 2012), he followed a sample of 998 kids from ages eleven through twenty-four. His team looked at the quality of the kids' environment when they were eleven through thirteen and its influence on their subsequent development. They found strong evidence of harm from stressful environments. Young people were more likely to get involved with deviant peers by age fourteen if they came from poor families, were disliked by other children, and lived in a family with high levels of conflict, where parents weren't supportive and didn't set limits on their involvement with deviant peers.

The dry statistics of Dishion's analysis of deviant peer development tell a precise and compelling story of why youth grow up to cause trouble for themselves and those around them. The 998 children in this study lived in Portland, Oregon. Dishion first met them when they were in sixth grade, mostly age eleven. His study showed that many of them came from families that were stressed due to poverty. That meant they often didn't have enough to eat, wore shabbier clothing than other children, had vehicles that broke down, had to move due to evictions, or lived in cars or homeless shelters. Their poverty was one reason that other kids rejected them. Kids, especially in middle school, are very sensitive to status and readily tease and bully others in an effort to establish that they have higher status (Rusby et al. 2005). Dishion's study tells us that, in 1998, sixth- and seventh-graders in Portland were getting teased and bullied. Some children woke up every morning dreading going to school.

Due to the stresses they experience, poor families are less likely to be warm and loving and more likely to have conflict and coercion. Thus, many of the poor children who were living through the hell of peer harassment at school probably didn't have help from their family in coping with it. This is understandable when you consider the standpoint of these parents. People who are trying to cope with the threat of unemployment, homelessness, or discrimination may find it hard to support their children in many ways. Learning that their child is being harassed may simply further threaten and stress them. They may feel powerless to do anything about it. Their reaction may be to blame the child, which simply adds family difficulties to the stress the child is experiencing at school. So it's likely that, in 1998, many of the children in Dishion's study experienced threats and slights at school and anger, criticism, and abuse at home.

By 2001, a group of fourteen-year-olds in Dishion's sample who were angry, hurt, frightened, and rejected began to cluster together, or self-organize. The social influence process that Dishion documented in his earlier study began. Kids whose parents paid little attention to what they were doing or whom they were hanging out with got together to talk about and do the things that we call "delinquent acts" and they call "fun!" Virtually all delinquent acts are committed by two or more young people acting together, with the kids richly reinforcing each other's behavior.

By the time these kids were sixteen and seventeen, many were using drugs, stealing, getting into fights, and having sex. In 2001, Portland had more than three thousand violent crimes and more than twenty-eight thousand property crimes. The kids in Dishion's study committed some of those crimes.

Between 2009 and 2011, Dishion and his colleagues assessed these young people at ages twenty-two through twenty-four. They found that young people who had highly stressful and uncaring lives at ages eleven or twelve were much more likely to have had children by their early twenties. This line of research shows a clear path from stress during early adolescence to friendships with other rejected kids at age fourteen to sexual promiscuity at age sixteen or seventeen to early reproduction.

The Source of the Problem: Nonnurturing Environments

In our punitive and disapproving society, in which we customarily hold people personally responsible for what they do and punish them for transgressions, it is easy to fall into a stance of blaming these kids for how they turned out. But if anything deserves blame, it is their environments—though, truth be told, blaming is a worthless activity.

Can we blame their parents? In most cases, they presumably did some things they shouldn't have done and failed to do some things that they should have done. But Dishion's later study (Dishion, Ha, and Véronneau 2012) shows that the "guilty" parents probably were themselves the victims of similar environments. After all, how do people become poverty-stricken, stressed, aggressive, nonnurturing parents? They typically grow up in environments that are coercive and rejecting, get into trouble, fail in school, and have children early. (Dishion views this dynamic too from an evolutionary perspective. In a threatening world, it may be prudent to have children early, since you might not survive to have them later.)

Only when we transform young people's family and school environments to minimize coercion, teach and richly reinforce prosocial behavior, and stave off the development of deviant peer groups will we end this intergenerational propagation of poverty, academic failure, delinquency, and teenage pregnancy. As I hope I have convinced you in earlier chapters, the means for doing so lie within our grasp.

Not Every Troubled Teen Becomes a Delinquent

In writing about youth with multiple problems, I sometimes worry that I will promote negative and unsympathetic views of young people that will increase support for punitive approaches to dealing with them. I hope I have conveyed that it isn't their fault that they are having these problems. Rather, their environments created their problems. Moreover, it is possible to intervene at any point along their life course to reduce the problems they're facing and prevent future ones.

I didn't have to go far to find an example of a young person who reversed course in this way. Tom Dishion once led the kind of life he often describes in his research. He and his friends experimented with many behaviors, including drug use. When he was in high school he was arrested at school for possession of marijuana. That resulted in his transfer to an alternative high school. There he saw firsthand how schools and programs for troubled youth brought delinquent kids together, creating a context in which they further reinforced each other's problem behavior. He and his friends were on their way to a life of failure.

However, sometimes it just takes a little nurturance to steer a kid in a different direction. When Tom's older brother moved to Santa Barbara, Tom moved there as well. He found an apartment and attended the city college, where he discovered a group of young people who were enthusiastic about learning. That started him down the road to becoming, in my estimation, one of the most innovative and productive behavioral scientists I know. All it took was a nurturing social environment.

Preventing Deviant Peer Influences

The frequently repeated tragedy of young people joining a deviant peer group and developing multiple problems can be prevented. When children are young, they can learn the social and self-regulatory skills they need so that their peers don't reject them. And even when kids are having problems as they enter adolescence, we can prevent them from traveling down a troubled pathway by monitoring their peer associations and limiting their opportunities to get involved in peer groups that reinforce problem behavior.

Establish Good Peer Relations at an Early Age

A toddler who doesn't get his way is likely to cry. A toddler who has a toy grabbed away from him by another child is liable to hit or push the other child. But it is probably a safe bet that last time someone was rude to you, you didn't cry or hit him. One of the most important skills young children must develop is emotion regulation: the ability to control emotions and restrain themselves from impulsively attacking others. This is a basic building block of a civil society. Fortunately, we have learned a lot about how to help young children develop this skill.

One of the most basic methods is what psychologist John Gottman (1997) calls *emotion coaching*. In chapter 4, I described how my wife, Georgia, talks to our granddaughter, Ashlyn, about her emotions when she seems upset. It is a technique that Georgia's preschool adopted based on Gottman's writing. When a child becomes distressed, adults approach her sympathetically and try to match the type and intensity of the child's emotion empathically: "Oh, you are angry!" By labeling the emotion, they help the child learn to understand her emotions in the same way they might help a child to learn to name colors. They also say something about the situation that apparently evoked the emotion so the child learns to understand what evokes her emotions: "He took your toy." This empathic approach helps children begin to calm down. Then adults can suggest ways of resolving the situation: "Why don't you tell him that you didn't like how he took your toy and that you want to play with it? Then he can have a turn after you."

This whole approach is a departure from traditional behavioral strategies that sought to avoid reinforcing children's negative emotions. The fear was that children would use these emotions to get what they wanted and escape from the demands of adults. But I have repeatedly seen Grandma Georgie stick with whatever request she is making of Ashlyn while also showing great empathy for the frustration Ashlyn feels at having to, for example, stop an activity she is enjoying. By doing this and giving Ashlyn choices within the context of the request (for example, "Do you want to put on the green socks or the pink ones?"), many struggles are avoided. Instead, cooperation begins to grow.

Prevention scientists Mark Greenberg and Celene Domitrovich have developed a systematic program for teaching these emotion regulations skills in preschools and elementary schools: Promoting Alternative

Thinking Strategies (PATHS). It is designed to teach children directly about each emotion and appropriate ways to express it. Children learn to understand the emotions others are feeling by taking the other person's perspective. That initially involves seeing what the other sees. As their sophistication grows, they develop the ability to infer what someone else is feeling. PATHS also helps children learn to use problem solving in emotionally difficult situations so they can better resolve conflict with other children. In addition, it directly teaches and reinforces basic skills such as sharing and cooperating. The program is in widespread use in schools, and randomized experimental evaluations show that it improves children's social competence, reduces social withdrawal, and prevents the development of aggressive social behavior, anxiety, and depression (Domitrovich, Cortes, and Greenberg 2007; Kam, Greenberg, and Kusché 2004).

Monitor and Set Limits with Adolescents

As children move into adolescence, they seek much more autonomy. At this stage, parents must achieve a delicate balance between granting adolescents autonomy and making sure they don't get into situations where problematic or even dangerous behavior could occur. To establish a strong foundation for navigating this period, it is helpful if parents have already established effective, regular communication with their children about what they are doing each day and have nurtured their children's prosocial values and academic interests. This makes it likely that their children are involved with other teens who are enthusiastic about school and not into risk taking. Yet even these parents must be watchful for situations that could encourage experimentation with problem behavior. An example would be the findings of Jean Richardson and her colleagues (1993). They discovered that ninth-grade students who were at home unsupervised by a parent were significantly more likely to experiment with drugs, be depressed, and get poor grades. Such kids had even greater problems if they were hanging out with other teens after school.

This is why every effective parenting program for families with teenagers focuses on getting parents to monitor what their teenager is doing when they aren't around and establishing rules to make sure the teenager engages in appropriate activities when not under adult supervision. Programs such as the Family Check-Up (Dishion, Nelson, and Kavanagh

2003) encourage parents to talk with their teens each day about what they have been doing and to make and enforce rules about the time teens need to be home, where they can go when they are out, and whom they can be with. In this way, a program like the Family Check-Up can prevent teen delinquency, drug use, and declining grades for as long as five years after families participate in the program.

Do Not Congregate Troubled Youth!

Despite all the evidence about how peers influence each other's deviant behavior, our society routinely deals with delinquency by bringing troubled youth together. Tom Dishion found this out the hard way. He did a randomized trial of the impact of a parenting intervention (an early version of the Family Check-Up) versus a program to teach kids good self-management and study skills (Dishion and Andrews 1995). He randomly assigned families of at-risk youth to either participate in the parenting intervention or not, and randomly assigned the youths to participate or not participate in the self-management program. He expected that the best outcomes would be for those who received both programs.

The parenting program worked as expected, but to Dishion's surprise, the self-management program led to *increases* in youth smoking. When he coded videotapes of the interactions of youth in self-management training groups, he discovered that those who were talking about deviant activities were most likely to get others' attention. This was exactly the process he showed in the research I described earlier in this chapter (Dishion et al. 1996): peer social approval reinforces deviant behavior.

Additional evidence has accumulated that raises serious questions about many of the things our society does in efforts to deal with at-risk or delinquent youth. We routinely put students who are doing less well academically on a different academic track than those who are doing well. In the process, we stigmatize them and bring them together, where they become friends and have little contact with students who embrace prosocial norms and behaviors. If at-risk kids have trouble in school, they are often transferred to alternative schools where the student body consists almost entirely of kids who experiment with drugs and other forms of risk taking. If they are arrested, they are locked up with other problem youth or treated in groups of adjudicated youth.

We need to change all of these practices. Of course, the best way to do so would be to intervene earlier with the approaches I described in chapters 2 and 3. This would allow families and schools to do what is necessary to prevent problems from developing in the first place.

Create Numerous Opportunities for Prosocial Activities

Most American communities don't have enough opportunities for youth to recreate in safe settings that support positive social behavior. This deficit was brought home to me when I attended a conference on mental health in Helsinki, Finland, several years ago. My colleague Hendricks Brown and I bought a basketball and went to a nearby park to play. We had been there maybe half an hour when suddenly several hundred teens showed up with a number of adults. They proceeded to play basketball and many other games. I didn't see a single instance of conflict. Unfortunately, I have never seen anything like that in a US community.

Offering numerous opportunities for young people to play a greater role in civic life and governance is another way that we can enhance prosocial development and prevent problems. Starting in preschool, children can be given meaningful roles in their school—roles that give them responsibility and pride. Examples include setting up equipment for an assembly, taking roll, or photographing prosocial activities. Evidence indicates that assuming such roles increases young people's prosocial behavior (Embry and Biglan 2008).

Action Implications

Research clearly shows that we need to cultivate prosocial peer relationships among youth to prevent deviant behavior and nurture their development. If left to their own devices, young people who are at risk for problems typically reinforce each other's deviant tendencies. Thus, families and schools need to be sensitive to the importance of peer relationships in young people's development. And while peer influences are especially important in adolescence, ensuring that adolescents have friends who support their positive social development ideally begins in early childhood, when children learn to regulate their emotions and cooperate with others.

For Parents

- Monitor your children's activities by talking to them about what they are doing in school and with friends. If you establish routine conversations with them when they're young, they will continue to tell you what is going on in their lives. This also creates numerous opportunities for you to show your appreciation and approval of the good things they do, and to guide them away from risky activities and toward prosocial choices.

- If you haven't established good communication with your children before adolescence, it is still possible to monitor and set limits on what they are doing. Tom Dishion and Kate Kavanagh's book *Intervening in Adolescent Problem Behavior: A Family-Centered Approach* (2003) offers guidance to parents of adolescents that you may find helpful.

- Set limits on your teenagers' opportunities to hang out with youth who get into trouble. If they are home alone after school, make sure they don't have friends over. As they get older and you become more confident that they will engage in safe, productive, or enjoyable activities alone with friends, you can gradually grant them more autonomy. Establish a routine in which they use after-school time to do their homework, household tasks, or solitary recreational activities. Be sure to show great interest and approval for the positive things they do after school.

For Schools

- Reduce or eliminate the practice of putting students into tracks based on their academic performance because this congregates and stigmatizes at-risk students and contributes to problem development.

- Implement evidence-based, school-wide systems of positive behavioral support to reduce social rejection of students by other students. (Chapter 3 describes several such programs.)

For Policy Makers

- Eliminate practices that congregate at-risk youth, such as incarceration and group treatment of those who are delinquent.

- Eliminate academic tracking in schools.

- Increase the availability of settings and activities that provide opportunities for young people to engage in prosocial behavior, such as participation in community betterment and social and recreational activities, as well as recognition for prosocial activities within the community.

CHAPTER 5

The Behavioral Revolution in Clinical Psychology

Chapters 2 through 4 largely focused on applying behavioral principles to nurturing children and adolescents. But what about the psychological and behavioral problems of adults? Can the principles of behaviorism be used to develop effective treatments for problems such as anxiety and depression among adults? They can, as a quick review of the history of behavior therapy reveals.

Although clinical psychology was practiced as early as the end of the nineteenth century, this work—treating people for psychological problems—began in earnest the 1940s. At first, Freudian theory dominated the work. Neuroses were seen as being due to deep-seated, unconscious problems that could be treated only through years of daily psychoanalysis. There was no empirical basis for this treatment. Nor was there a tradition of empirically evaluating the effectiveness of treatments.

That began to change in the 1950s, when psychiatrist Joseph Wolpe reported on a new technique for treating phobias, which he called systematic desensitization. Up to that point, people crippled by fear of specific stimuli, such as spiders (arachnophobia) or public places (agoraphobia), only had the option of a long course of psychoanalysis—if they could afford it.

Wolpe believed that phobias arose because of a conditioning history in which the thing a person feared had repeatedly been paired with high levels of anxiety. He believed he could decondition the fear by pairing the presence of the feared stimulus with relaxation. His method involved creating a hierarchy of situations ranging from mildly distressing (such as seeing a spider across the room) to highly distressing (such as holding a spider in one's hand). Using a deep muscle relaxation technique that Edmund Jacobson (1938) had developed, he taught clients to relax deeply. Then he had them imagine feared situations while remaining relaxed, starting with the least fear-arousing situations.

Wolpe used this technique with a large number of clients and kept a careful record of his results. His publication of *Psychotherapy by Reciprocal Inhibition* (1958) led to the first randomized experimental evaluation of a clinical intervention when Gordon Paul, a psychologist at the University of Illinois, evaluated the effects of systematic desensitization for treating anxiety associated with public speaking (Paul 1966). What followed was an explosion of research on the treatment of phobias and other anxieties. This work, combined with the advances made by psychologists who were applying Skinner's principles, marked the beginning of the development of behavior therapy. The two distinctive features of behavior therapy were its application of behavioral principles to the study of human behavior, and its insistence on empirically evaluating the impact and effectiveness of treatment procedures derived from these principles.

My Own Journey

I began my career as a social psychologist. However, by the time I got my doctorate in 1971, I was disillusioned. Social psychology had become boring to me. A new generation of social psychologists that craved the prestige of "real sciences" like physics had banished the practical and socially relevant aspects of social psychology from the field. Doing research that smacked of anything applied had become verboten. Prestige went to those who conducted obscure and clever studies of "nonobvious" phenomena. If something was obvious, such as prejudice or conflict, it was regarded as too trivial. This didn't appeal to me. Whenever I tried to read the latest "hot" study in the *Journal of Personality and Social Psychology*, I fell asleep.

Meanwhile, because of the Vietnam War, the sizzling sixties had turned into the radical seventies, with talk of free love and socialist revolution. I was living in Seattle and still studying social psychology at the University of Washington, a hotbed of radical activity. I was more committed than ever to changing the world, but social psychology and its fascination with fame and prestige no longer seemed a good vehicle for accomplishing that task.

I decided to get retreaded as a clinical psychologist. It was the time of the counterculture movement, with its emphasis on personal growth, mind expansion, and consciousness raising. I was a child of the times. I began to embrace the personal growth movement, along with free love and revolution. I found it exhilarating to get inside people's heads, advise them, and guide them on their journeys.

Ned Wagner, the head of the clinical psychology program at "U Dub," agreed to give me a year of postdoctoral training in clinical psychology if I would teach a course on social psychology. He gave me an office across from Bob Kohlenberg, and eventually Bob introduced me to B. F. Skinner's work in behaviorism. By the time I finished my clinical training and got an internship at the University of Wisconsin Psychiatry Department, I was engrossed in the developing field of behavior therapy. By the end of my Wisconsin internship, I'd read virtually all of the extant works on behaviorism, behavior therapy, and the philosophy of science that underpins them.

Establishing the Behavior Change Center

By 1977, I had cofounded a storefront clinic in Springfield, Oregon, with three friends from the University of Oregon: Jane Ganter, the administrative assistant at the University of Oregon Psychology Clinic; Nancy Hawkins, a psychologist trained at the university; and David Campbell, the director of the Psychology Clinic.

We called our new clinic the Behavior Change Center. It was the first behavior therapy clinic in Oregon. As of 1975, behavior therapy researchers had accumulated enough knowledge that we could offer behavioral therapy to the public. We saw adults with depression or anxiety, families that were having problems with their children, and people who wanted help with specific behaviors, such as smoking, procrastinating, or literally pulling their hair out, which is known as trichotillomania.

For that time, we were pretty good at what we did. We helped people develop goals about what they wanted in their lives, and we used their sessions to help them take specific steps in the direction of their goals. Unlike traditional therapies, with their focus on treating deep-seated, underlying neuroses through extensive talk therapy, we simply helped people change behaviors they wanted to change, and we tried to do it in as few sessions as possible at as low a cost as possible. Initially, we charged seven dollars for fifteen minutes.

In people's first session, we asked them to tell us what would be different if, six months from that day, they looked back and could say, "Things are much better." Most people said they wanted to feel less anxious or less depressed, and many said they wanted to improve their relationships with others.

Our focus was always on what people could do in specific situations that came up in the daily course of their lives. I liked to say, "You could have a wonderful time in our sessions, but it wouldn't mean much if things 'out there' were still a problem. We need to use our sessions to plan the steps you can take to move in the direction you want to go out there." As a result, we focused on helping people try new behaviors in the daily situations that challenged them. We taught people who had problems with anxiety how to relax in practice sessions. But rather than simply have them practice once a day, we had them do "comfort checks" five times a day to get good at relaxing in all circumstances of their daily lives.

Although we based our approach on behavioral theory, our fundamental commitment was to use empirically based practices. One set of findings that informed our work but didn't come from behavior theory involved the way in which therapists interact with clients. Carl Rogers, who had developed what he called client-centered therapy, argued that therapists were most effective when they provided empathy, genuineness, and warmth to clients (1951). A review of evidence supporting this approach (Truax and Carkuff 1967) convinced my colleagues and me that we could more effectively help people if we were genuinely warm and empathic. This wasn't hard to do. After all, we were in this line of work because we wanted to help people.

Learning to Take the Long View

Peter Lewinsohn, who had developed a behavioral approach to treating depression at the University of Oregon, suggested I read a book by Alan Lakein called *How to Get Control of Your Time and Your Life* (1973). I did and found it very helpful in my own life and began using it with clients. Following Lakein's approach, I asked people to brainstorm the things they wished to achieve in life at three different times: their whole lives, the next five years, and if they had only six months to live. I then had them pick the most important ones from each period and ultimately boil them down to five or so things they most wanted to focus on.

Lakein argued that the day-to-day demands we all encounter typically crowd out attention to important things that might take hundreds or even thousands of little steps to achieve. This insight was one of the most important things I ever learned. I made a list of my major goals using Lakein's approach, then reviewed and revised it annually. At the beginning of each week, I chose some concrete things I could do that week to move forward on important goals, and then I made a task list for each day.

People who are struggling with anxiety and depression—and in truth, I was one of them—can get so focused on how they are feeling that they become stuck. They make not feeling bad the central theme of their lives, thinking they can't move on with their lives until their emotional problems end. Lakein's approach of setting goals and breaking them down into small steps did a great deal to help people begin to move out of their depression or anxiety.

It certainly worked for me. I have used variations on this approach to organize my work throughout my career. It not only guided me to get projects done but also helped me calm down. I eventually got to the point where, if I woke up on a Monday morning sky-high with anxiety and worry about all the things I needed to do, I could simply make my list for the week and the day and calm down. I didn't need to worry about all the things I had to do: I only needed to do the things on that day's list. In fact, I often told my clients, "Rather than having to worry about what you need to do, you can have your list worry for you."

This system worked quite well for most of our clients at the Behavior Change Center. They learned to relax in common stressful situations and began to accomplish things that moved them out of the miasma of depression and anxiety. In six to ten sessions, most clients began to feel better and do the things that moved them toward a more satisfying life.

However, some clients didn't improve. With them, it seemed that everything I suggested only amplified their feelings of anxiety, worry, and depression. Typically, they were people who had already been through a lot of therapy. While I was increasingly confident that the behavioral approach was helping many people, it was clear that there was still much to learn.

The Schism in Behavior Therapy

One thing missing from early behavior therapy was an effective analysis of cognition and verbal behavior. Although Skinner had inspired a generation of psychologists to consider the possibility that people's behavior is influenced by its consequences, virtually all of the research involved directly observable behavior. What people were thinking and feeling hardly entered into the early research. This produced a schism within the behavior therapy movement. A number of prominent people began to advocate for *cognitive* behavioral therapy.

It was undeniable. People talk and think, and what they say and think has enormous influence on what they do. For Skinner, however, the ultimate causes of behavior were found in the environment. He labeled explanations in terms of thoughts and feelings as "mentalism."

For centuries, the standard way of explaining what people did was to point to their desires, intentions, beliefs, and feelings, which were said to be the causes of their behavior. This was the so-called doctrine of autonomous man. In this view, people, not their environment, determined their behavior. Skinner saw this way of thinking as the biggest obstacle to a science of human behavior. If people continued to believe that the causes of our behavior are inside us in the form of wants, wishes, and so on, we would never examine how the environment affects behavior. Only when people stopped being satisfied with mentalistic explanations would they be willing to explore environmental influences on behavior.

In addition, the cognitive movement stemmed from resistance to the notion that people's behavior was determined by their environments. As with prior paradigmatic revolutions in science (Kuhn 1970), the behaviorist revolution was threatening to those who held the view that humans had a privileged place in the universe. Humanity's fall from its pedestal had begun with Copernicus, who argued that the earth was not the center of the universe, and Galileo, who ended up under house arrest for agreeing with him. Darwin's assertion that humans were just another species that had evolved as the result of the same processes that produced every other species was another blow to our primacy. Now Skinner was saying that even our understanding that we freely choose our behavior was mistaken, claiming instead that our behavior was shaped by the same laws that accounted for the behavior of pigeons and rats. I found his line of thinking quite compelling. In particular, if humans evolved according to the same processes as all other species, and if resistance to prior Copernican revolutions had been due to the conceit of humans, why should it be any different for human behavior?

But it didn't help that Skinner had a penchant for putting his claims in strident terms. Perhaps as a result, his critics tended to attack in rather nasty ways. Among the most prominent of those critics was Albert Bandura, who published papers and books attacking the view that human behavior was shaped by the environment. Using pejorative terms, he wrote about "odious imagery, including salivating dogs, puppetry, and animalistic manipulation" (1974, 859) and a wholly robotic view of humans.

I never quite understood why Bandura felt salivating dogs were odious, but he certainly found an eager audience within the behavior therapy movement. Many people who would laugh at any rejection of Darwinian evolution were relieved to encounter a view that preserved the autonomy of humans, and they latched on to it.

For my part, I felt quite threatened by these developments. Most of the people who embraced the cognitive movement hadn't read Skinner, but they were comfortable being dismissive of his theories. On more than one occasion, I encountered sneers from other psychologists. I felt a bit like a persecuted minority.

Research with children, especially children with developmental disabilities, continued to make use of behavioral consequences. But cognitive behavioral therapy largely dominated research with adult humans. Peter Lewinsohn's behavioral approach to depression prompted people to increase reinforcing activities (Lewinsohn 1975). But according to the cognitivists, "depressogenic" thoughts caused depression. Therefore, their treatment approaches emphasized getting people to modify dysfunctional beliefs and distorted thinking. Twenty years later, Lewinsohn's approach was vindicated. Studies that compared the cognitive components of depression treatment with components that prompted people to get active showed that the activation component was what made a difference (N. S. Jacobson et al. 1996).

At the Behavior Change Center I tried to help my clients modify their dysfunctional beliefs, but I was never very good at it. I couldn't deny that people's thoughts influenced their behavior. However, in my view, a different underlying process was at work—one in which thoughts, including private thoughts, were a form of verbal behavior. After all, when I encouraged clients to identify what they most wanted to accomplish in life and make to-do lists to help achieve their long-term goals, I was helping them make choices and influence their subsequent behavior. And Skinner had convinced me that the functional influence our plans have on subsequent behavior is due to a long history of getting reinforcement for doing what we say we will do and getting punishment when we fail to do so.

Furthermore, I could see the consequences at play in my clinical work. As a therapist, my social support, encouragement, and attention were consequences that helped people establish their ability to make a plan and carry it out. If that was successful, my clients would continue to engage in sequences of planning and doing because of positive consequences in their lives. Meanwhile, ample empirical justification for this view was emerging. Research with children included the "say-do" literature, which showed that children learned to do what they said they would do thanks to reinforcement for doing so (Ballard 1983).

Psychological Flexibility and the Third Wave of Behavior Therapy

In 1986, I received a book chapter from a psychologist by the name of Steven Hayes. I had never heard of Hayes, and to this day, neither he nor I know why he sent me the chapter. The chapter was titled "A Contextual Approach to Therapeutic Change" (Hayes 1987). When I read it, I realized that Hayes was describing all of the clients I had been unable to help: people who were so locked into their struggle with anxiety or depression that they couldn't escape.

Hayes argued that the cognitive behavioral therapy approach to controlling unwanted thoughts was counterproductive. Efforts to control troublesome thoughts, rather than getting rid of them, actually amplified them (Hayes 1987). This resonated with my experience with clients who didn't benefit from relaxation training. Although they practiced a procedure that worked for many other people, it just seemed to heighten their anxiety.

For example, I sometimes worked with people suffering from panic attacks, most of whom had gradually limited their lives by avoiding new situations that seemed to trigger panic. If they experienced panic attacks in movie theaters, they stopped going to movies. If they became anxious driving on bridges, they stopped driving across them. They were acutely aware of their bodily sensations and monitored them to detect whether panic was arising. Their philosophy was that they could proceed with their lives only after getting rid of these terrible feelings and thoughts. Then they could see a movie, drive to work, or go shopping.

Hayes described a new method of helping people change their orientation toward frightening thoughts and feelings. Rather than supporting people in efforts to get rid of such experiences, he encouraged them to be willing to have those experiences—to let go of efforts to control them. He called this approach comprehensive distancing. Using metaphors and experiential exercises, he helped clients step back from thoughts and feelings they had been attempting to control and start doing the things they had been avoiding.

He also developed methods, including the use of metaphors, for helping people see that the things they had been doing to feel good were actually part of the problem. In one such metaphor, he asked clients to imagine that they have fallen into a hole. They discover that they have a shovel, and being highly motivated to get out of the hole, they use the only tool they have available to try to get out. The only problem is, shovels are for digging, and that just makes holes bigger. Then he posed a question: Hadn't the client been digging for many years to avoid this terrible anxiety, depression, or panic? Perhaps the first thing to do is to put down the shovel and stop trying to dig yourself out of the hole. Hayes described impressive successes with this approach, although he had not yet tested the intervention in randomized trials.

A Contextual Account of Human Behavior

To me, the most exciting thing about Steve Hayes's approach was that it was completely consistent with Skinner's orientation. Hayes too had embraced the Skinnerian idea that the environment shapes human behavior. For Skinnerians, people's thoughts and feelings are not causes of behavior—they are simply other behaviors.

The practical goal of this approach is to be able to predict and influence behavior. It is undoubtedly true that my thinking can influence other things I do. I make a plan, and then I follow it. I remember something I said I would do, and then I do it. But what about all the times my thoughts don't result in action? For example, among procrastinators, simply saying they are going to do something may almost guarantee that they don't do it. We can't simply assume that thoughts cause other actions. We need to understand why they sometimes influence other actions and sometimes don't.

The answer is to look to the environmental context that influences not only what we think and what we do, but also the relationship between our thoughts and our actions. In my work with clients at the Behavior Change Center, I helped people strengthen the relationship between their plans and their actions by supportively reinforcing this consistency—for example, by discussing how they had done on following through with the plans we made in the previous session. The same process is involved when a parent praises a child for doing what she said she would do or admonishes her for not doing so.

The problem with traditional cognitive behavioral therapy is that it doesn't consider how the context affects the relationship between thoughts and other actions. It just tries to help people get rid of thoughts that seem to cause problematic actions or obstruct effective action. In Hayes's approach, on the other hand, the goal is to change the context that maintains the power of words over action. Rather than help people get rid of problematic thoughts, his approach focuses on loosening the relationships between thought and actions that cause people trouble. People don't need to get rid of these thoughts; they need to get to a point where they can be less influenced by them so they can consciously choose a course of action and follow through.

As I got to know Steve and studied his improvements to Skinner's behaviorism, I realized that his contextual approach was not just generating powerful new methods to help people with their psychological problems, but also providing a general account of how the environment shapes all aspects of human behavior. This includes not simply people's thoughts and feelings, but the relationships between their thoughts and feelings and the rest of their behavior. His approach has since been developed and elaborated on by a large and growing number of behavioral scientists around the world, and it is proving to have profound implications for what it means to be human and how we can build a more caring and effective society that nurtures everyone's well-being.

Acceptance and Commitment Therapy

Hayes's treatment approach came to be known as acceptance and commitment therapy, or ACT (said as one word). It involves helping people develop more of the psychological flexibility I described in chapter 1. Russ Harris, one of the most prolific writers about ACT, suggests that we think of psychological flexibility as involving three things: making room for our thoughts and feelings without judging or struggling with them, being in the present moment, and doing what matters most to us (2009a).

Treating Schizophrenia with ACT

As of this writing, more than eighty randomized trials have shown the benefit of ACT with problems as diverse as schizophrenia, epilepsy, depression, and quitting smoking. To give you a feel for it, I will tell you about Patty Bach's work with people with schizophrenia (Bach and Hayes 2002).

Schizophrenia is the most damaging and difficult mental illness. It usually strikes in late adolescence or early adulthood and involves becoming overwhelmed by hallucinations or delusions. Patients have sometimes described it as a descent into hell. Hospitalization and heavy medication are typical treatments. But while this helps people gain some control over their bizarre experiences, they usually don't resume a "normal" life. Bach, a clinical psychologist in Chicago, told me the story of one woman's descent into hell, which I'll summarize here.

Emma was a thirty-year-old white woman whose early life held great promise. She was a bright, attractive teenager and an outstanding student in high school. In college she met a guy she really cared for, and soon they married. She seemed to be headed toward a wonderful life.

She had her first psychotic episode while still in college. She began withdrawing from her husband, family, and friends. She started skipping classes frequently because she believed other students were talking about her. Then she became convinced that one of her professors was delivering messages to her through his lectures and stopped attending his class altogether. Her husband took her to the emergency room after an episode in which she accused him of trying to harm her, called his parents, and told them they had raised a monster. She was treated with antipsychotic medication and released after a four-week hospitalization. Her husband tried to be supportive, but it was difficult. He hadn't bargained on having a schizophrenic wife and living with constant fear about what she might do, and they eventually divorced. He remarried but continued to provide financial and social support. Eventually, however, he moved away.

For a while Emma coped reasonably well. She didn't return to college but did occasionally hold down a job—usually until she quit due to some suspicion about her employer or coworkers. She received treatment at a community mental health center and took her medication most of the time. She had some money from a trust fund, which covered her basic costs of living. But when the money in the trust fund ran out, she began to deteriorate.

In a conversation one day, her landlady mentioned that her husband had been sick but she had taken care of him. Emma somehow concluded that her landlady had murdered her husband, and this developed into an unyielding delusion that occupied most of Emma's life. She reported it to the police, but they did nothing about it. She began interpreting everything her landlady did as a threat directed at her. Emma began posting signs that said things like "Murderer!" She was eventually evicted and moved into a nearby hotel. In her continuing efforts to get someone to do something about this "murder," she contacted the FBI, the police, and the circuit court. At some point she stopped getting treatment and quit taking her medication. She was eventually homeless and living on the street.

Emma came to Bach's attention when she was arrested for harassing personnel at a courthouse where she was trying to get someone to do something about the "murder." Realizing that she was paranoid, the police brought her to the psychiatric hospital where Bach worked. At this point, a typical outcome would be: Emma gets back on her meds, damping down her paranoid delusions, but no one is able to talk her out of the delusions. She is unable to hold a job, and will cycle in and out of mental hospitals for the rest of her life.

Schizophrenia is like a huge boulder. It often seems as if there is no way to move it. However, scientific breakthroughs often involve finding a lever and a fulcrum that no one has seen before. When these forces align properly, even big boulders can be moved with ease. That is what happened for Emma, because Bach had received ACT training from Steve Hayes.

To see how ACT exerts a different and more effective force on schizophrenia, we need first to take a deeper look at this devastating illness.

Imagine that one day you have a hallucination. You are quite frightened, both by what you hallucinated and by the fact that you had a hallucination. You know this is very bad. Perhaps you tell a loved one, who also becomes frightened. You don't want this, and neither does your loved one. You consult a psychiatrist, who joins you in trying to make sure that these things don't happen. Your psychiatrist puts you on medication. Now your life has become about not having any more hallucinations. That is the absolute imperative, so you're constantly alert to the possibility that you might be having one.

Delusions are a bit different; unlike a hallucination, the individual experiencing a delusion is not aware that the delusion isn't real. Emma's life became focused on dealing with the "murder," and because there had been no murder, everyone tried to get her to give up her delusion. But that just made her even more dedicated to getting people to understand and take action. For Emma, the defining issue in her life was this "murder," and little else was going to happen in her life until it was dealt with.

Bach focused on helping Emma take a different tack: beginning to move forward in other areas of her life anyway. Rather than trying to talk Emma out of her delusion, Bach guided Emma in exploring her values. What was important to her? What did she want her life to be about? She said she wanted a job and wanted to work with developmentally delayed children. She even named specific agencies she wanted to work for. As a result, she focused on how to get a job.

Emma never gave up her delusion, even after she was back on her medications. But in their work on values, Bach and Emma clarified that, for Emma, justice was an important value. Emma was able to come to the resolution that she had done her part to try to see that justice was served. The cost for her had been high, and it was time for her to move on. So she stopped talking about her landlady and began to focus on other things.

Emma was in the hospital for four months. Toward the end of that time she got day passes to apply for jobs. Bach and her colleagues helped Emma practice for job interviews and other social interactions. She got a job in a health care setting as a janitor. Bach's team arranged for Emma to live in a residential facility, and Emma developed a plan to get her own apartment eventually. The last time Bach saw Emma, she was moving forward in her life.

If you don't know much about schizophrenia, this may seem like a sad story. Compared to how Emma was doing before she began to have delusions, working as a janitor and living in a residential facility may not seem like much of a life. But compared to the way many people with schizophrenia live—with a constant focus on delusions or hallucinations, in and out of hospitals, and living on the street—it is actually quite a bit. Emma had begun to focus on things that she valued and worked toward making her life about those things. As a result, her delusions were no longer torturing her.

A Randomized Trial of ACT for Schizophrenia

Bach was one of Steve Hayes's graduate students when she came up with the idea of trying ACT for people with schizophrenia. ACT had proven effective for depression, anxiety, and a number of other problems, and she wondered whether it might be useful for this intractable psychiatric problem. Based on initial work with a few patients at a Reno psychiatric hospital, she began to think it could.

She and Hayes decided to test this in a randomized controlled trial. They identified eighty people who were hospitalized with a psychotic disorder and randomly assigned them to get treatment-as-usual or treatment-as-usual augmented with ACT. The ACT intervention consisted of four sessions with Bach, each forty-five to fifty minutes long.

In the first session, Bach encouraged patients to talk about how they had been trying to deal with their symptoms. They usually described continual efforts to suppress or control problematic thoughts. She then tried to help them adopt a new perspective: that instead of struggling with these thoughts, they could simply notice and accept them without doing anything about them. To do this she used a classic ACT intervention: taking their mind for a walk (Hayes, Strosahl, and Wilson 1999).

In this intervention, Bach would ask a patient to walk around the hospital as she walked just behind him, talking to him as if she were his mind. She provided a running commentary on whatever the patient encountered, evaluating, analyzing, predicting, and recommending various actions. Prior to beginning the exercise, she asked the patient to just notice what his "mind" was saying without acting on it and to behave however he chose, without regard to what his mind said. The purpose was to give these patients some experience with not taking their thoughts literally or needing to do anything about them. ACT therapists call this process *defusion*, in a reference to not being fused with thoughts. From a defused stance, you don't see the world through your thoughts; you see that you are having thoughts.

In the second session, Bach worked on helping patients accept their symptoms even if they didn't like them. She did this using another classic ACT intervention, the polygraph metaphor (Hayes, Strosahl, and Wilson 1999). It is typically presented along these lines:

> *Imagine that you're hooked to a very high-quality polygraph. It can detect the slightest increase in any type of fear or arousal. It has meters that show different aspects of arousal, such as heart rate, breathing, sweating, and blood pressure. So if you get upset, I'll know about it! Your job is to stay calm. In fact, it is essential that you stay calm. Think of it as a matter of life or death. In fact, just to make sure you're motivated, I'm going to put a gun to your head and pull the trigger if any of these meters move. Do you think you can stay calm?*

This metaphor is designed to help people *experience* the paradox that focusing on not having unwanted feelings actually makes them worse. In terms of Bach's study, the patients clearly couldn't control the unpleasant thoughts and feelings their schizophrenia generated, so it was important to help them understand that trying to control those thoughts and feelings actually makes them more intense and frequent.

In the third session, Bach talked to patients about their valued goals and questioned whether their efforts to control their symptoms were working to get them what they valued. Many patients said they wanted to live independently. Then Bach asked them to look at how they'd tried to control their symptoms. For example, yelling at voices or using illicit drugs might stop some symptoms for a while, but these behaviors could be a barrier to living independently. In ACT, clients aren't cast as being right or wrong for trying these things; rather, the point is to determine what works.

The fourth session in the experimental intervention took place upon a patient's discharge from the hospital. In that session, Bach reviewed what they had covered in the previous three sessions.

The results of this intervention were some of the best ever seen in research on the treatment of schizophrenia. Four months after patients left the hospital, 40 percent of those who received treatment as usual had been rehospitalized, as opposed to only 20 percent of the patients who received the additional ACT intervention.

In addition, those who received ACT and were rehospitalized stayed out significantly longer than those in the other group. You might think this occurred because those who received ACT had fewer symptoms. However, one of the most surprising things about the study is that the people who received ACT reported *more* symptoms. But ACT had helped many of them develop a new relationship to those symptoms. Instead of fighting to control symptoms, they had become more accepting of them. Those who received ACT and were rehospitalized tended to be people who continued to deny their symptoms. Apparently, they had not benefited from ACT in the sense that they were continuing to struggle to control their symptoms.

Perhaps most significantly, all of this was achieved with less than four hours of treatment. Most of the people in this study had already undergone countless hours of other forms of treatment without the same beneficial effects. These results are not a fluke. A second study, done by different people, produced similar results (Gaudiano and Herbert 2006).

A Universal Approach

Bach's success is an especially striking example of the strides that behavioral scientists have made in helping people change their behavior. But there are many other success stories. ACT practitioners have shown the value of this approach for a surprisingly diverse number of problems. Tobias Lundgren and JoAnne Dahl applied these principles to treating people with severe epilepsy (Lundgren et al. 2008). They helped patients practically eliminate their seizures—not by trying to stop the seizures, but by helping patients accept what they didn't seem able to change and start living in the service of their values.

Several ACT researchers have achieved dramatic improvements in helping people quit smoking (for example, Bricker et al. 2010). Instead of supporting smokers' beliefs that they could stop smoking only if they didn't have cravings, they helped them accept their cravings while choosing to act in the service of their value of living longer. Barbara Kohlenberg is a clinical psychologist who has done some of the research on smoking cessation using an ACT approach. She told me that many of these ex-smokers reported that they also started using ACT principles to change many other aspects of their lives.

Other studies have shown the value of ACT for treating depression, anxiety, drug addiction, chronic pain, and obesity. It is also useful in helping diabetics keep their disease under control. In addition, it is proving helpful in reducing prejudicial thinking, preventing burnout in work settings, and decreasing stigmatizing attitudes that health care providers sometimes have toward patients. (For a thorough, searchable listing of empirical studies into the effectiveness of ACT, visit http://www.context ualscience.org/publications.)

ACT has changed my life and the lives of many others. It has helped me to become more patient, empathetic, and caring. It has made me less materialistic. It has helped me cope more effectively with the stresses I now realize are simply a part of life.

Implications of the Progress in Clinical Psychology

The progress made in clinical psychology in the past fifty years is unprecedented in human history. This doesn't mean we have the ability to "cure" every psychological or behavioral problem. Indeed, the ACT work indicates that rather than getting rid of all of the difficult and unpleasant things involved in the human experience (which the word "cure" implies), our well-being improves when we learn to live flexibly despite, and *with*, these difficulties. This means accepting our emotional and cognitive reactions to our experience while continuing to live in alignment with our values.

These developments in clinical psychology have important implications for how we can build a better world. We need not wait until people develop psychological and behavioral problems such as depression, aggression, or drug abuse. Instead, we can foster psychological flexibility and a commitment to acting on values within families, schools, workplaces, and communities. In the process, we can significantly reduce human suffering and help make our world the best it can be.

B. F. Skinner argued that science tends to develop by focusing on the places where it can gain traction, moving on to more complex problems only after work with simpler problems has provided tools to help us tackle more intractable ones. In part 2 of this book, I hope I've shown you how much we have learned about human behavior and how much we can use this science to help people live more productive and caring lives.

Yet to enhance human well-being on a broad scale, we must use what we know about individual behavior to build the more nurturing larger social system we need. These problems have seemed insurmountable. However, in part 3 of the book, I will explore how we can apply what we have learned in studying the behavior of individuals to large organizations and cultural practices. By employing the same contextualist principles of prediction and influence to society on a broader scale, we can achieve transformations unlike any previously seen in human history.

Action Implications

The progress made in clinical psychology has important implications for how all of us can live our lives more effectively. It also has implications for public policy.

For Everyone

- Cultivate psychological flexibility, perhaps using one or more of the many recent ACT books for the general public:

  - To develop more psychological flexibility, *The Happiness Trap* (Harris 2007)

  - For overcoming psychological problems in general, *Get Out of Your Mind and Into Your Life* (Hayes 2005)

  - For depression, *The Mindfulness and Acceptance Workbook for Depression* (Robinson and Strosahl 2008)

  - For anxiety, *Acceptance and Commitment Therapy for Anxiety Disorders* (Eifert and Forsyth 2005)

  - For strengthening partner relationships, *ACT on Love* (Harris 2009b)

For Policy Makers

- Make evidence-based clinical interventions available to all who need them. Although I think ACT has made advances over cognitive behavioral therapy, I don't suggest that CBT is ineffective. The Evidence-Based Behavioral Practice website (http://www .ebbp.org/index.html) provides extensive information about the efficacy of CBT for many psychological problems. Similarly, the website of the Association for Contextual Behavioral Science (http://www.contextualscience.org) provides information about the efficacy of ACT.

- Fund further research on clinical interventions. Much progress has occurred in research on clinical treatments for psychological and behavioral problems. One of the most important areas of future research will be to investigate how clinical interventions can be available to more people through online programs and smartphone apps.

PART 3

The Larger Social Context Affecting Well-Being

I hope I've convinced you that advances in behavioral science make it possible to help families and schools become more nurturing. However, this still needs to be translated into approaches that can benefit entire populations. Evolving a society in which virtually every family and school is nurturing is partly a matter of making effective programs available to all families and schools that need them. But it also requires that we change the larger social system within which families and schools exist.

Families and schools exist within communities. Mass media and the state of the economy affect those communities; public policies may either support or stress them. Families and schools also exist within a network of for-profit, nonprofit, and government organizations that can have a huge influence on their functioning and the well-being of individuals. To realize the vision of a society that nurtures the well-being of every member, behavioral science needs to understand these larger social systems and their effect on families, schools, and individuals. It must provide principles to guide the evolution of larger social systems so their practices benefit everyone.

In this part of the book, I'll explore how the public health framework can guide such efforts, describing the major, society-wide factors that undermine well-being and showing how we can understand most of these factors in terms of the influence of recent developments in the evolution of corporate capitalism. Then, in part 4, I'll describe a strategy for evolving a system, based on the public health framework, that restrains capitalism's worst excesses while maintaining its many benefits.

CHAPTER 6

From People to Populations

The public health framework organizes how we can translate recent advances in prevention and treatment into widespread benefits. By applying the principles of this framework not just to physical health, but also to the gamut of physical, psychological, and behavioral problems that plague us, we can evolve societies that nurture everyone.

The goal of public health is to increase the incidence and prevalence of well-being in entire populations. It has five key practices:

- Targeting the incidence and prevalence of specific indicators of well-being

- Making use of epidemiological evidence to identify the major risk factors that contribute to the targeted aspect of well-being

- Setting up a surveillance system to monitor the incidence and prevalence of the target problem

- Pragmatically implementing programs, policies, and practices that can diminish the incidence or prevalence of the targeted problem

- Establishing an effective advocacy system to effect the changes in norms, policies, and practices required for population-wide improvements in well-being

We can use these principles to create a comprehensive public health movement that will evolve a society that nurtures the well-being of every person. The tobacco control movement is a great example of what we can accomplish. If you are under forty, you may not be aware that in the 1960s more than half of US men and about 35 percent of US women smoked

(CDC 2011). People smoked everywhere. In 1963, I was an orderly in the Emergency Department at Strong Memorial Hospital in Rochester, New York; we and our patients regularly smoked in the ER.

In this chapter, I describe the key features of an effective public health effort, provide examples of these efforts drawn from the tobacco control movement, and show how public health principles could be applied to increasing the prevalence of a nurturing environment in families and schools. I believe this could be the most significant intentional cultural change humans have yet achieved.

Targeting Incidence and Prevalence

Public health practice evolved from sometimes desperate efforts to control epidemics. One of the first and most disastrous was the bubonic plague. It arrived in Europe in 1347 when Genoese sailors arrived in Sicily from the Crimea. Many were already sick. They—or the fleas on the rats that accompanied them—proceeded to infect all of Europe, killing as many as twenty-four million people. That was one-third of the population.

More localized epidemics continued to erupt over the next three centuries.

It wasn't hard to define success in dealing with these terrifying epidemics. Authorities needed to reduce the *incidence* of a disease (the rate of occurrence of new cases) and thereby reduce its *prevalence* (the proportion of the population with the disease).

Although public health developed as a way to control infectious diseases, its practices are relevant to addressing anything that affects human well-being, including behaviors and environmental conditions. Public health agencies now monitor the incidence and prevalence of most diseases. And as they identify factors, such as smoking, that cause disease, they develop systems for monitoring the incidence and prevalence of those factors.

Unfortunately, the typical approach is to treat each problem as though it is unrelated to other problems. As a result, we pay little attention to environmental conditions that contribute to multiple problems. One of the most important things we could do to accelerate the improvement of human well-being would be to shift our focus from individual problems to the prevalence of environments that contribute to most of our problems.

Epidemiology

Epidemiology is the study of the patterns and causes of diseases in populations. Once reducing the incidence and prevalence of a disease is established as a public health goal, epidemiologists try to figure out what is causing the disease.

A classic example of this process was the discovery that contaminated water causes cholera. In *The Ghost Map* (2006), Stephen Johnson tells the story of John Snow, a London surgeon who developed the theory that contaminated water, not bad air, caused cholera. On four occasions between 1831 and 1854, there were outbreaks of cholera in London. On August 31, 1854, an outbreak began in the Soho area. By September 10, it had killed five hundred people. In an exhausting process, Snow and a local pastor interviewed the surviving victims of this outbreak and found that most lived in proximity to a pump at the corner of Broad and Cambridge Streets. Those living closer to another pump in the neighborhood had a much lower incidence of the disease. Snow convinced the Board of Guardians of St. James Parish, which controlled the pump, to remove the pump handle. When they did, the outbreak of cholera ended. (One building in the neighborhood—a brewery—had no cholera deaths. Guess what they were drinking.)

The episode stands as the first clear victory for the fundamental elements of public health. Careful observation led to a hypothesis about a risk factor for disease. Removal of that risk factor—the water—ended the epidemic.

Once a risk factor for a disease is identified, it becomes a target of public health efforts. Once we learned that cigarette smoking caused lung cancer, it became imperative to reduce the prevalence of smoking. That in turn led to identifying and targeting the prevalence of major influences on smoking behavior, such as the marketing of cigarettes to young people.

This way of thinking can be extended to any problem that confronts humans. Consider how it applies to nurturing environments. There is clear evidence that diverse psychological, behavioral, and health problems result from family and school environments that fail to nurture prosocial development (Biglan et al. 2012). This is ample justification for establishing a society-wide goal of increasing the prevalence of nurturing families and schools.

Embracing such a goal could help organize and integrate the disparate efforts of health care providers, educators, researchers, and policy makers, who are often working on individual problems, such as crime, drug abuse, or academic failure, but are not taking into account the fact that all of these problems stem from the same nonnurturing environments.

Once you embrace the goal of increasing the prevalence of nurturing families and schools, the natural next question is which factors can help effect these outcomes. In the following chapters, I describe how poverty and many corporate practices directly affect the development of youth and the quality of family life and school environments. In chapter 7, I describe corporate marketing practices that have a deleterious effect on well-being and suggest ways that these harmful influences can be reduced. In chapter 8, I describe how poverty and economic inequality in the United States increase the stress that families experience. I also describe the public policies that have contributed to the huge economic disparities that have arisen over the past forty years. In chapter 9, I trace these policies to the recent evolution of capitalism, wherein advocacy for such policies has emerged from their benefits to the economic well-being of the wealthiest among us. This analysis has direct implications for how we might reverse these harmful trends.

Good Surveillance

Public health practitioners refer to monitoring a disease as *surveillance*. People unfamiliar with that use of the term sometimes comment that it has a creepy connotation of spying on people. But this is good surveillance. It helps us know if we are reaching our goals for improving health and well-being.

You cannot know whether you are making progress in combating a disease or problem behavior unless you carefully measure its incidence and prevalence in the population. The practice of counting the number of people who contract a disease dates back to the monitoring of plague epidemics in the sixteenth century, when each summer the plague descended upon the cities of Italy. These days, all infectious diseases are routinely monitored.

Now the practice is slowly being extended to monitoring psychological and behavioral problems. The National Institute on Drug Abuse funds

Monitoring the Future, a system for assessing drug use and related behaviors in a representative sample of students throughout the country annually. It provides invaluable information about rates of alcohol consumption, adolescent smoking, and illicit drug use. In the 1990s, when data showed that adolescent cigarette smoking was increasing, Monitoring the Future triggered successful efforts to combat the rise (Johnston et al. 2013).

The tobacco control movement has been shaped and guided by evidence about how its actions and policies affect smoking prevalence. When policy initiatives such as ensuring clean indoor air proved helpful in motivating people to quit smoking, advocacy for such policies accelerated. Similar monitoring of psychological problems has lagged behind. For example, we still have no system to monitor rates of depression and anxiety among adults.

Ultimately, a surveillance system suited to creating a culture of nurturance would extend beyond monitoring problems. As almost all psychological, behavioral, and health problems are influenced by environments that either do or do not nurture healthy, prosocial development, we should be monitoring the quality of our environments. I would start with families and schools, and eventually move to tracking the quality of workplaces and public spaces.

A system for monitoring the prevalence of nurturing families and schools can be built on existing systems that monitor youth and adult well-being, such as Monitoring the Future and the Center for Disease Control's Youth Risk Behavior Surveillance System (Eaton et al. 2012). We could begin by monitoring nurturance in families through adolescent surveys. The Behavioral Risk Factor Surveillance System (Li et al. 2011), which assesses a wide range of health conditions and behaviors, obtains data on health and well-being from representative adult samples. However, although conflict-filled stressful environments are a major contributor to most psychological, behavioral, and health problems, the Behavioral Risk Factor Surveillance System obtains no data on conflict in homes.

Most surveillance systems provide good estimates of the rates of problems at the state level but do not have large enough samples to provide estimates at the community level. However, some communities are beginning to get data at this level (Mrazek, Biglan, and Hawkins 2005). Ultimately, every community should have accurate and timely data on the proportion of families and schools that are nurturing.

Now let me address a "Yes, but…" you may be having—namely that it is inconceivable that we would ever devote the resources needed to accomplish such surveillance. I've even heard such skepticism from people who conduct Monitoring the Future and the Youth Risk Behavior Surveillance System. Yet consider this: every mass-produced product you purchase is manufactured in a system that carefully monitors the quality of each item produced. The quality assurance procedures that have evolved in manufacturing over the past fifty years have increased the quality and durability of material goods enormously. For example, my son Mike still drives a Toyota Camry we purchased in 1994. In the 1960s it was rare if a car lasted more than five years.

Given this level of care in monitoring the quality of manufactured goods, surely it makes sense to be just as vigilant about the development and well-being of our fellow humans. And in the unlikely event that you have no interest in the well-being of young people, you should still value a system that monitors family and school nurturance. The benefits may reduce the taxes you pay and the chances that you or a loved one will be harmed due to failure to provide nurturing environments.

Programs, Policies, and Practices

Public health researchers and practitioners are pragmatic. They will implement any intervention that seems likely to promote a desired outcome in a population, and they will evaluate its impact in terms of creating the desired change, as measured by the surveillance system. There are three main routes to delivering such interventions: programs, policies, and practices.

Programs

I've already described many family and school programs that can improve these two environments and promote prosocial development. The family programs were developed mostly for delivery to individual families or small groups of families. However, as we adopt the goal of increasing the prevalence of nurturing families, we need to find more efficient methods to ensure that we reach every family that would benefit.

One of the first people to embrace the goal of affecting an entire population of families was Matt Sanders, a New Zealander who is now at the University of Queensland in Brisbane, Australia. Like me, Sanders has a background in behavior analysis. He began developing behavioral interventions for families in the late 1970s and has an especially pragmatic approach. Early on, he realized that intensive home-based coaching of parents could be effective but wouldn't reach many parents. Then he visited the Stanford Heart Disease Prevention Program and was impressed by their effort to reach the entire population in several California communities. This inspired him to spend the next ten years developing the interventions that now comprise his multilevel program, the Triple P–Positive Parenting Program. It makes use of mass media, offers ninety-minute seminars for parents, and provides parents with tip sheets for specific problems, such as getting a young child to go to sleep at night. It also provides more intensive support for families that need it.

Sanders also teamed up with Ron Prinz, from the Psychology Department at the University of South Carolina, to see if they could affect the prevalence of behavioral problems among children in an entire population. They randomly assigned eighteen South Carolina counties to either offer or not offer Triple P. In the nine counties that offered the program, they trained about six hundred people who were likely to be in contact with parents of young children and therefore in a position to give parents advice about common behavioral problems, if the parents wanted advice. They trained preschool staff, child care providers, health care workers, and providers of mental health and social services.

At the time of the study, child maltreatment had been increasing throughout South Carolina. However, in the counties with the Triple P program, rates of child maltreatment did not rise, and further, they were significantly lower than in the control counties (Prinz et al. 2009). The intervention also significantly reduced foster care placements, which often result after abuse is detected. The Washington State Institute for Public Policy independently determined that the intervention produced a $6.06 return on each investment dollar (Lee et al. 2012).

The era of developing and evaluating family interventions seems to be winding down, having resulted in a substantial number of family interventions that have proven benefit. Research and practice are now turning to the question of how to reach families with brief, efficient, and effective programs that prevent or ameliorate the most common relationship problems they encounter.

There are also impressive examples of community-wide interventions to implement family and school-based interventions in entire communities. David Hawkins and Rico Catalano, at the Social Development Research Group at the University of Washington, created Communities That Care, a program that helps communities identify and address major risk factors for youth. In a randomized trial, the program helped communities significantly reduce usage of tobacco, alcohol, and other drugs, as well as delinquency (Hawkins et al. 2014). Prevention scientists Richard Spoth of Iowa State University and Mark Greenberg of Pennsylvania State University have teamed up to test a community intervention that provides both a family intervention and a school-based intervention. Their randomized trial showed that the intervention helped communities reduce substance use (Spoth et al. 2013).

Policies

In this book, I use the term *policies* to refer to laws and regulations that affect health or behavior, or conditions that affect either one (Wagenaar and Burris 2013). Examples include taxation of harmful products, prohibitions on marketing harmful products, and requirements to provide incentives for desirable behavior.

At the outset of the tobacco control movement, many of us hoped we could develop effective cessation and prevention programs that would reduce the prevalence of smoking. But despite all the work I've done on smoking prevention (for example, Biglan et al. 2000), I have to confess that policies, public advocacy, and education have been far more important than programs in reducing smoking.

Researchers with a public health orientation often argue that policies are the most efficient way of affecting entire populations. For example, Harold Holder, who worked at the Center for Advanced Study in the Behavioral Sciences as I did, often said something along the lines of "You wouldn't have to reach every parent with a program if you had policies that directly affected adolescent drinking." He pointed out that simply raising the price of alcohol has helped to reduce youth use, alcohol-related car crashes, and the development of alcoholism (Biglan et al. 2004).

Fortunately, there is no need to choose between policies and programs. No single intervention can be entirely successful, so we should take public health victories wherever we can get them.

Since working with Harold, I've had the pleasure of working with Kelli Komro, another advocate of policy interventions. She and her husband, Alex Wagenaar, who are at the University of Florida, collect policy studies the way some people collect baseball cards. Komro worked with me and twenty other behavioral scientists on the Promise Neighborhood Research Consortium, leading our efforts to identify evidence-based policies that are beneficial for child and adolescent development. The consortium's website (http://www.promiseneighborhoods.org) lists more than fifty such policies.

One example of an effective and beneficial evidence-based policy is taxation of alcoholic beverages. Komro's review concluded that doubling the tax on alcoholic beverages could produce all of the following benefits:

- A 35 percent reduction in alcohol-related morbidity and mortality

- An 11 percent reduction in traffic crash deaths

- A 6 percent reduction in sexually transmitted diseases

- A 2 percent reduction in violence

- A 17 percent reduction in beer consumption

- A 25 percent reduction in wine consumption

- A 25 percent reduction in distilled spirits consumption

Recently Alex Wagenaar and Scott Burris edited an excellent book on policies, titled *Public Health Law Research: Theory and Methods* (2013). It provides numerous examples of policies that are benefiting public health, along with information about how the impact of policies can be evaluated. We also have to be concerned with policies that harm well-being. In chapter 8, I'll describe how numerous policy changes in the United States over the past thirty years have harmed families and young people.

Practices

In addition to developing programs and policies, behaviorists and other interventionists have come up with a large number of simple techniques for influencing behavior. These are valuable resources for anyone engaged in efforts to help people develop their skills. In earlier chapters, I've mentioned Dennis Embry and his work in developing the Good Behavior Game. A voracious reader, he has been tracking the development of simple behavior-influencing techniques for many years and has identified more than fifty techniques proven to affect one or more behaviors of children, youth, or adults. He calls the individual techniques *kernels* (Embry and Biglan 2008).

Many kernels involve providing reinforcement for behavior you want to increase. Examples include praise notes, which teachers can write to students and students can write to each other, and "the mystery motivator" or "prize bowl," where people draw prizes of varying values for behaviors as diverse as completing homework or having drug-free urinalysis results.

Kernels exert their effects in different ways. Examples of kernels that reduce reinforcement for a problem behavior or increase the cost of such behavior include time-outs and higher taxes on cigarettes or alcohol. Other kernels affect behavior through *antecedent stimulation*, meaning establishing a signal that elicits a desired behavior. For example, you can establish nonverbal transition cues that guide students from one activity to another. Many teachers establish a cue such as flipping the lights on and off or raising a hand to signal that it is time for the class to pay attention to the teacher. This might seem trivial, but studies have shown that orderly transitions from one classroom activity to another can free up a week or more of instructional time across a school year.

Some kernels affect behavior by changing the way people think about things. For example, when people make a public commitment, it is more likely they will do what they said they would do. This is because we all have a history of reinforcement for doing what we said we would do, along with a history of social disapproval when we failed to follow through. Finally, some kernels affect well-being by affecting physiology. For example, considerable recent evidence indicates that supplementing diets with omega-3 fatty acids can reduce aggression, violence, depression, bipolar disorder, postpartum depression, and borderline personality disorder (Embry and Biglan 2008).

People like kernels because they are simple, easy-to-implement practices that usually produce immediate results. Parents, teachers, child care workers, and managers can use these positive techniques to nurture prosocial behavior in others and replace nagging, criticism, and cajoling. Spreading awareness of these techniques and promoting their use is another way we can help entire populations become more nurturing.

Advocacy

Returning to the tobacco control movement: As evidence about the harm of smoking grew, it mobilized people who had been harmed by smoking to create advocacy organizations that supported further investigation of the health consequences of smoking and the factors that influence smoking. In what I like to call a virtuous cycle, researchers learned more and more about the harm of smoking, advocates spread the word about these detrimental effects, and this generated further support for research and advocacy about the harm of smoking and ways to reduce smoking.

Surgeon General reports, National Cancer Institute monographs, and Institute of Medicine reports systematically marshaled evidence about specific aspects of the smoking problem to generate support for antismoking policies. For example, a series of Surgeon General reports documented how cigarettes cause heart disease, strokes, aneurysms, chronic obstructive lung disease, asthma, low birth weights of babies, premature births, sudden infant death syndrome, and most kinds of cancer (US Department of Health and Human Services 1980, 1981, 1982, 1983, 1984, 1988, 1989). A Surgeon General report on the effects of secondhand smoke showed that as many as fifty thousand people a year die due to exposure to other people's cigarettes (US Department of Health and Human Services 1986). That enlisted support among nonsmokers for restricting smoking and getting smokers to quit. Another report showed that tobacco is an addictive product, which undermined tobacco industry arguments that smoking was simply a lifestyle choice (US Department of Health and Human Services 1988).

The tobacco control movement has been enormously creative in finding ways to persuade people that cigarette smoking should be treated as an epidemic. To dramatically illustrate how many people cigarettes kill each year, we often say that it is as if two Boeing 747s crashed every day of the year, killing everyone on board. If two 747s crashed today, the FAA would probably ground all other 747s until it had thoroughly investigated the problem and determined the cause. Can you imagine such carnage going on for a week without government taking action?

A similar effort could convince millions of Americans that their well-being and the well-being of the nation depend on making families, schools, workplaces, neighborhoods, and communities more nurturing. Non-nurturing environments contribute directly to most of the psychological, behavioral, and health problems of society. We need to find creative ways to communicate evidence of this via many avenues, from government reports and news stories to blogs and social networks to entertainment media.

Action Implications

I envision—and hope you can envision—a society-wide movement working to increase the prevalence of nurturing environments. I think we should start with a focus on families and schools because they are the most important environments for youth, and because most psychological, health, and behavioral problems begin in childhood or adolescence.

For Policy Makers

- Create an umbrella organization focused on nurturing families—a coalition of advocacy organizations and foundations dedicated to alleviating one or more of the most common and costly psychological, behavioral, or health problems.

- Produce Institute of Medicine or Surgeon General reports on how to ensure that families and schools are nurturing.

  - In the report on families, merge all of the evidence on the detrimental impact of family dysfunction on all aspects of well-being. Describe the policies, programs, and practices now available to reduce the prevalence of dysfunctional families, thereby contributing to preventing an entire range of psychological, behavioral, and health problems. This would provide an agenda for future research and policy making.

- In the report on schools, review the evidence regarding how conflicts between students and adult-to-student punitiveness both contribute to academic failure and the development of psychological, behavioral, and health problems. Review the evidence supporting specific policies, programs, and practices to reduce these conditions. Also call for the research and policy making needed to increase the prevalence of nurturing schools.

- Create policies that target increasing the prevalence of nurturing families and schools, such as the following:

  - Assessing the prevalence of nurturing environments in both families and schools

  - Making evidence-based family interventions available to families that need them

- Requiring schools to monitor levels of punishment and student conflict, and requiring them to implement evidence-based social behavior programs to address these problems

- Adopt policies that reduce stress on families and schools. (See chapter 8 for details.)

For People Working on Family Support

- Create a unified profession that unites all the disparate professions and organizations that work to improve family functioning.

- Instead of relying on agencies that only detect and intervene in cases of child abuse, build a system that, like Triple P, attempts to reach every family with as much or as little help as they need to deal with common problems in child rearing. The resulting agency or network of agencies should have the responsibility to contact parents and support their success from before the birth of their first child through their children's adolescence.

For Educators

- Identify and implement one or more of the evidence-based programs that have proven benefit in reducing conflict and punitiveness and promoting prosocial behavior.

- Join and support the Association for Positive Behavior Support, which is already advancing nurturing practices in our schools.

For Parents and Other Community Members

- Examine your own environments. Consider your immediate and extended family, your workplace, your circle of friends, your neighborhood, the organizations you belong to, and the civic activities you are involved in.

  - For each environment, ask yourself how nurturing it is. Are people kind and caring, or do they tend to be critical and argumentative?

  - Think about your own behavior in each environment. Do you add to conflict and discomfort, or do you model and reinforce kind and caring behavior?

  - Are there small things you can do to make these environments more nurturing?

  - Notice any tendencies you may have to blame others for things they do that increase your stress or that of other people. You may be correct about that, but you can choose to step back from such thoughts and find ways to act that, over time, can move you and those around you toward more compassionate behavior.

- Join organizations that support policies and programs to increase nurturance in families and schools.

- Advocate that your elected officials implement family support policies and programs.

- Inquire about whether your child's school is implementing evidence-based programs to prevent conflict and bullying.

CHAPTER 7

Harmful Corporate Marketing Practices

Imagine, if you will, that you raise your children carefully, using all of the love, patience, and skills described in part 2 of this book. Would you be satisfied if your kids got a good education, got married, had kids, had a good job, and then died of a smoking-related illness at age forty-five? Of course not.

Successful nurturance includes protecting our children from everything that could damage their health and well-being throughout life. One of the influences that is most important yet also most difficult to control is the marketing of harmful products. If you've ever been in a supermarket with a young child, you've probably had the experience of your child demanding candy at the checkout counter and getting upset when it wasn't forthcoming. Of course, stores put candy there because they know how little kids work—and because they know how hesitant most parents are to refuse and risk a tantrum.

Even the most competent and motivated parents are challenged to protect their children from the risks modern marketing poses to healthy child development. For example, John Pierce and his colleagues at the University of California, San Diego, studied a group of 894 early adolescents whose parents used effective parenting practices: they were warm, they monitored their kids' activities, and they did a good job of setting limits. Yet even among these well-parented teens, those who were interested in and liked cigarette ads were more likely to start smoking over the next three years (Pierce et al. 2002).

In this chapter, I describe some of the most harmful marketing practices, along with the behavioral principles that underlie successful marketing, and propose guidelines for restricting marketing practices that undermine efforts to nurture children's healthy development.

Marketing

Products are marketed by associating the product or brand with things the consumer desires. Through advertising, promotions, store displays, distribution of branded paraphernalia, and placement of products in the media, marketers try to get potential consumers to feel that the product will give them something they'd rather have than their money. It might be something tangible, like the ability to cut grass; or it could be emotional, like the feeling you get when you wear new clothes and someone compliments you on them. This is not to say that marketing is inherently evil. It actually has many benefits, including telling us about things that genuinely improve our lives. But sometimes it can cause great harm.

Marketing Cigarettes to Teens

I began to realize the importance of corporate practices on well-being when the US Department of Justice asked me to study the tobacco industry's youth marketing. Before I was finished, I had read more than twenty thousand pages of tobacco company documents and reviewed thousands of cigarette ads. As I studied the documents, I began to see how the tobacco companies were systematically recruiting young people to become addicted to cigarettes.

And for good reason. Numerous documents showed that tobacco companies had carefully analyzed the cigarette market and knew that very few people would start smoking after their teen years. In the ninety-six pages of testimony I submitted regarding the tobacco company R. J. Reynolds, I cited numerous documents showing that the company understood that recruiting underage teens to smoke was vital in maintaining their market share. In a memo to Reynolds executives, an R. J. Reynolds employee, Dianne Burrows, nicely summarized the situation: "*Younger adult smokers have been the critical factor in the growth and decline of every major brand and company over the last fifty years. They will continue to be just as important to brands/companies in the future* for two simple reasons: The renewal of the market stems almost entirely from eighteen-year-old smokers. No more than 5 percent of smokers start after age twenty-four. The brand loyalty of eighteen-year-old smokers far outweighs any tendency to switch with age" (Biglan 2004, p. 292; emphasis in the original). (Other documents showed that "eighteen-year-old smokers" was in fact code for those under eighteen. It came into use after tobacco companies stopped talking openly about those under eighteen due to concerns about accusations they were marketing to underage teens.)

Over at Philip Morris, the analysis was pretty much the same. As one executive put it, "It is during the teenage years that the initial brand choice is made: At least part of the success of Marlboro Red during its most rapid growth period was because it became *the* brand of choice among teenagers who then stuck with it as they grew older" (Biglan 2004, Demonstrative 8, p. 3).

The resulting marketing has had devastating consequences. John Pierce, Betsy Gilpin, and Won Choi (1999) calculated that Marlboro's marketing between 1988 and 1998 would eventually lead to deaths of 300,000 young people who became addicted as teens. Camel marketing eventually contributed to the deaths of even more young people— 520,000—thanks to the success of the Joe Camel campaign, which Philip Morris implemented during this period.

The best available estimates are that smoking currently kills about 400,000 smokers in the United States each year, along with about 50,000 people who don't smoke but are exposed to others' smoke (CDC 2008).

If smoking kills, then anything that induces people to smoke makes a direct contribution to death and is itself a killer. Tobacco industry marketing should be treated in the same way we treat the cause of an infectious disease.

The Behavioral Processes Involved in Marketing

In chapter 1, I described human verbal relational abilities. This capacity has a great deal to do with why marketing can be so effective. Human valuing of things is a function of the relational networks in which those things are embedded. In marketing cigarettes to young people, corporations utilize this by starting with some things young people already value and associating them with the product to be sold. Through brand identities, logos, and repeated messages, consumers come to associate valued outcomes with the product. If a company can get the consumer to relate the brand to valued outcomes, they can make having that product highly reinforcing.

Consider the red chevron on Marlboro packs of cigarettes. What kinds of things do young people value that the company could get them to relate to the Marlboro brand? The most basic and important thing for most adolescents is social acceptance. Therefore, it isn't surprising that adolescents who are having trouble academically or experiencing social rejection are particularly likely to be susceptible to advertising that suggests they will be accepted by their peers if they smoke a particular brand of cigarette (Forrester et al. 2007; National Cancer Institute 2008). My review of hundreds of Marlboro ads showed that they routinely associated the brand with popularity. They also associated it with things related to popularity, such as being rugged and physically attractive, being tough, being an independent adult, or being someone that people admire. Many young people—especially those most likely to take up smoking—crave excitement and taking risks. Thus, many Marlboro ads associate the brand with bronco busting and auto racing (National Cancer Institute 2008).

So why do young people take up smoking despite the evidence that it is harmful? One thing to consider is that not all young people are susceptible to tobacco advertising. The susceptible kids are those struggling for social acceptance and excitement. For these kids, the risk of getting a disease many years later is much less important than getting a chance to gain social acceptance in the short term. And for many, the risk associated with smoking may actually make smoking more attractive. This is why, in my most recent work on smoking prevention programs, we have almost entirely abandoned associating smoking with health risks. Instead, we associate *not* smoking with social acceptance, fun, and excitement (Gordon, Biglan, and Smolkowski 2008).

In sum, marketers can make it reinforcing to buy and use a harmful product simply by getting people to relate the brand to things that are already important reinforcers for them. The brand and logo of the product can come to have powerful evocative effects, thanks being associated with multiple images of things the person already values.

Seeing the Harmfulness of Cigarette Advertising

Tobacco industry practices have directly harmed public health in several other ways. As concerns mounted about the dangers of smoking, the industry developed so-called low-tar and low-nicotine cigarettes and marketed them as safer alternatives to regular cigarettes. They did this to persuade smokers to switch to "light" cigarettes rather than stop smoking. However, their own research showed that these cigarettes were not safer.

When concerns were raised that cigarette marketing was enticing young people to smoke, the industry's public relations arm, the Tobacco Institute, created a program supposedly aimed at preventing smoking among youth. But the review of their programs that I did for the Department of Justice showed that it was designed to create the impression that the companies didn't want youth to smoke and that youth smoking was due to lax parenting (Biglan 2004). Internal documents of the Tobacco Institute showed that it typically announced these programs in state capitals and briefed editorial boards and legislators on them. These contacts and their effectiveness in deterring legislation that would restrict tobacco marketing carefully monitored legislative action and reported to the industry. However, I could find no evidence that the industry ever tested whether the programs reached parents or had any impact on smoking among young people.

In a landmark decision in 2006, in *United States v. Philip Morris et al.*, Judge Gladys Kessler found that the tobacco industry knew that cigarettes caused cancer, hid these facts from the public, marketed to youth, and marketed so-called low-tar and low-nicotine cigarettes to prevent people from quitting, even though they knew that these cigarettes were not safer. For the first time, an industry was found culpable for marketing that influenced people to engage in unhealthy behavior.

Marketing Alcohol to Adolescents

Your efforts to raise healthy, successful young people would come to a tragic end if your teen died or received grave injuries in an alcohol-related car crash. According to the Centers for Disease Control and Prevention, in 2010 about 2,700 teens age sixteen to nineteen died in car crashes and

282,000 sustained injuries (CDC 2012). About a quarter of the car crashes are alcohol related, and alcohol marketing plays a significant role in the problem of youth drinking.

When Judge Kessler ruled the tobacco industry was to blame for people becoming addicted to cigarettes and remaining addicted, the implications of this ruling were immediately obvious to the alcohol industry. Therefore, if you search the bottom of most TV ads for alcoholic beverages these days, you'll find a statement like, "Drink Responsibly." If the tobacco industry could be held accountable for the death and disease of young people who were addicted due to cigarette advertising, might the alcohol industry also be liable if it could be shown that their marketing influences young people to drink as minors or to drink to excess? The evidence is mounting that this is the case, although it isn't yet as solid as it is for tobacco marketing.

Alcohol use contributes to death in a variety of ways. In the United States, it accounts for 41 percent of all traffic fatalities—more than seventeen thousand deaths annually (National Highway Traffic Safety Administration 2008). It also contributes to deaths through drowning, falls, hypothermia, burns, suicides, and homicides (CDC 2013). One analysis, carried out by the Bureau of Justice Statistics (Greenfeld 1998), estimated that 40 percent of all crime is committed under the influence of alcohol. Alcohol use, however, is not invariably harmful as tobacco use is. It is a part of most cultures, contributes to social relations, and, in moderation, may have some health benefits.

On the other hand, binge drinking—defined as having five or more drinks at a time—is a major problem, especially among young people. Binge drinkers have more alcohol-related car crashes and are more likely to become alcoholics (CDC 2013). The Harvard School of Public Health College Alcohol Study, which looked at 120 college campuses, found that 44 percent of students reported binge drinking (Wechsler and Nelson 2008). Nearly 20 percent reported such episodes more than once every two weeks. Students on campuses with high rates of binge drinking reported more assaults and unwanted sexual advances. Binge drinking is also a problem among high school students. In Oregon, we found that 10 percent of eighth-graders and 25 percent of eleventh-graders reported binge drinking in the last thirty days (Boles, Biglan, and Smolkowski 2006).

My friend and colleague Joel Grube has summarized evidence on the impact of alcohol advertising. Although the alcohol industry pledged that it wouldn't advertise on TV shows or in magazines where more than 30 percent of the audience is teens, that standard is functionally meaningless because their ads still reach most youth. You see, the industry concentrates its marketing in venues chosen to reach the 30 percent maximum, rather than selecting those likely to reach very few young people. The average teen sees about 245 alcohol ads on TV each year, and the 30 percent who view the most see as many as 780 per year. As a result, young people actually encounter 45 percent more ads for beer and 65 percent more ads for alcopops, or coolers, than adults do. By the way, if you aren't a teen, you may not know that alcopops are alcoholic beverages that are sweetened to make them appealing to those who aren't accustomed to drinking.

(Lest you think that all this concern about alcohol comes from a bunch of prissy teetotalers, each year Joel Grube sends me a fine bottle of California wine. If the California Golden Bears ever beat the Oregon Ducks in football, I will send him an even finer bottle of Oregon wine.)

Although alcohol marketers will tell you that their advertising targets only adults, the evidence shows otherwise. Youth who see more alcohol ads know more about alcohol and are more familiar with brands (Pechmann et al. 2011). And some experiments have shown that when young people see ads for alcohol, they become more interested in drinking (Grube, Madden, and Friese 1996). Finally, some studies, but not all, have shown that communities with more alcohol advertising have more young people who drink and more alcohol-related motor vehicle fatalities (Grube and Nygaard 2005).

Marketing Junk Food

Now the food industry also has reason to worry. The US obesity rate has been steadily increasing, and evidence is mounting that food marketing is one reason.

The definition of obesity is a body mass index (BMI) of 30 or more. BMI is a calculation based on height and weight; for example, an adult who is five foot nine and weighs 203 pounds would have a BMI of 30; for the average person of that height, this would be at least 35 pounds overweight. Figure 3, which comes from the CDC Behavioral Risk Factor Surveillance System, shows the rate of obesity for US states in 1990, 2000, and 2010. In most states for which there was data, less than 15 percent of the adult population was obese in 1990. In 2010, just twenty years later, over 20 percent of adults were obese in every state; in twelve states, more than 30 percent were obese (CDC 2014).

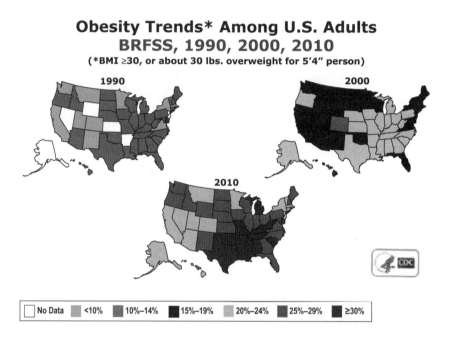

Figure 3. Obesity trends among US adults. (Reprinted from "Overweight and Obesity: Adult Obesity Facts," an Internet-based fact sheet by the CDC, available at http://www.cdc.gov/obesity/data/adult.html.)

In her book *Food Politics* (2002), Marion Nestle (no relation to the food company) has described the role of food processing and marketing in increasing obesity. Food companies spend more than $11 billion annually on advertising, and the foods most heavily marketed are those that are most profitable. Unfortunately, many are high in fat or calories and have little nutritional value.

Television ads for food and beverages on Saturday morning children's shows more than tripled between 1987 and 1994, and by the end of that period, about 57 percent of the ads were for foods of little nutritional value, such as sweetened breakfast cereals and candy. More recently, a study looked at what percentage of TV food ads in 2003 and 2004 targeted to children were for foods high in fat, sugar, or sodium (L. M. Powell et al. 2007). Among two- to eleven-year-olds, 97.8 percent of ads were for such foods, and among twelve- to seventeen-year-olds, 89.4 percent of ads were for such foods.

TV viewing is associated with obesity in children (Dennison, Erb, and Jenkins 2002). Although inactivity is certainly one reason for this link, exposure to ads for fattening foods is another (Borzekowski and Robinson 2001; Dixon et al. 2007). Both broadcasters and the food industry put the onus for this problem on parents, saying that parents need to guide their children. This is the same argument that the tobacco companies make. It may work to prevent unwanted restrictions on broadcasters and advertisers, but as a practical matter, childhood obesity will remain a problem as long as marketing unhealthful foods to children continues.

In 2006, the Institute of Medicine reviewed 123 empirical studies of the influence of food and beverage marketing on the diets and health of children and adolescents (IOM Committee on Food Marketing and the Diets of Children and Youth 2006). Studies involving children ages two to eleven led an Institute of Medicine committee to conclude that there is strong evidence that TV ads influence children's food and beverage preferences and moderate evidence that it affects their beliefs about food and beverages. The committee concluded that food marketing influences children to prefer and request unhealthful foods. The evidence regarding the influence of television marketing on teens was less clear, partly because there have been fewer studies. The committee concluded that exposure to television advertising is associated with childhood obesity. However, despite the fact that the committee reviewed experimental studies showing the causal effect of advertising on children's food preferences, it was unwilling to state conclusively that exposure to food advertising caused childhood obesity.

Even if we reach every family and school with information about the things they need to do to encourage healthful eating and exercise patterns among children, this won't be enough to address the problem of obesity (or drinking and smoking) among young people. We have to reduce the effects of marketing.

Free Speech and Corporate Marketing

Any proposal to restrict marketing by these industries must contend with long-standing principles of free speech. In the United States, we have constitutional protections of speech that extend even to "commercial speech," such as advertising. Restrictions on such speech start us down a slippery slope that could result in substantial governmental suppression of any speech the current government doesn't like.

In the United States, the current constitutional principles regulating commercial speech were articulated in a 1980 US Supreme Court case, *Central Hudson Gas & Electric Corp. v. Public Service Commission*, which established criteria for allowing government regulation of commercial speech. Truthful advertising for legal products is protected. Any restriction must advance a substantial interest of the government, and there must be clear evidence that the regulation serves that interest. Finally, the regulation should be narrowly tailored to restrict only the problematic speech.

This issue has been litigated regarding cigarette advertising. In 2001, the US Supreme Court overturned Massachusetts regulations that prohibited cigarette advertising within one thousand feet of schools (Koh 2002). Massachusetts had enacted the regulations based on evidence that cigarette advertisements appeared more often in areas that reached children than in others. That fact concurs with much other evidence that the tobacco industry has targeted young people (Biglan 2004). However, the court ruled that, although the ban advanced a legitimate state interest—preventing youth smoking—and the restriction would advance that interest, such advertising was truthful and for a lawful purpose. The court concluded that the ban was not narrowly tailored, as it would prohibit most current tobacco advertising in Massachusetts.

Apparently, both sides in the case agreed that the cigarette advertising was truthful and for a legal purpose. I think they were mistaken. The legal analysis in this case points to the need to bring the law into line with what the behavioral sciences have learned about human behavior.

The courts considered the advertising truthful in the sense that it accurately indicated the brand being sold and its price. However, that analysis fails to consider the functional effects of cigarette advertising. Research conducted both by the tobacco industry and by public health researchers shows that advertising for cigarette brands that are popular among youth influences many young people to believe that those who smoke certain brand will be seen as popular, tough, exciting, adventurous, and so on. My testimony in *United States v. Philip Morris et al.* cited nine studies that showed this (Biglan 2004). For example, one study (Pechmann and Knight 2002) found that when ninth-graders were exposed to cigarette advertising, they rated smokers more positively on adjectives such as "fun," "well liked," "sexy," "desirable to date," "successful," "smart," "intelligent," and "cool." In other words, the ads influenced these adolescents to view smokers more favorably. Other studies show that when adolescents view smokers more favorably, they are more likely to take up smoking.

The tobacco companies' own research also shows that their advertising conveys positive images of smokers. For example, one extensive study of the Marlboro image indicated that the brand evoked the following images and concepts: all-American; hardworking and trustworthy; rugged individualism; and being a man's man, as defined by being experienced, sure of oneself, confident, in charge, self-sufficient, down to earth, and cool and calm (Biglan 2004). Cigarette advertising convinces vulnerable adolescents that they can achieve this desired image by smoking a brand popular among youth. And so they smoke.

So is cigarette advertising truthful? In a sense, it is. Many adolescents come to see the Marlboro smoker as tough and popular. So there is some truth to their notion that if they smoke Marlboros, they will appear this way to their peers. Yet this is a Faustian bargain for which adolescents are ill informed. They get an image that may contribute to their social acceptance, and the tobacco company gets an addicted smoker. As one R. J. Reynolds executive put it, "Attract a smoker at the earliest opportunity and let brand loyalty turn that smoker into a valuable asset" (Biglan 2004, 290).

But from another perspective, the advertising is deceptive. It portrays smoking as an activity that will lead to substantial social benefit and says nothing about the fact that an adolescent who takes up smoking will have a difficult and expensive addiction and a one-in-three chance of dying of a smoking-related illness. The law needs to catch up with the behavioral sciences and look at not simply what an ad says but how it functions. Cigarette advertising functions to get young people to take up smoking and to keep current smokers from quitting. As a result, it currently contributes to 450,000 deaths in the United States each year.

Targeting marketing practices because of their impact on public health will seem controversial to many. And any industry worth its salt will try to keep it controversial by sowing doubts about the evidence and arguing that encroachment on their marketing practices unduly restricts freedom of speech. As long as influential citizens can be convinced that altering marketing to improve public health is a radical and unwarranted idea, harmful marketing will continue.

This situation may seem disheartening. But recall the evolution of sanitary practices. It was once nobody's business what people did with their sewage. When it became clear that raw sewage was killing people, standards changed. A similar process is underway for marketing practices that endanger health. If the legal system can stop your neighbor from doing as he pleases with his sewage, why should we not have a legal system that prohibits marketing that systemically contributes to death? The day will come when we will look back and marvel that we ever allowed the cigarette, alcohol, or food industries to market in ways that contribute to disease and death.

Guidelines for Restrictions of Marketing Practices

I am well aware that legal regulation of marketing runs the risk of excessive government control of free speech. If the principle is simply that the government can prohibit advertising that contributes to harm to people in any way, where might we end up? Would we prohibit ads for high-fat food? How about peanuts, which can cause deadly allergic reactions in some people? Reclining chairs encourage inactivity. Perhaps recliner ads should target only those who already exercise. Libertarian op-ed writers could have a field day with this issue.

Epidemiological research can provide guidance. Public health targets disease, health behaviors, and risk factors based on their demonstrated harm to human well-being. Public health officials have the power to restrict or limit practices that contribute to significant disease, injury, or death. For example, they can recall tainted products, quarantine infected people, and prohibit the marketing of dangerous drugs. However, our society has not given the government a blank check to prohibit anything deemed harmful by some passion of the moment.

As applied to marketing tobacco, alcohol, and unhealthful foods, particularly to young people, limitations must be based on clear and convincing empirical evidence that advertising influences a substantial number of people to engage in a behavior that results in death for a significant number of them. And to be clear and convincing, at least some of the evidence would need to be experimental. That is, it would need to show that advertising is a direct influence on the behavior when other sources of influence are controlled.

As an example of how this comes about, in five studies on the effects of cigarette advertising on youth that I reviewed in *United States v. Philip Morris et al.* (Biglan 2004), adolescents were randomly assigned to see or not see the ads, and their attitudes and intentions to smoke were subsequently measured. By randomly assigning adolescents to these two conditions, the studies controlled for other possible explanations of the link between exposure to ads and smoking, such as the possibility that adolescents who were already interested in smoking were more likely to look at the ads. These experiments showed that exposure to the ads significantly increased positive attitudes toward smoking and toward those who smoked the brand advertised, and increased intentions to smoke. Numerous studies have shown that these attitudes and intentions do influence young people to start smoking.

Then there is the question of how to define a "substantial number" of people and a "significant number" of deaths. One way to think about this is in terms of what we would deem substantial or significant in other parallel situations. Research by Betsy Gilpin and colleagues (1999) estimated that about 2,933 people under the age of twenty-one become regular smokers each day. Estimates in the CDC's *Morbidity and Mortality Weekly Report* indicate that about one-third of young people who begin smoking will eventually die of a smoking-related illness (US Department of Health and Human Services 2014). So every day, cigarette advertising lures nearly one thousand people to an early death. We currently prohibit food production practices that have far less serious outcomes. For example, the CDC has mounted a major effort to combat contamination of food by *E. coli*, which kills about sixty people a year (Rangel et al. 2005).

In my view, there currently isn't sufficient *experimental* evidence showing that specific practices in marketing alcohol and food contribute to ill health, injury, and death, although considerable correlational evidence shows that they do. Therefore, experimental studies are needed to determine whether exposure to ads for alcoholic beverages or unhealthful foods increases young people's motivation to drink or to eat those foods. A series of studies showing this would be sufficient reason to restrict such advertising.

Once you begin to consider marketing in terms of its impact on public health, you may wonder whether other corporate practices are also damaging to health and well-being. I am convinced that corporate advocacy for certain economic policies contributes to poverty and economic inequality, which cause substantial harm to well-being. Therefore, in the next chapter, I'll describe how poverty and inequality harm well-being. Then, in chapter 9, I'll analyze how the evolution of economic policies has created the huge income disparities evident in the United States and examine the role that corporate advocacy has played in this evolution.

Action Implications

Research on the impact of cigarette, alcohol, and food advertising could better inform policy makers, parents, and citizens in general. By preventing young people from exposure to harmful advertising, we can significantly reduce the risks to their health.

For Policy Makers

- Fund further research on the impact of food and alcohol marketing practices to obtain experimental evidence on the harm to public health from certain marketing practices.

- Enact laws that establish standards for assessing whether marketing practices are harmful to health, replacing the standard established in *Central Hudson Gas & Electric Corp. v. Public Service Commission* with one that assesses not simply the literal truth of an ad but also the functional effects of ads on unhealthful behavior.

For Parents

- Limit your child's exposure to advertising for tobacco, alcohol, and unhealthful food—if you can. I wish I could provide tips on how to inoculate children against the effects of such advertising. Unfortunately, research has not found media literacy training to reduce the persuasive influence of such advertising. However, I strongly recommend that you take advantage of new technologies that can help reduce children's exposure to TV ads. For example, you might record a show your child watches and fast-forward through the advertisements.

For Citizens

- Support legislation to fund research on the impact of marketing on the well-being of young people, and legislation to limit children's exposure to advertising for tobacco, alcoholic beverages, and unhealthful foods.

CHAPTER 8

Poverty and Economic Inequality

In previous chapters, I've described the nurturing conditions that are important for young people to thrive. Children need warm, patient, attentive, and skilled parents and teachers who provide instruction and reinforcement for all the diverse behaviors and values they need to become productive and caring members of society. They need parents and teachers who minimize punitive, critical, and demeaning behavior toward them and limit their opportunities to engage in dangerous or counterproductive behavior. Ultimately, they must be able to flexibly pursue their values, even when doing so requires considerable persistence and the acceptance of strong negative feelings.

Poverty is a major obstacle to creating these nurturing conditions. I hope I have demonstrated the effectiveness of interventions to improve young peoples' chances in life. Although these interventions can benefit children in poor families and neighborhoods, poverty makes it harder for these programs to help. If we can reduce poverty and economic inequality, we will produce benefits for poor families even if we never reach them with interventions.

Imagining Being Poor

When we hear about the misfortunes of others, it is a natural, psychologically protective mechanism to think of reasons why similar misfortunes couldn't happen to us. See if that process isn't operating as you read this chapter. Watch for thoughts like *It couldn't happen to me.*

Consider a study done in 2007, before the 2009 recession (Himmelstein et al. 2009). It found that medical problems led to 62 percent of bankruptcies. Among people filing for medically caused bankruptcies, 75 percent had health insurance, and most were well educated and owned homes. This study indicates that even if you are middle-class, should you suffer a heart attack or stroke, between the cost of medical care and an inability to work, you could quickly lose your life savings and your home.

What would it be like to be poor? The official poverty level for a family of four is $23,050. Perhaps you earn more than that, or you're a student with good prospects for making more than that in the near future. Imagine living for just one month on a little less than $2,000. If you lived alone you could probably afford an apartment and enough to eat. But what if you were supporting three others? The federal minimum wage is $7.25 an hour. If you worked full-time at that wage, you would earn about $14,500 a year: not enough to afford an apartment almost anywhere in the country.

The Damage Done by Poverty

Psychologist Lisa Goodman and her colleagues at Boston University (2013) summarized the consequences of poverty that make it so stressful. There are the challenges of securing food and housing. Imagine that you haven't yet figured out where you're going to sleep tonight. Poverty is also stigmatizing. If you were poor, there is a good chance that people would apply negative labels to you, such as "unmotivated," "uneducated," "unpleasant," "dirty," "angry," "stupid," "criminal," "violent," "immoral," "alcoholic," and "abusive." As you might imagine, people who have thoughts like this about you wouldn't be very warm or respectful. As a result, you would have many stressful interactions. You would also have very little power. If you felt that a merchant, professional, or bureaucrat had treated you unfairly, how likely is it that you could prevail in a dispute?

Poverty is especially harmful to children, affecting most aspects of their development and making them generally less healthy (McLoyd 1998). They may have lower birth weights, potentially resulting in a variety of conditions affecting cognitive development. Poor children are more likely to be exposed to lead, which affects neurological functioning and reduces school achievement. They often face dangers and victimization in their neighborhoods, stigmatizing attitudes from teachers and other adults, frequent moves or changes to living situation, and homelessness. Such experiences make children hypervigilant and prone to aggression and depression.

Poverty is most harmful to young children. They develop fewer cognitive and verbal skills than other children and are more likely to fail in school. In chapter 2, I described a study that showed that parents on welfare, compared to families of professionals, speak as many as twenty million fewer words to their children during their first three years of life (Hart and Risley 1995). Poor parents don't read to their children as much or teach them as many of the rudimentary facts they need in order to be ready for school—for example, colors, shapes, and the names for common objects. These differences arise partly because poorer families have fewer toys and books, and partly because many poor parents simply have less time to interact with their children due to working two jobs or being a single parent. You might think that some of these effects of poverty arise simply because poor parents are less well educated; but some studies have controlled statistically for parents' education and found that, given two families where parents have the same level of education, the family in greater poverty is more likely to have children who fail in school (McLoyd 1998).

Poverty undermines children's development because it hampers effective parenting (McLoyd 1998). Poor adults have many more stressful life experiences, such as layoffs, evictions, forced moves, conflicts with neighbors, and hostile and discriminatory behavior from others. As a result, they experience more anxiety and depression. Poorer parents are also more likely to be sick, not only because of poorer health habits and inadequate health care, but also because poverty is a physical stressor. Of course, physically ill parents are less able to care for their children and more likely to sink deeper into poverty. So it shouldn't come as a surprise that poor parents are less involved with their children, less positive, more critical and angry, and more punitive.

To see how financial stress affects parenting, imagine two days you might have in your life. On one day, you have just lost your job. On the other, you got a raise. On which day would you take some time to play with your kids? On which would you be short-tempered and unwilling to do anything with them?

The farm crisis of the 1980s provides a dramatic example of the impact of economic hardship on families. During the 1970s, the prices of US corn and soybeans soared largely because of Soviet purchases of these commodities. This led to increases in the value of farmland and more borrowing against the value of that land—factors involved in a classic economic bubble. When prices dropped in the 1980s, the bubble burst and suddenly many farmers were deeply in debt. People who had seen their incomes growing were losing their farms. The results were devastating for many families. A nine-county area in southern Iowa had a 10 percent increase in child abuse. Divorce and alcohol abuse soared. In Hills, Iowa, a farmer killed his banker, his neighbor, his wife, and then himself (Manning 2008).

Rand Conger was a scientist at Iowa State University when he studied a sample of families during this period. He documented how economic hardship had a cascading effect on family well-being (Conger and Conger 2008). Parental stress and depression increased, as did marital conflict. As a result, parents were increasingly hostile and coercive toward their children. This made their children more anxious, depressed, and aggressive. Parents didn't do as good a job of setting limits on their adolescents' behavior, and delinquency increased as a result.

I have only recently encountered research on the impact of poverty on physical illness. In a briefing paper from the National Center on Health Statistics (Fryar, Chen, and Li 2012), researchers reported that among those whose income was 130 percent of the poverty level or less, more than 60 percent had at least one of three risk factors for cardiovascular disease (high cholesterol, high blood pressure, or smoking), while among more affluent Americans, fewer than 40 percent had at least one risk factor.

I was particularly disturbed to discover that children raised in poverty have a significantly greater risk of heart disease *as adults* (Galobardes, Lynch, and Smith 2004, 2008). Even if people escape from poverty, as adults they still have a 20 to 40 percent greater risk of heart disease. One study (G. E. Miller et al. 2009) looked into the mechanisms leading to this situation and found that because poverty increases stressful interactions among family members, it permanently alters the stress reactions of young people in ways that lead to inflammatory processes. However, it need not be this way. The same researchers also found that poverty didn't raise the risk of cardiovascular disease for people who were raised in poverty but had nurturing mothers (G. E. Miller et al. 2011).

Poverty is, of course, not just a problem for children. A Gallup study of 288,000 adults found that those who were poor had significantly higher rates of depression (30.9 percent versus 15.8 percent), as well as higher rates of asthma, obesity, diabetes, high blood pressure, and heart attacks (A. Brown 2012).

Sadly, the United States is a world leader in raising poor children. More than 20 percent of our children live in poverty. Of the thirty developed countries tracked by the Organisation for Economic Co-operation and Development, only three (Poland, Turkey, and Mexico) have higher child poverty rates than those in the US.

American policies that maintain such high levels of family poverty are typically advocated on the theory that social welfare programs undermine individual initiative and take money away from individuals and companies that would spend the money more wisely on business investments. But the empirical facts have brought us beyond the point where such general theories should determine public policy. Poor families cost society. As outlined above, they have higher health care costs due to higher rates of obesity, diabetes, cardiovascular disease, and cancer, and they are more likely to have children who fail academically, become delinquents, and have higher rates of depression.

The US obsession with limiting government spending is myopic. At the same time that we are limiting social welfare costs, we are incurring huge costs in medical care, criminal justice, productivity, and quality of life. The situation is contrary to both sound values and good sense.

Finally, poverty simply isn't good for the economy. People with minimal income cannot fully participate in the economy because they don't have sufficient resources to buy the goods and services they need to be fully productive (Whiting 2004). If even half of the families living in poverty were better off, how many more customers would American business have?

The Damage Done by Economic Inequality

It isn't difficult to see that poverty is extremely damaging—not just for the poor, but also for our society. However, a related but less obvious problem is economic inequality, which exerts ill effects that appear to be distinct from those of poverty. UK epidemiologist Richard Wilkinson has taken the lead in looking at this (1992). He and his colleague Kate Pickett reviewed 155 studies of the relationship between economic disparity and health and found that in countries where the lowest proportion of the country's total income went to the poorest 70 percent of families, life expectancy was significantly lower. As indicated in figure 4, the United States did not fare well in comparison to most other countries.

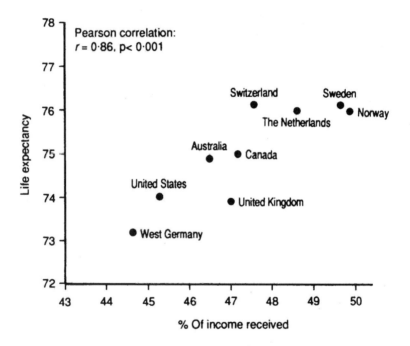

Figure 4. Relation between life expectancy at birth (male and female combined) and percentage of total post-tax and benefit income received by the least-well-off 70 percent of families in 1981. (Reprinted with permission from R. G. Wilkinson. 1992. "Income Distribution and Life Expectancy." *British Medical Journal* 304: 165–168.)

Along similar lines, the US death rate is significantly higher in states where the least-well-off 50 percent have a smaller share of total income (Ross et al. 2000), as indicated in figure 5. This isn't the case in Canadian provinces.

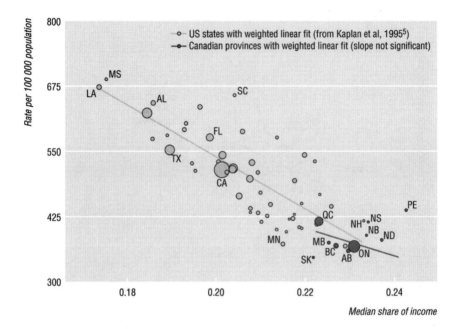

Figure 5. Mortality in working-age men by proportion of income earned by the less-well-off 50 percent of households in US states (1990) and Canadian provinces (1991). (Reprinted with permission from N. A. Ross, M. C. Wolfson, J. R. Dunn, J.-M. Berthelot, G. A. Kaplan, and J. W. Lynch. 2000. "Relation Between Income Inequality and Mortality in Canada and in the United States: Cross-Sectional Assessment Using Census Data and Vital Statistics." *British Medical Journal* 320: 898–902.)

Higher death rates are not the only consequence of inequality. Figure 6 shows the relationship between economic inequality and a host of social and health problems, including mental illness, life expectancy, obesity, children's educational performance, teenage births, homicides, imprisonment rates, social mobility, and level of trust. As you can see, the United States has the highest rate of inequality as measured by the ratio of the income of the top 20 percent of earners to that of the bottom 20 percent.

There is clearly a strong relationship between economic inequality and these diverse social problems.

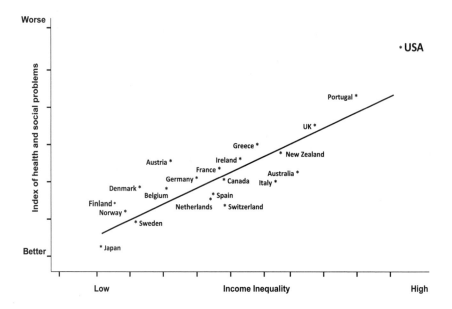

Figure 6. Health and social problems are closely related to inequality in rich countries. (Reprinted with permission from R. Wilkinson and K. Pickett. 2009. *The Spirit Level: Why Greater Equality Makes Societies Stronger*. London: Bloomsbury Press.)

Although health is worse and death rates higher for poorer people than for those who are better off, even wealthier people suffer ill effects from living in unequal societies. Figure 7 shows the rates of various diseases in England and the United States. For each group of three bars, the one on the right represents the group with the highest income, while the one on the left represents those with the lowest income. As expected, disease rates are higher for poorer people. But notice that rates of disease are consistently higher in the United States than in England, where there is less economic inequality—though England is still one of the three countries with the greatest economic inequality.

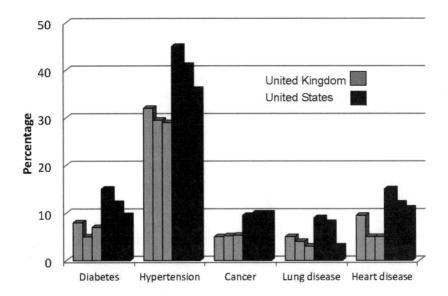

Figure 7. Rates of serious disease in England and United States. (Reprinted with permission from R. Wilkinson and K. Pickett. 2009. *The Spirit Level: Why Greater Equality Makes Societies Stronger.* London: Bloomsbury Press.)

Why would this be? Richard Wilkinson and Kate Pickett (2009) suggest that in societies where social status is important, people measure status by comparing what they have with what others have. They point out that countries with greater economic inequality have higher rates of advertising, which increases people's desire to have things that others don't have. Moreover, countries with greater economic inequality also have more people with materialistic values (Kasser 2011). In essence, people are competing to be richer than those around them.

This is a losing battle. Say you make having a nice car a measure of your worth. You'll start paying attention to cars. You'll soon know the prices of various models and which are deemed better. You can work hard and get yourself a Lexus—well, not the LX at $82,000, but the GX at $49,000. In this scenario, you have spent a bunch of money to enhance your feeling of self-worth, and yet you still don't have the highest-status vehicle. If we measure our worth by money and possessions, we will always be able to find someone who has more. And because we live in a country with greater economic inequality, most of us will always be surrounded by people who are wealthier (unless you are Bill Gates or Warren Buffett). If wealth is your measure of your status, having less than others becomes a source of stress.

The Benefits of Improving Families' Economic Well-Being

Reducing families' economic stress could greatly improve young people's well-being. One study estimated that a $1,000 increase in annual family income would produce a 2.1 percent increase in math scores and a 3.6 percent increase in reading scores (Dahl and Lochner 2012). This effect is probably due to families that are better off having more books and intellectually stimulating toys, as well as more time for interactions between parents and children. If these differences seem small, consider what $10,000 could achieve.

Jane Costello and her colleagues at Duke University provided a dramatic example of the benefits of increasing family income. I got to know Costello when we were serving on an Institute of Medicine committee on prevention. She is one of the most careful researchers looking into what influences the development of mental disorders. She spearheaded the Great Smoky Mountain Study, which focused on what influences children to develop mental disorders (Costello et al. 2003). Her team recruited 1,420 families in western North Carolina and, for each, interviewed a child and a parent every year for eight years.

Their sample included 350 families from the Eastern Band of Cherokee Indians, who lived in two of the counties in North Carolina. The study began in 1993. In 1996, the tribe opened a casino. As a result, every tribal member started receiving payments, including the children, whose money went into trust funds. By 2001, each tribe member was receiving $6,000 annually. In addition, the casino and hotel hired numerous workers, many of whom were members of the tribe.

This was a great natural experiment. Costello and her colleagues could look at the effect of this sudden increase in wealth on the psychological and behavioral problems of the children whose families were lifted out of poverty. Before the casino opened, the poorer children had higher rates of psychiatric symptoms than more well-off children. After the casino opened, the Cherokee children who were lifted out of poverty had no more symptoms than the kids who hadn't been poor initially. Reducing poverty had a direct impact on children's well-being.

In sum, our society's callous disregard for the harm that poverty does to the environments in which families find themselves guarantees a steady stream of poorly raised children—young people who will face challenges in learning and who are less likely to become productive members of society. Instead, they are likely to develop the problems that burden our entire society today—increased crime, drug abuse, unwanted pregnancies, and yet another generation of children who will face the same difficulties. Reducing the number of children who are raised in poverty has clear benefits—not just for them, but for everyone.

Policies That Have Increased Poverty and Economic Inequality

If you are under forty and grew up in the United States, you may never have lived in a country that made reducing poverty a high priority. But there was a time when the most prominent US political leaders made this a high priority—and the majority of Americans supported them. The most passionate and inspiring leader of that era was Robert F. Kennedy. I recall a visit he made to Mississippi in 1967 to call attention to the fact that children were going hungry. It was described in the article "With RFK in the Delta," in the journal *American Heritage* (Carr 2002). The writer of that article, John Carr, was a reporter for the only liberal paper in Mississippi at the time. He describes how Kennedy led reporters to a village of very poor black sharecroppers, where, thanks to recent reductions in pay, many children were malnourished (2002, 93):

The first house we walked into had a refrigerator in a big room. Kennedy opened it. The only item inside was a jar of peanut butter. There was no bread. We walked outside, and he held out his hand to a bunch of young, filthy, ragged but thrilled kids. In a minute or two he was stopped by a short, aging, very heavy black woman in old, baggy clothes. I regret to say that I'd become inured to poverty by a childhood and young adulthood in the Delta, but this poor woman was in awful shape even for Mississippi.

She thanked Senator Kennedy for coming to see them and said that she was too old to be helped by any new program but she hoped the children might be. Kennedy, moved, softly asked her how old she was. "I'm thirty-three," she said. Both he and I recoiled.

When Robert Kennedy ran for president in 1968, I became president of Students for Robert Kennedy at the University of Illinois. It was a time of great hope and inspiration. We were determined to change the terrible conditions less fortunate people faced. If someone had told me then that poverty would be a significant problem in the United States in 2012, I would have dismissed the idea and considered that person to be out of touch with the direction the nation was clearly headed.

But I would have been wrong. Figure 8 shows US Census Bureau data on the rates of poverty in three different age groups: those under eighteen, those eighteen to sixty-four, and those sixty-five and older (DeNavas-Walt, Proctor, and Smith 2010). As you can see, poverty rates declined dramatically between 1959 and about 1970. Then they continued to decline among older Americans, while climbing slightly among eighteen-to sixty-four-year-olds and increasing rather substantially among those under eighteen. In addition, the more recent rates are distinctly higher for young people. And, as I said earlier, the United States has one of the highest child poverty rates among developed countries.

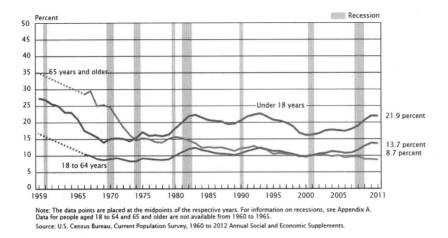

Note: The data points are placed at the midpoints of the respective years. For information on recessions, see Appendix A. Data for people aged 18 to 64 and 65 and older are not available from 1960 to 1965.
Source: U.S. Census Bureau, Current Population Survey, 1960 to 2012 Annual Social and Economic Supplements.

Figure 8. Poverty rates (by percentage) for various age groups in the United States. (Reprinted from DeNavas-Walt, C., B. D. Proctor, and J. C. Smith. 2010. *Income, Poverty, and Health Insurance Coverage in the United States: 2009.* Washington, DC: US Government Printing Office.)

Nor has American society reduced economic inequality. In fact, inequality has steadily climbed. According to the Congressional Budget Office (2011), after-tax income of the top 1 percent of earners increased more than 250 percent between 1979 and 2007, while it increased less than 20 percent for the poorest 20 percent of the population. According to economist Andrew Leigh (2009), the share of total income that goes to the top 1 percent of earners in the United States rose from 8 percent in 1973 to 1975 to nearly 16 percent in 1998 to 2000. By 2007, the Working Group on Extreme Inequality reported that the richest 10 percent of Americans own more than 70 percent of the nation's wealth, with the top 1 percent owning 34 percent of the wealth. In contrast, the bottom 50 percent hold only 2.5 percent of the wealth.

Political scientists Jacob Hacker and Paul Pierson (2010a) have detailed the policy changes over the past forty years that have produced the current situation, wherein the level of inequality in the United States is greater than at any time since 1928. A sizable portion of the disparity resulted from reductions in taxes on the wealthiest. Between 1970 and 2000, the top 0.1 percent of earners increased their share of total national after-tax income from 1.2 percent to 7.3 percent. Had federal policy not reduced their taxation, their share would have increased to only 4.5 percent (Hacker and Pierson 2010a). Other changes in tax policy that have disproportionately benefited the very richest Americans include reductions in the estate tax, changes in the alternative minimum tax, and reduction in the number of IRS audits of the highest earners.

Failure to change outdated policies, including tax policies, has also contributed to the disparity. For example, as unregulated hedge fund activity has expanded, the incomes of hedge fund managers have exploded, with the top twenty-five averaging $600 million *in income* in 2006. Yet due to the way laws were written before hedge funds became a significant activity, these managers are able to treat their income as capital gains and pay income tax at a rate of just 15 percent.

Economic disparity also grew because political leaders failed to update policies in keeping with changes in the economy. Here are some of the most noteworthy examples:

- Failure to index the minimum wage to inflation

- Failure to update or enforce laws regulating the formation of unions

- Failure to adopt health care reforms that could have dealt with the increasing costs of health care for individuals and companies

- Failure to regulate the compensation of CEOs, who, in the United States, earn more than twice the average of their peers in other developed nations

- Failure to regulate new financial instruments, such as derivatives

- Failure to prevent the erosion of company-provided pension plans

Clearly, poverty and economic inequality have grown in the United States over the past forty years in part because public policy has favored these changes. For me, the natural next question is why policies have changed so dramatically in favor of the wealthiest while undermining the well-being of the middle class. These changes must be understood within the broader context of the recent evolution of corporate capitalism, the topic of the next chapter.

Action Implications

If you think the situation is hopeless, you may find the ACT perspective described in chapter 5 helpful. After all, why do we feel distressed about these facts and want to turn away from them? It is because facing them puts us in contact with others' distress and the threat that we too could experience these terrible life outcomes. ACT encourages us to accept these feelings and see that they will not harm us. Indeed, these feelings reflect our empathy for others. If we take action to try to change this situation, that is an example of living and affirming our values, regardless of how much progress we make.

So for anyone who wishes to take action against poverty and economic inequality, the first step is to accept difficult feelings about the situation, rather than struggling with them. The second step is to identify concrete actions we can take to move our society in directions we value.

For Policy Makers

- Request that the Institute of Medicine or the Surgeon General create a report that articulates the epidemiological evidence on the harm of poverty, and that identifies policies that increase or decrease poverty and economic inequality. Such a report would make reducing poverty and economic inequality clear public policy goals. If we are serious about having a society that ensures everyone's well-being, we need to think about these issues in the same way that we think about harmful infectious agents.

- Enact laws that require economic policies to be evaluated in terms of their impact on poverty and inequality. Because poverty and economic inequality are so harmful to well-being, we need to create a system for routinely evaluating how any proposed policies affect them. This would be analogous to policies that require environmental impact analyses before major infrastructure projects can be implemented.

For Citizens

- Campaign for political leaders who will support policies that reduce poverty and economic inequality. It isn't enough to vote for such leaders; we need to work to get them elected in order to create the society we want.

- Join (or create) and generously support organizations aimed at working in favor of policies needed to reduce poverty and inequality.

CHAPTER 9

The Recent Evolution of Corporate Capitalism

If we truly want to ensure the well-being of everyone, we can't stop at providing strong family, school, and community interventions. We also must be concerned about economic policy.

A profound example comes from a study that examined the impact of the 2008 recession on US suicides (Reeves et al. 2012). The suicide rate increased four times faster between 2008 and 2010 than it had in the eight previous years. The researchers estimated that the increase led to an additional 1,500 suicides. Because the recession occurred because of public policies, including banking deregulation and failure to regulate financial vehicles such as credit default swaps (McLean and Nocera 2010), it appears that economic policy had a direct impact on how many people killed themselves. And while suicide is a devastating and tragic outcome, it is only one way in which the recession harmed well-being.

I am sure no one involved in these policies set out to cause suicides. But once we know that a public policy does harm, we need to factor that knowledge into our policy making. First, however, we need to understand what drives policy making.

A Contextual Approach to Policy Making

It might seem that studying the influences on policy making requires entirely new conceptual tools. And in terms of both science and practical action, we know far less about how to influence corporate practices that affect policy making than we do about influencing the behavior of individuals. However, the behavioral science revolution is lapping at the door to this problem. Thanks to David Sloan Wilson's leadership, an increasing number of scientists working in diverse areas of the human sciences are coming to see that their efforts are best organized within an evolutionary framework. B. F. Skinner's notion that behavior is selected by its consequences is simply the application of evolutionary thinking to the evolution of behavior, rather than to organisms.

That same principle of selection by consequences is useful for understanding corporate behavior. Corporate practices are selected and maintained by their consequences in the same way that the behavior of individuals is selected by reinforcing consequences (Biglan and Cody 2013). For both people and corporations, the ultimate consequence is survival. People and corporations don't survive if they don't achieve outcomes that enable them to survive. In a capitalist system, a corporation's survival is a matter of achieving profits.

Let's revisit what I said about the development of the behavioral science revolution in the 1960s and 1970s. Initially, there was virtually no evidence that reinforcing consequences shapes human behavior. But a small group of scientists felt compelled to explore this possibility based on strong evidence from animal studies indicating that consequences affect animal behavior. In addition, evolutionary theory led early behaviorists to doubt that humans were somehow exempt from the effects of reinforcement. What ensued was an incredible accumulation of evidence and practical strategies for influencing behavior.

I believe we are at a similar place with respect to the behavior of organizations. Evolutionary principles suggest that it is extremely likely that organizational practices are selected by their material consequences. Indeed, David Sloan Wilson and his colleagues have enumerated many examples of the selection of group practices from realms as diverse as eusocial insects, such as bees and ants, to the Good Behavior Game to the evolution of religions (D. S. Wilson 2003, 2007).

Just as a person will continue to engage in a behavior that has had favorable consequences, a corporation will continue and expand a practice that results in revenue growth. For example, consider the marketing practices of the tobacco industry discussed previously. That industry innovated in the marketing of cigarettes, and when they found a campaign that worked, they continued it and then refined it. When a campaign failed, they abandoned it and tried something else.

Unfortunately, the fundamental role of selection by consequences is obscured by myriad other ways of thinking about corporations and their practices. I submit that analyzing and testing the impact of consequences on corporate practices would give policy makers and citizens the tools they need to influence the further evolution of corporate practices (Biglan 2009, 2011; Biglan and Cody 2013). Therefore, in this chapter, I provide a brief history of the evolution of corporate practices relevant to the developments I described in chapters 7 and 8. I hope to convince you that both harmful marketing practices and economic policies have evolved as a function of the completely understandable efforts of corporations and wealthy individuals to maximize their gains.

The Powell Memo

Jacob Hacker, a political scientist at Yale, and Paul Pierson, a political scientist at the University of California Berkeley, recently provided a thorough analysis of the political and policy developments that increased poverty and inequality in the United States over the last forty years (Hacker and Pierson 2010a). They credit a 1971 memo from Lewis F. Powell for inspiring a massive redesign of corporate America's advocacy for business-friendly policies. Powell wrote the memo for his friend and neighbor Eugene Sydnor, Jr., the chairman of the US Chamber of Commerce Education Committee. The memo, dated August 23, 1971, argued that there was a growing attack on the free enterprise system (1971, 2–3):

> The most disquieting voices joining the chorus of criticism come from perfectly respectable elements of society: from the college campus, the pulpit, the media, the intellectual and literary journals, the arts and sciences, and from politicians. In most of these groups the movement against the system is participated in only by minorities. Yet, these often are the most articulate, the most vocal, the most prolific in their writing and speaking.
>
> Moreover, much of the media—for varying motives and in varying degrees—either voluntarily accord unique publicity to these

"attackers," or at least allow them to exploit the media for their purposes. This is especially true of television, which now plays such a predominant role in shaping the thinking, attitudes, and emotions of our people.

The business community's concerns were well justified. During the 1960s and early 1970s, many people were highly suspicious of business. Young people were loath to pursue careers in business, and the public strongly favored policies that were hostile to business. Powell was simply describing, in a dispassionate way, some of the reasons that business was viewed so negatively.

Powell said that the business community's response to the problem involved "appeasement, ineptitude, and ignoring the problem" (1971, 8). Rather than each company simply pursuing its own business interests, Powell argued that companies needed to be "equally concerned with protecting and preserving the system itself" (10). He called for an effort to accrue political power through "united action and national organizations [that would engage in] careful long-range planning and implementation [and] consistency of action over an indefinite period of years, [with a] scale of financing available only through joint effort" (11).

In the memo Powell proposed specific steps the business community could take. The first was to increase support on college campuses for conservative intellectual efforts. He argued that top colleges were producing graduates who held strong antibusiness views and were moving into influential roles in the media. If the business community could strengthen support for conservative points of view on college campuses, they could create a cadre of well-trained advocates of conservative viewpoints who would increase public support for conservative values when they graduated and moved into leadership positions in society.

Second, Powell recommended creation of a group of "eminent scholars, writers, and speakers, who will do the thinking, the analysis, the writing, and the speaking" (21), as well as personnel "who are thoroughly familiar with the media, and how most effectively to communicate with the public" (21). Third, he recommended that conservative scholars be encouraged to publish in scholarly journals, popular magazines, and books. Fourth, he proposed that businesses be encouraged to devote some of their advertising budgets to advocacy of the free enterprise system, rather than simply promotion of their products or company. Fifth, he urged more vigorous pursuit of political power (25–26):

> Business must learn the lesson, long ago learned by Labor and other self-interest groups. This is the lesson that political power is necessary; that such power must be assiduously cultivated; and that when necessary, it must be used aggressively and with determination—without embarrassment and without the reluctance which has been so characteristic of American business.

The sixth thing Powell advocated was to develop organizations that would litigate on behalf of the interests of conservatives. He cited the American Civil Liberties Union as a model for well-organized efforts to influence judicial decisions on behalf of a point of view. Seventh, he suggested that the business community help stockholders organize and advocate for the free enterprise system.

Powell noted that the strategy he outlined would require substantial investment from the business community. The money was forthcoming. Through their foundations, a number of very wealthy individuals and families have funded the development of a network of organizations that support all of the conservative efforts that Powell proposed. These backers include Richard Mellon Scaife, the Coors family, Smith Richardson, and John Merrill Olin. Lewis Lapham, writing in *Harper's* in 2004, estimated that the resulting foundations were worth about two billion dollars. He cited Rob Stein as estimating that these foundations had contributed more than three billion dollars to conservative advocacy efforts over the previous three decades.

All of the things Powell advocated are now in place. A system of scholarships supports conservative scholars at America's elite universities. Lapham estimated that scholarships amounting to $39 million were available to support conservative students in 2001, $16 million of that at Harvard, Yale, and the University of Chicago. There is financial support for writing, publishing, and promoting books, magazine articles, op-ed pieces, and scholarly articles that advocate conservative viewpoints. A network of think tanks supports conservative scholarship and advocacy and produces reports, newsletters, briefing papers, and op-ed pieces that dominate public discussion. The network includes the Heritage

Foundation, the American Enterprise Institute, the Cato Institute, the Hoover Institution, the Hudson Institute, the Manhattan Institute for Policy Research, Citizens for a Sound Economy, the National Center for Policy Analysis, the Competitive Enterprise Institute, the Free Congress Foundation, and the Business Roundtable. Lapham estimated that the 2001 annual budgets of the major think tanks totaled $136 million. These organizations supply a steady stream of conservative opinion leaders who regularly appear on television news and talk shows. This system of organizations exerts considerable influence on public opinion, making it more favorable to the needs and interests of business.

Leftist discussions of the Powell memo often characterize it as sinister. But, in truth, it is a fairly balanced and dispassionate analysis of the reasons why, in 1971, public support for policies favoring business was at a low point (15):

> Few things are more sanctified in American life than academic
> freedom. It would be fatal to attack this as a principle. But if
> academic freedom is to retain the qualities of "openness," "fairness,"
> and "balance"—which are essential to its intellectual significance—
> there is a great opportunity for constructive action. The thrust of
> such action must be to restore the qualities just mentioned to the
> academic communities.

Powell simply laid out the avenues that are available in a free society to promote policies favorable to business. These interests had huge amounts of money available to them, but the basic principles they employed are applicable to any group's efforts to influence public policy making.

The results of these efforts have been remarkable. Compare the political landscape of 1964 with that of 2014. In 1964, both the federal government and public opinion were decidedly liberal. Lyndon Johnson won the election with 61 percent of the vote. Democrats picked up two Senate seats and thirty-six House seats and had a two-thirds majority in both houses of Congress. Indeed, from 1933, at the height of the great depression, through 1995, a period of sixty-two years, the Democrats controlled the House of Representatives for all but two years. For fourteen of the eighteen years after 1995, the Republicans were in control. In 2014 Republicans controlled the House of Representatives, with 233 Republicans to 199 Democrats. They also controlled 45 Senate seats. Although the latter isn't a majority, it is sufficient to allow them to block legislation and appointments by threatening filibusters.

There have also been huge changes in the nature of public discussion and in public policy making since 1964. Whereas the majority of Democrats considered themselves liberals in 1964, only about one-third of Democrats do so now, and the term "liberal" has become an epithet. The Republicans in leadership positions are all conservatives, and the party is far more conservative than it was in 1964. Furthermore, a Democrat, Bill Clinton— whose policies included welfare reform, balancing the budget, and reducing the federal workforce by about 350,000—declared in his 1996 State of the Union address that the era of big government is over. Finally, government regulation of business has dwindled significantly since the 1960s.

In sum, recognizing that generalized advocacy for conservative points of view would serve their interests, a number of wealthy people invested in creating an infrastructure to influence public opinion and policy making. As the benefits of these efforts became noticeable, increasing amounts of money flowed to the network of organizations working for conservative causes. Major financial instruments such as derivatives were completely unregulated, and as a result, we experienced the worst economic downturn since the great depression (McLean and Nocera 2010).

If the evolution of these corporate and business practices was due to the economic consequences to the individuals and organizations that engaged in them, we should find that businesses benefit from the changes in policy. And indeed they did. As discussed in chapter 8, between 1970 and 2000 the top 0.1 percent of earners increased their share of total national after-tax income from 1.2 to 7.3 percent (Hacker and Pierson 2010a). Moreover, in 1980, chief executives of American corporations made forty-two times what the average blue-collar worker earned. They now make 331 times what the average blue-collar worker earns (Dill 2014).

Capitalism from an Evolutionary Perspective

The changes I've documented are among the most important cultural events of the last forty years. Understanding how and why practices and policies evolved in this way could help us influence the further evolution of policy making and politics in directions that will benefit more people.

You might think of capitalism as evolution on steroids. Just as the behavior of individuals is selected by the consequences of that behavior, the practices of corporations and other businesses are selected in a process that is finely tuned by the marketplace. Quarterly profits quickly reveal whether a company is succeeding. Profitable activities are expanded both through the influx of funds to the company and as other companies adopt a successful company's profitable practices. Variation is assured due to new people entering the marketplace and the continuous invention of new products and services.

These factors result in selection of organizations that are increasingly skilled at discerning what will enhance their profits. The contingencies select *any* practice that contributes to profits, regardless of whether it is beneficial more broadly. Improving products and services is certainly a critical practice, and it is generally beneficial. However, many other practices are detrimental. These include the marketing practices I described in chapter 7, as well as lobbying for favorable government policies or contracts, minimizing costs of labor and materials, and undermining the success of competitors. Indeed, over the past one hundred years, all of these practices have been refined by their economic contingencies.

Marketing and lobbying deserve particular attention in relation to our concern for nurturing human well-being. Since the early 1900s, marketing has expanded enormously thanks to its contribution to profits. In the tobacco industry—a leading innovator in advertising over the last century—advertising has been critical to the expansion of markets. Few women smoked before Lucky Strike began its "Reach for a Lucky Instead of a Sweet" campaign in the mid-1920s.

Lobbying has greatly expanded in the past twenty years, particularly because it has proven increasingly profitable to invest in getting government to change policies and contract with private companies for work the government traditionally conducted. In 2009, registered lobbyists reported spending nearly $3.5 billion, a record amount (Hacker and Pierson 2010b).

Just as marketing and lobbying practices of individual corporations have evolved, a cooperative network of business and advocacy organizations has evolved over the last forty years. This network has been shaped and maintained by its economic consequences, including increased profits, increased political influence that helps maintain profitability, and increased income for the people who lead these organizations.

In essence, the network of business and advocacy organizations has changed the public perception of the value of government, regulation, and redistribution policies. Effective advocacy for business-friendly beliefs and policies led to deregulation of corporate practices. As government regulation of unsafe, unhealthy, or economically disastrous practices has declined, practices have increasingly been determined by the marketplace, which selects whatever works to increase short-term profits. Throughout, general well-being has steadily receded as a value that influences policy making.

I want to stress that this is not a critique of capitalism per se. The benefits of the evolutionary process that is capitalism are evident in all of the products and services that have evolved in the last two hundred years, including the computer on which I am writing this book. However, we need to evolve a system that retains the benefits of capitalism while also restraining its worst excesses.

Increasing Materialism

Substantial changes in the goals and values of Americans have accompanied changes in the political and economic structure of US society. For the past four decades, the Higher Education Research Institute has been surveying incoming freshmen at 1,201 colleges and universities (Astin 2002). These surveys show that the percentage of freshmen who said that being very well-off financially was essential or very important hovered around 40 percent in the late 1960s and early 1970s and then rose steadily to more than 70 percent by the mid-1980s, remaining at that level ever since. In the 1960s, more than 80 percent said that developing a meaningful life philosophy was important, and that number declined steadily until the mid-1980s, at which point it leveled off in the 40 to 50 percent range (Astin 2002).

Jean Twenge, a social psychologist at San Diego State University, has worked with colleagues around the country to analyze changes in the values and aspirations of high school and college students across the years (Twenge 2009; Twenge and Campbell 2008). Her analysis of data from

Monitoring the Future, an annual survey of high school students, found sizable increases in the proportion of youth who say that money is important, buying things you don't need is okay, and doing your own thing is a good idea. Twenge also studied the extent of narcissism, or inflated self-absorption, among college students across the country and found that between 1985 and 2006 the level of narcissism increased significantly (Twenge and Campbell 2009; Twenge and Foster 2010; Twenge et al. 2008).

Other researchers who analyzed data from Monitoring the Future (Wray-Lake, Flanagan, and Osgood 2010) found that the proportion of youth who said that wealth was important rose from 45 percent in 1976 to 63 percent by 2005. In addition, the percent of young people who said that most people can be trusted dropped from 31.5 percent in 1976 to 19.7 percent in 2001.

Is Materialism Beneficial?

Given the unquestionable benefits that capitalism has provided in improved technology, transportation, health, and wealth, it might seem good that people are becoming more materialistic. The more people desire material goods, the harder they will work for them, and the more productive society will be.

However, research on materialism shows that there is a decidedly dark side to pursuing this value. Tim Kasser, a social psychologist at Knox College in Illinois, has been studying materialism for the past twenty years. He and his colleagues have identified two clusters of goals: one involving being popular, financially successful, and attractive, and the other centering around having satisfying relationships with others, improving the world through selfless action, and accepting oneself. In a series of studies (for example, Kasser 2004; Schmuck, Kasser, and Ryan 2000), Kasser and his colleagues found that people tend to endorse one or the other cluster, rather than both. So some people are motivated to have fame and fortune, while others want to make their lives about self-development, caring relationships, and helping their community.

It turns out that people who endorse materialistic goals aren't very happy. In fact, they have many problems (Kasser and Ryan 1993, 1996). College students who endorse materialistic values are more likely to be depressed and anxious and less satisfied with their lives. They report more unpleasant emotions, fewer pleasant emotions, and more physical symptoms and drug and alcohol use. Adolescents who aspire to be rich are more aggressive and uncooperative. Parents with a strong focus on having money and status are less warm and more controlling toward their children. People with materialistic goals are less empathetic, less cooperative, and more greedy when playing a game that involves the sharing of resources. Not surprisingly, they are also more likely to live an environmentally damaging lifestyle.

Given all these downsides, why do people embrace materialism? One answer lies in a study involving three experiments that exposed people to various kinds of threats; in it, Kasser found that threat increases people's materialistic tendencies (Sheldon and Kasser 2008). In the first experiment, half of the subjects were asked to briefly describe their emotions in response to the thought of their own death and to briefly describe what they imagine will happen to them after death. The other subjects answered similar questions about their experience of listening to music. The people who thought about their death were significantly more likely to endorse goals about being rich and famous.

In the second experiment, Kasser's team simply asked people to imagine that a year later they would be either employed and financially secure or unemployed and on shaky ground financially. Those who imagined being insecure endorsed materialistic goals more strongly. The third and final experiment found that people were more likely to endorse materialistic values when they were asked to think about someone "who clearly likes you, tends to be very evaluative of you, and seems to accept you only to the extent that you live up to certain standards of performance" (Sheldon and Kasser 2008, 42).

If you think about this from an evolutionary perspective, it makes sense that when people feel threatened, they focus on having the material and social resources they need to survive. These are the reinforcers they need and seek. Thinking about your own death or financial insecurity naturally focuses the mind on having safety and security. This may be one reason why poorer people are more likely to endorse materialistic values. Similarly, thinking about people who only like you if you measure up to their standards makes the possibility of being rejected more salient, which will probably increase your desire to be accepted.

You may be entertaining the possibility that, for all its harm to individuals, maybe this is just a cost we must endure to have a society with high levels of material well-being. Yet here too, Kasser has found just the opposite, using data on the values of people in twenty different countries (Grouzet et al. 2005; Kasser 2011; Schmuck, Kasser, and Ryan 2000). The countries differed in how much people endorsed values having to do with harmony and egalitarianism versus mastery of the environment and hierarchical relations among people. As it turned out, the more a country's population valued harmony and egalitarianism, the greater the well-being of the country's children, as measured by a UNICEF index of forty indicators of well-being. In addition, the countries that endorsed harmony and egalitarianism had more generous parental leave policies and lower carbon dioxide emissions. The strongest relationships, however, had to do with the amount of advertising to children. Countries that endorsed mastery and hierarchical relationships had much more advertising targeting children. I suspect that this is because advertising increases not only people's desire for material goods, but also their concern about whether they have high social status.

Evolution in the Wrong Direction

Evidence seems to be converging that, for at least the past fifty years, cultural evolution in the United States has been taking us where we don't want to go. As detailed in earlier chapters, research by economists, sociologists, and psychologists indicates that more children are being raised in poverty, and that poverty contributes to family conflict. Psychologists, including Jerry Patterson, have shown that the moment-to-moment interactions within stressed families are marked by conflict and coercion that put children on the road to aggressive social behavior, crime, drug abuse, academic failure, and early childbearing (Biglan et al. 2004). Neuroscientists have delineated the physiological processes that underpin the effects of conflict and threat and wire people to be biased toward aggression, materialism, and all of the just-mentioned problems (Bardo, Fishbein, and Milich 2011). Research by social psychologists, including Tim Kasser, suggests that threatening conditions in families and schools tilt people toward the endorsement of self-aggrandizing, materialistic values (Sheldon and Kasser 2008). These values, in turn, contribute to societies that place a high premium on materialism, do a poorer job of ensuring children's well-being, and fail to sustain the environment. Thus, we have a classic vicious cycle in which harsh, nonnurturing conditions produce a large number of threatened, self-focused, materialistic people who support policies that maintain these harsh and nonnurturing environments.

It is virtually impossible to say whether conservative advocacy influenced the increase in materialism, whether materialism increased support for conservative policy, or whether each increased the other. What is clear, however, is that over the past fifty years, the United States has become a more ideologically conservative, more materialistic, and less trusting place—and a nation that is not providing the material support for families or the programs, practices, and policies that behavioral science shows can improve the well-being of most Americans.

Changing the Consequences for Corporate Practices

If a corporate practice is shown to have a negative impact on well-being and our goal is to improve individuals' well-being, it makes sense to establish a goal of ending or limiting that practice. Yet on a practical level, what do we know about changing the practices of corporations? To some extent, contingency management of corporate behavior is already in place to accomplish this, but not as much as it should be, given the central role of consequences. For example, we can make harmful practices less desirable by taxing them or levying fines on them. The government could fine cigarette companies for every smoker under the age of twenty-one who became addicted to their brand. Or there could be a fine for every alcohol-related car crash among those under twenty-one, levied against the company that produced the beverage involved in the crash. Product liability lawsuits can also produce negative consequences for companies, although the National Restaurant Association has been able to encourage several state legislatures to pass what are deemed "commonsense consumption" laws, which prevent individuals from pursuing obesity-related litigation (Strom 2011).

However, a thorough analysis of selection by consequences suggests more innovative strategies, in particular, using positive consequences to shift corporate practices. Positive strategies could reduce corporate resistance to efforts to change harmful practices. For example, given the growing evidence for the value of foods high in omega-3 fatty acids, food companies could receive tax incentives for marketing such foods. If we want an industry to agree to change a practice, it may initially be more effective to make it profitable to adopt the new practice than to punish the industry for a problematic practice. We could then slowly withdraw incentives for the change once it has been widely enough adopted. Among the many merits of this approach is that it takes into account that corporations are currently very skilled at influencing policy making, and that they are much more likely to fight policies that punish certain practices than policies that offer remuneration for favorable practices.

The Critical Role of Advocacy Organizations

The major obstacle to altering any of these contingencies is, of course, the power of companies to control public opinion and influence government regulatory practices. The most promising strategy I can see for countering the influence of entrenched and powerful organizations is to strengthen the practices of organizations working for change. I've already described how a system of tobacco control organizations evolved and became more effective in influencing the culture of tobacco use. Similar systems are evolving with respect to alcohol problems, although they are only beginning to address marketing practices.

Mothers Against Drunk Driving (MADD) provides an excellent example of what we can accomplish. Thanks to MADD, the rate of drunk driving and alcohol-related car crashes has declined substantially. Since 1980, when MADD was founded, the number of alcohol-related motor vehicle deaths declined by 53 percent, with as many as 150,000 deaths being prevented by reductions in drunk driving (National Transportation Safety Board 2013).

MADD was created by Candy Lightner, whose thirteen-year-old daughter was killed by a hit-and-run drunk driver. Prior to MADD, drunk driving wasn't seen as harmful in quite the way it is today. Then MADD mobilized thousands of victims of drunk driving and the families of victims to form hundreds of chapters around the country, all demanding stronger laws against drunk driving. They were extremely effective. For example, in 1984 the drinking age was raised to twenty-one in all states. Studies have shown that this significantly reduced alcohol consumption by young people and, with it, alcohol-related car crashes (Wagenaar and Toomey 2002). In essence, MADD created a virtuous cycle in which advocacy influenced both the adoption of stronger laws against drunk driving and people's beliefs about the appropriateness of drunk driving. As the public heard about the changes in laws and about people being prosecuted for drunk driving, they became more likely to disapprove of drunk driving and less likely to do it themselves.

A Comprehensive Strategy

The work of the tobacco- and alcohol-control organizations demonstrates that specific corporate policies can be shifted by changing the consequences of corporate behavior. Unfortunately, the influence of corporations on public policy, and thereby human well-being, as described earlier in this chapter, calls for more comprehensive efforts to reform capitalism. We need to evolve a network of advocacy organizations that promote policies, norms, and practices that will enhance well-being.

We also need an umbrella organization that can lead and coordinate the efforts of this network of organizations. Most nonprofit organizations currently working to increase human well-being focus on a narrow range of problems, and concentrate on the major influences on those problems; in doing so they fail to focus on fundamental underlying conditions that affect most problems of human behavior. For example, Mothers Against Drunk Driving has done an excellent job of getting policies enacted that reduce drunk driving. However, to my knowledge they haven't done anything to address family conflict or poverty, both of which contribute to the development of alcoholism.

An umbrella organization could support the efforts of all the individual organizations by coordinating joint action when doing so is likely to be helpful. Perhaps more importantly, it could advocate for changes that would affect fundamental conditions in ways that increase nurturance of and in families, schools, workplaces, and communities, thereby addressing virtually all of the psychological, behavioral, and health problems that are so costly to our society.

One of the obstacles to creating such umbrella advocacy organizations involves the limits on what nonprofit organizations can do. Despite the fact that nonprofit organizations and foundations have evolved to provide benefits to society that neither for-profit companies nor government provide, current regulations limit their ability to work for changes in public policies that are critical to reducing poverty and economic inequality or to moderating other harmful corporate practices.

We need to develop a model policy for the creation of a new type of advocacy organization that is chartered to advocate for those policies, programs, and practices that have been empirically proven to increase human well-being. Such a policy would identify a set of health, behavioral, and economic outcomes that have been shown to increase the prevalence of well-being in the general population. Under this policy, nonprofit organizations would be able to specify one or more of these outcomes to target. Harking back to the early days of capitalism, when corporations were chartered by governments for a fixed time and a fixed purpose, these corporations would be chartered by the government and required to specify a plan of action over a fixed time—say, ten years—and that plan would have to be deemed likely to advance beneficial policies and practices by a panel of experts. The plan would also need to include evaluation of its impact, with renewal of the organization's charter depending on evidence of success.

For example, if an umbrella advocacy organization seeks to create a network of supportive organizations, it could test its strategy for doing so by applying that strategy to successive sets of organizations, measuring how many join the effort at each stage and refining its approach with each iteration. If a policy to restrict a marketing practice is adopted, its impact can be evaluated by assessing its success in achieving the intended outcome. Only through empirical evaluation can we effectively strengthen advocacy organizations and influence problematic organizational practices.

Action Implications

The major policies that will affect whether families and schools are nurturing include those that target the redistribution of wealth, those with a focus on providing programs that support nurturing environments in families and schools, and those that restrain corporations from engaging in financial and other practices that harm individuals, the entire economy, or the environment. Both policy makers and individuals can play a role in enacting such policies.

For Policy Makers

- Develop a model policy for the creation of a new type of advocacy organization that is chartered to promote policies, programs, and practices that have been empirically proven to improve human well-being.

- Require these advocacy organizations to conduct empirical evaluations of their effectiveness in order to retain their charter.

- Fund further research on the impacts of marketing practices on child and adolescent health and well-being.

For Citizens

- Make a list of two or three changes that you would like to see in your community. Then identify one or two local, state, or national organizations that you think are making a difference or could do so. Join those organizations. Support them and advocate that they take helpful actions.

- Join and support organizations that work on one or a few societal problems or on the reform of corporate capitalist practices.

PART 4

Evolving the Nurturing Society

Can we translate all that we have learned about human behavior in the past forty years into truly revolutionary changes in society? I think we can.

In part 2 of this book, I enumerated how much we have learned about how to help families and schools nurture the successful development of children and adolescents and the powerful methods that have been created to help adults with psychological and behavioral problems. In part 3, I described the changes we need in the larger social system of corporate capitalism in order to fully realize the well-being of every member of society.

Here, in the final part of the book, I pull all of this together to describe how we can use our accumulated scientific knowledge about human behavior to produce improvements in human well-being that go beyond anything ever achieved in human history. If that seems like hyperbole, remember how long it took to communicate with someone on the other side of the world in 1850—before science created telephone networks and the Internet.

In chapter 10, I discuss how and why achieving caring relationships is foundational for progress in every facet of society, from families to corporate boardrooms. Then in chapter 11, I envision the movement we can create to make nurturing environments a reality throughout society.

CHAPTER 10

In Caring Relationships with Others

As I mentioned in chapter 1, the Institute of Medicine's report on prevention envisioned a society that we could achieve in which virtually all young people "arrive at adulthood with the skills, interests, assets, and health habits needed to live healthy, happy, and productive lives in caring relationships with others" (IOM and NRC 2009, 387). Imagine what it would be like if we put all of our energies into building caring relationships among people. Suppose we let instructional practices in schools stay as they are, didn't work on changing policies that affect economic well-being, and didn't directly work on reducing global warming; rather, we concentrated solely on cultivating a society in which the highest value and most important priority was that people care for each other. Suppose we were to achieve a society in which, in every contact, we first paid attention to how the other person was doing, and when we saw situations that could harm others' well-being, we worked to alter those situations. What would it be like if, each day, we got up and tried to contribute to the comfort, safety, skill, and success of those around us?

I am convinced that caring relationships are the fundamental building blocks for creating the nurturing environments that are vital to everyone's well-being, and thus achieving the larger goals to which we aspire. In part 2, I focused on relationships in families, schools, and young people's peer groups. As the programs, policies, and practices I described become more widely available, our young people will increasingly go out into the world with the values and skills needed to live in caring relationships with others. However, it is much more likely that we will support this trend if caring relationships become foundational—not only to families and schools, but to all other relationships in society.

Imagine that Fortune 500 companies supported policies that enhanced the nurturance of families and schools because the executive leadership of these companies embraced the value of caring relationships. Would the materialism that so distorts our values and policy making recede? Would everyone insist on economic policies that ensured all members of society had their basic material needs met? How much more likely is it that young people's caring would be nurtured if people throughout society—from grocers, policemen, and physicians to religious leaders, coaches, businesspeople, and neighbors—all embraced and acted on the value of caring for others?

If the well-being of others were at the forefront of our daily thinking, might we also be more likely to work for policies to reduce climate change and other environmental problems? And while successful pursuit of caring relationships might not result in the lion lying down with the lamb, if it became a worldwide feature of human relationships, it would certainly make war a bit less likely.

As a reminder of what I mean by "caring," a good approximation is provided by the four features of nurturing I described in chapter 1: In caring relationships, we minimize toxic conditions, from coercive behavior to biological toxins such as cigarette smoke. We richly reinforce other people's prosocial behavior. We limit negative influences and opportunities. And we promote psychological flexibility.

I'll elaborate on psychological flexibility later in this chapter. But I'd like to begin by exploring the opposite of caring relationships—namely, coercive relationships. Understanding how and why coercive relationships arise illuminates what is needed to cultivate caring relationships.

Coercion: The Main Obstacle to Caring

In chapter 1, I argued that coercion—the use of aversive behavior in an attempt to terminate someone else's aversive behavior—is the fundamental process driving human conflict. There is no shortage of types of conflict and coercion: war, genocide, murder, harassment, bullying, cheating, child abuse, marital conflict, discriminatory behavior; the list goes on. All of this cruelty is rooted in the kind of moment-to-moment coercive interactions I described in chapter 1. Humans are finely tuned to learn strategies that reduce others' aversive behavior, and we readily learn to counteraggress to get immediate relief.

Unless we are fortunate to have people around us who patiently ignore our most irritating behaviors and richly reinforce our prosocial behavior, we end up living in a world where people use aversive means to ward off others' aversive behavior. Conflict-ridden families, schools, and communities are crucibles that create a constant stream of threatened, hostile, and aggressive children and send them out into the world as adults. These damaged people often raise their own children using the same coercive practices their parents used on them. Blaming them simply adds more aversives into the mix. It is also unfair. Recent research on epigenetics shows that being raised in a threatening environment can wire people to have a heightened sensitivity to threat and more aggressive reactions to others—traits they pass on to their children (Jablonka and Raz 2009).

The Evolutionary Roots of Coercion

Unfortunately, just as our inherited preference for high-fat foods and sugar leads to heart disease and diabetes in the modern era, inherited tendencies for dealing with aversives don't serve us well in the modern world. Evolutionarily speaking, organisms that were quick to respond to threat were a bit more likely to survive, and we therefore inherited a propensity to counterattack. While this may often produce short-term gain, it causes us to live in a world filled with people who have a hair-trigger response to anyone else's threatening behavior. In fact, the hair trigger is itself a biologically created bias toward seeing others' behavior as threatening.

One of the biggest dangers to humans is other humans, and not just because other humans may harm or attack us. There is also the threat that our own group may exclude us. Unlike cougars, humans are ill equipped to survive on their own. Thus, even a frown of disapproval constitutes a threatening stimulus.

As humans evolved, being quick and effective in attacking those who threatened us had great survival value. We have gotten very good at counteraggression thanks to our capacity to be reinforced by anything that terminates others' aversive or threatening behavior or by signs that those who are threatening us are harmed or frightened. Combined, our sensitivity to threat and the success of coercive behaviors in producing immediate, albeit temporary, cessation of others' aversive behavior have led to humans developing coercive relationships quite readily.

As I recounted in chapters 1 through 3, reducing coercive relations in families and schools is critical to nurturing the development of prosocial behavior and preventing patterns of problematic behavior. But reducing or eliminating coercion is also critical in most every human relationship. A physician who is quick to be defensive or irritable with a patient may keep that patient from complaining, but this isn't good for either the patient or the physician. Coercion may help a husband in getting his wife to not complain about his behavior, but it is likely to contribute to constant or escalating conflict and, ultimately, the dissolution of the relationship. A prison guard using coercive tactics to keep a prisoner "in line" may further motivate him to be angry and aggressive. Coworkers may coercively damp down each other's aversive behavior, but it may come at the cost of effective cooperation. A coach may think he is teaching his players to be "tough," but his constant criticism will turn many young people away from sports entirely.

Human verbal relational abilities further extend our tendency to develop and maintain coercive relationships. We can remember being slighted by someone years ago. We can anticipate future harm and may treat others badly simply because we think they intend to harm us.

Our social, cooperative tendencies and our language abilities are intertwined in ways that further support coercive interactions. In work organizations, I've often observed a tendency for two people who are in conflict to recruit social support for their own sides of the argument. We are naturally avoidant of confrontation. If someone isn't treating us well, we fear (often with good reason) that confronting the person will simply bring on more aversive behavior. As a result, we often tell a friend, who naturally will listen sympathetically and probably try to help us feel better about it. Unfortunately, this often leads to mutually hostile cliques, because it is highly likely that the other person also has friends in whom she confides.

In the projects I have directed, my policy regarding hostility between coworkers has always been to bring the two people together to discuss their concerns. Boy, do people resist such conversations. But my experience has virtually always been that people get along better if they talk to each other directly in a context of organizational norms that favor cooperation and respect.

The Physiological Costs of Coercion

Robert Sapolsky's book *Why Zebra's Don't Get Ulcers* (1994) explains the physiology involved in interpersonal conflict. Say your toddler gets upset because her brother hit her. This stressor causes her hypothalamus to release corticotropin-releasing hormone, which stimulates the anterior pituitary to release adrenocorticotropic hormone, which in turn stimulates the adrenal gland to release cortisol. This cascade of hormones raises blood pressure, heart rate, and blood glucose and mobilizes the child to either fight or flee—even though neither option may be the best in this circumstance. She cries and screams, which sets off the same cascade of stress responses in *you*, mobilizing you to fight or flee, neither of which is the best move for you or your family.

In his book, Sapolsky reveals how chronic stress reactions contribute to a wide range of physical illnesses, including insomnia, colds, irritable bowel syndrome, ulcers, miscarriages, memory impairment, major depression, hypertension, cardiovascular disease, adult-onset diabetes, osteoporosis, immune suppression, drug addiction, and stunted growth.

The most important stressor we humans typically face comes in the form of coercive interactions with other humans. For example, one study (Eaker et al. 2007) found that married women who self-silenced during conflict, keeping their feelings to themselves, had four times the likelihood of dying than women who didn't self-silence, even when other risk factors, such as blood pressure, body mass index, cigarette smoking, diabetes, and cholesterol levels were controlled statistically.

The implication is clear: if you want to keep your stress-response system from being chronically aroused, it will be helpful if the people around you aren't coercive. When I do workshops with teachers, I point out that it is in their own interest that everyone around them be safe and calm. I might say, "Imagine that one of your students runs into a street gang that threatens him, and arrives at school shaking and upset, but can't explain what happened. How would you like to have twenty-five kids coming in like that every day? It is in your interest—as well as theirs—that their relationships and environments help them be more calm."

The Imperative of Reducing Coercion

There is a simple message in all of the evidence outlined above and in earlier chapters: we need to reduce coercion in *all* of our environments—not just homes and schools, but workplaces and neighborhoods. Parents who feel coerced at work or in a conflict with a neighbor typically coerce their children. Children who are coerced usually pick on each other and act defiantly toward teachers. Coworkers who feel threatened are likely to act in angry and uncaring ways toward each other, often escalating the threatening behavior of those around them. It doesn't take much. One study of young adults showed that their brain functions were harmed even if the only form of abuse their parents subjected them to was verbal (Choi et al. 2009).

We need to replace all of this coercive behavior with behavior that calms, supports, and teaches—the kind of behavior that helps others thrive. Imagine that policy makers, teachers, parents, the grocer down the street—everybody—began to understand that people are harmed by the stressful things that happen to them. That aggressive driver you flipped off the other day got angrier. He went home and yelled at his kid. His kid acted out in school the next day, so his father grounded him for a week. And because that acting out took the form of bullying, the coercion spread, like a disease, to another child and another family. It goes on and on.

Stressing other people makes it more likely that they will be aggressive to you and everyone else. And so we keep conflict going. Unfortunately, due to the American predilection for punishment, the natural answer to this is typically to punish people for being so aggressive. Yet that's just more of the same.

If we could get everyone to begin by thinking about reducing everyone's stress, maybe we would live in a world where school board members say, "Maybe we should think about how much we're punishing kids in school. And are we mostly punishing teachers when kids do poorly? Does that work?" Maybe we could get people in the criminal justice system to look at current practices in terms of how much we punish and stress people and see that this makes them *less* able to reform their ways. Maybe we could get companies to consider whether the stress they expose their workers to undermines productivity and increases health care costs (as, indeed, it does).

If people in public health, psychology, medicine, sociology, and neuro-science joined together to underscore the message that coercion is the culprit underlying most of society's problems, we might get policy makers, health care practitioners, parents, teachers, and supervisors to look for ways to reduce coercive interactions and find better ways to motivate people. But where do we start? How do we influence the entire population to abandon coercive behavior and adopt more nurturing ways? How do we get governments to make human nurturance a goal of public policy? The public health perspective teaches us that we take gains wherever we can find them. We can build from the bottom up by implementing good family and school interventions in individual communities. But we can also work from the top down, creating public policies that require and fund the dis-semination of nurturing programs and policies to ameliorate poverty and coercive practices.

Cultivating Forbearance and Forgiveness

The world has struggled with how to deal with others' aversive behavior for centuries. The fundamental problem is to get people to not respond to others' aversive behavior with their own aversive behavior because, more likely than not, doing so will simply perpetuate coercion and conflict. Instead, we need to cultivate forbearance and forgiveness as cardinal fea-tures of our culture. We look with wonder at examples of such behavior:

- When Charles C. Roberts stormed an Amish school house and killed five young schoolgirls before he killed himself, the Amish community expressed its forgiveness by attending his funeral and raising money for Roberts's widow and three small children. Those three small children must live out their lives knowing that their father committed a horrendous act. They will face difficul-ties in any case. But which will be better for them: knowing that the families of their father's victims hate them, or knowing that those families have forgiven their father and care for them?

- When Mohandas Gandhi vowed to fast until all violence between Hindus and Muslims ended, a Hindu man came to him and con-fessed that he had killed a Muslim boy as revenge for the killing of his son. He implored Gandhi to end his fast because he didn't want to have Gandhi's death on his soul. Gandhi told him that he could atone for his sin by finding a Muslim child whose parents had been killed in the religious riots and raising that child as a Muslim (Gandhi 1998).

- In Matthew 5:38, Jesus says, "You have heard that it was said, 'An eye for an eye, and a tooth for a tooth.' But I tell you, do not resist an evil person. If someone strikes you on the right cheek, turn to him the other also. And if someone wants to sue you and take your tunic, let him have your cloak as well. If someone forces you to go one mile, go with him two miles. Give to the one who asks you, and do not turn away from the one who wants to borrow from you."

- During Martin Luther King's nonviolent movement to end segregation, civil rights activists subjected themselves to violent attacks. In so doing, they inspired the sympathy and support of enough Americans that segregation ended.

- In South Africa under Nelson Mandela's leadership, a Truth and Reconciliation Commission was created to address the many wrongs that had been done during apartheid. The commission invited victims of apartheid to give statements about their experiences. Perpetrators of violence were also invited to give testimony and could request amnesty from both civil and criminal prosecution. The process is generally credited with having prevented a great deal of retaliatory violence.

- A mother patiently changes the dirty diaper of a crying child.

I hope you see how this last example resembles the others. In every instance, the key is that people choose not to retaliate or otherwise respond with aversive behavior. In doing so, they make it a little more likely that peaceful behavior will replace aggressive or unpleasant behavior. When they succeed, they build the capacity of others to react to stressful situations calmly and perhaps even warmly.

You might be inclined to respond to this line of thinking by saying, "Yes, we know all this. It is all in the teachings of people like Gandhi,

Jesus, Martin Luther King, and many others." That is quite true. It is no accident that each of these leaders had an impact on millions of people. However, I'm also offering something I believe to be new and I hope helpful: that the behavioral sciences have developed systematic ways to aid people in controlling threatening or antisocial behavior without acting in ways that simply provoke further aggression.

Only when we spread these practices throughout society and reduce the number of people who arrive at adulthood with coercive repertoires will we achieve the kind of peaceful society that Jesus, Gandhi, and Martin Luther King envisioned. Spreading warm, supportive, caring interpersonal relations requires that people have skills for dealing with others' aversive behavior without further escalating it.

My admittedly behavioristic shorthand label for the skill we need is "stepping over the aversives of others." It might also be called forbearance, which means "patient self-control," "restraint," or "tolerance." Every one of the effective parenting programs developed over the past forty years helps parents get better at stepping over the aversive things that children naturally do: An infant cries and a mother who might otherwise respond abusively or neglectfully receives encouragement from a skilled nurse to step over this aversive behavior. The nurse teaches her to hold the infant and rock him, talking soothingly. The nurse makes it clear that the mother's frustration and distress are natural and understandable (which is an example of the nurse stepping over the distressed behavior of the mother). The nurse commiserates with the mother while also modeling more patient—and more effective—ways of soothing the child.

In numerous family interventions, parents learn a variety of strategies for helping children develop the self-care skills and routines they need to get through the day. These may include praising and rewarding what the child does, or simply doing things together. In essence, parents get a lot better at responding not with anger or impatience but rather with support, interest, and calm, patient guidance, and they thereby help their children develop an ever-expanding set of skills, interests, and, most importantly, the ability to regulate their own emotions and restrain angry or impulsive behavior. In short, parents learn to ignore the milder forms of their children's aversive behavior and simply do what it takes to comfort and soothe their children and guide them in developing new skills.

The same is true for couples who aren't getting along. Psychologists such as Bob Weiss and John Gottman have carefully observed the interactions of couples in conflict, who often escalate aversive behavior because it may make their spouse stop doing something aversive. Effective couples therapy helps both partners replace cycles of criticism, blaming, anger, and cold silence with forbearance, patience, and positive activities. It doesn't work in every case, but it does save many marriages.

Stepping over aversives is also useful in helping people who are depressed. Research I conducted with Hy Hops and Linda Sherman showed that depressed mothers got some respite from the aversive behavior of their family members by being sad and self-critical (Biglan 1991). When mothers acted this way, their husbands and children were just a little bit less likely to be angry or critical. No one was having fun, but the mothers occasionally avoided negativity from other family members. Based on that finding, other researchers tested whether reducing conflict between depressed women and their spouses would reduce their depression (Beach, Fincham, and Katz 1998). It did.

So what we need to do is to build people's repertoires of forbearance, forgiveness, empathy, and compassion. This will undoubtedly be a bootstrap affair. But every time we influence someone to replace coercive reactions with behavior that calms and supports others, we have one more person who is cultivating these same nurturing reactions in those around them. And a good place to start in this quest is with children.

Helping Children Develop Empathy

How do we cultivate the skills and values that people need to deal with others' distressing behavior patiently and effectively? If you look at how young children learn to be empathetic, you can see the key skills they need. The first skill is simply having an awareness of their own emotional reactions. In the Early Education Program in Lane County, Oregon—directed by my wife, Georgia—staff members use distressing experiences to do emotion coaching.

Imagine that four-year-old Carlos opens the lunch his mom prepared for him and starts to cry. One of the adults joins him and talks empathically about how Carlos is feeling: "Oh, are you feeling really sad?" In doing so, the teacher is helping Carlos learn the names for his feelings. When asked why he is upset, Carlos says that his mother promised to put a cookie in his lunch, but there isn't one. His teacher might commiserate with him, acknowledging that this would make her sad too and showing, through her tone of voice and facial expression, that she feels sad about his predicament. In addition to helping Carlos develop the ability to describe what he is feeling, their interaction helps him understand that feelings result from things that happen to us. And as he calms down and receives comfort from a caring adult, he is learning to accept and move through his emotions—a small step in the development of emotion regulation.

But empathy also requires being able to see things from someone else's perspective. If I am going to experience caring and concern about how you are feeling, I first have to know *what* you are feeling. Research on perspective taking suggests that young children learn that others see things from a different perspective—literally. As they become more adept at realizing that what others see isn't what they see, they become better able to discern the emotions that others are feeling.

A good illustration of this process is a test that three-year-olds usually fail but five-year-olds easily pass. A three-year-old watches a video of an adult putting a pencil in a green box while a child named Charlie watches. After Charlie leaves the room, the adult moves the pencil from the green box to a red box. When a three-year-old is asked what box Charlie will look in to find the pencil, she or he will say the red box. But in the same situation, a five-year-old will correctly say the green box. The three-year-old has not yet learned to see things from Charlie's perspective.

If children are able to notice and describe their own emotions and can take the perspective of another child, they may then be able to understand the emotions another child is feeling. Suppose Ryan notices that Kaitlin is upset and learns that her mother didn't put a treat in her lunch as Kaitlin had expected. Because of his earlier experience, Ryan may then understand and even experience some of the emotion that Kaitlin is feeling.

These experiences form the foundation for empathy—the ability to perceive and experience what another person is thinking or feeling—as well as loving-kindness, understood in traditions like Buddhism as the expression of love through goodwill and kind acts. But by themselves, such experiences don't guarantee development of the loving-kindness we need to build in our society. For example, a child who perceives that another child is upset about her lunch might use that as an occasion to tease the other child. To build a compassionate and caring society, we need to promote, teach, and richly reinforce loving-kindness.

I recently attended the fifth birthday party for our granddaughter, Ashlyn. At one point, as she and her friends were playing, one of girls, Sara, left the group and sat alone at a table crying. She was very sad. I didn't know why. A few minutes later, Ashlyn came over and, in the sweetest way, rubbed Sara's head and said something soothing. Sara clearly felt better.

I later learned that Sara was the only one of the girls who had not yet turned five, and she was upset and feeling excluded. I also learned that Ashlyn's mother, Jen, prompted Ashlyn to comfort Sara.

You might think that doesn't count as a genuine instance of compassion, since Ashlyn had to be prompted. But that is how these vital repertoires are built. This episode was just a step on the road to building the behaviors and values of compassion and caring.

I know how carefully Jen and Mike have worked to help Ashlyn learn to be considerate of the feelings of her brother and her friends. They interrupt aversive interactions and prompt more positive ways of relating. They richly reinforce instances when Ashlyn is considerate of others. Sometimes they prompt these reactions, but over time, Ashlyn increasingly often acts this way on her own. All of this was facilitated by a lot of labeling and describing the behaviors that count as patient or compassionate: "That was sweet," "You're being so considerate," "You're being really patient."

By cultivating patient, nurturing family and school environments, we can help young children learn to understand and regulate their own emotions, understand the emotions of others, and react to others' distress with empathy and caring. We help them go from automatic distressed and angry reactions to more patient, empathic, and skilled ways of dealing with the distressed and distressing behavior of others. In the process, we help them cultivate a value of nurturing themselves and others.

Helping Adults Develop Empathy

Even if we make great progress in increasing the number of families and schools that help children cultivate these nurturing skills, we will have to do the same for many adults. Recent research on mindfulness interventions offers insight into how adults can be aided in developing these skills and the inclination to use them. It seems that as people become more mindful, they also become more empathic and compassionate. For example, a review of research on the impact of mindfulness training on health care providers showed that mindfulness helped them create a more caring environment, increased their capacity for empathy and appreciation of others, and assisted them in becoming less reactive or defensive in their relationships (Escuriex and Labbé 2011).

Due to the quality of the studies they reviewed (most were not randomized trials), I am hesitant to make great claims based on their findings. However, based on the research I've reviewed and my own experience in working with clients from an ACT perspective, I am inclined to believe that when people become more psychologically flexible, as described in chapter 5, they also tend to become more empathic and less likely to respond to angry or aggressive people with their own anger and aggression. It seems that as people become better able to step back from their thoughts and feelings in a mindful way and be explicit about the values they want in their relationships, they aren't as quick to react negatively and are better able to act in pragmatic ways that strengthen relationships with others.

Why would psychological flexibility help people become more patient, empathic, and compassionate? It probably helps in four ways. First, it involves a mindful way of being in the world—simply being more attentive to what is going on around you in the present moment. If you actively attend to another person, you are more likely to notice how the person feels and discern what she might be thinking.

Second, psychological flexibility involves the ability to take another's perspective. If you become better at noticing what is happening in the present moment, you can also get good at noticing that *you* are noticing all these things. There is a part of us that simply observes but is none of the things we observe. It is what ACT therapists call the *observer self*. It is a safe perspective from which to observe your own thoughts and feelings and those of other people.

Third, if you get good at noticing that the things you see are not the *you* that is seeing, you become better able to experience others' emotions without becoming overwhelmed by them (Atkins 2014). From this perspective, you can experience others' distress without needing to avoid it or to deny that it is important.

Fourth, psychological flexibility involves being clear about our values and having a focus on behaving in ways that are consistent with those values.

In my view, such psychological flexibility is critical to creating a society that nurtures everyone. Think about the troubling people you see in your community. For example, when you see someone begging on a street corner or hear of a person arrested for assault, you may react with irritation, revulsion, or fear. That is understandable. I don't ask you to suppress those reactions. And research shows that it doesn't work to suppress them anyway. Instead, merely think about what that person's life has been like. More than likely, their environment failed to nurture the skills they needed. As children, they probably didn't learn emotion regulation and other self-regulation skills because they lived in stressful environments, and therefore struggled in school and had ongoing stressful experiences with family, teachers, and peers. Now, as adults, they continue to have daily experiences of rejection, derision, and threat.

So while accepting the fact that we are frustrated by many of the troubled people we see around us, we can also invest in making our communities places with far fewer troubled people. I am convinced that most of us value being part of a community that sees to the successful development and well-being of everyone. We all want communities with less crime, drug abuse, and welfare dependency. If we can convince more people that such communities are not only possible but also in everyone's interest, we can bring together the public and private resources to make it a reality.

We need a lot more research on this problem. Even if ACT interventions make individuals more empathic and forgiving, we have a long way to go in translating that approach into strategies that significantly increase the prevalence of caring and compassion in entire societies.

Action Implications

Hopefully I've convinced you that cultivating forbearance, forgiveness, and compassion is fundamental to achieving a nurturing society. Here are some effective actions that can advance these skills and values, whether undertaken individually or in organizations. After all, every organization is a place where people may either experience great conflict or enjoy the support and approval of those around them. And given all of the evidence that positive interpersonal relations benefit both individuals and organizations by increasing effectiveness and reducing stress and stress-related problems, public policies are also essential to promoting nurturing human relationships.

For Everyone

- See if, a few times each day, you can notice whether those around you seem comfortable, involved, and thriving, or tense, threatened, and fearful. Then look for ways to support those who seem troubled. Simply paying attention to people and expressing an interest can make a difference.

- When dealing with people who often act in angry and aggressive ways, try to put yourself in their shoes and see why they might feel threatened. Patient, warm reactions to their irritable behavior could set the stage for changing your relationship with such people. Of course, you will have to accept—but not believe or act on—all the thoughts you will experience about feeling threatened by them or needing to retaliate.

- My friends Peter and Susan Glaser have written a book that is helpful for developing the skills needed to deal effectively with people who are prone to anger and argument: *Be Quiet, Be Heard* (Glaser, Glaser, and Matthews 2006), which offers specific techniques for receiving criticism and raising difficult issues with others while also reducing conflict.

- Another valuable resource is the website of a good friend, Doug Carmine. It's called Feed Kindness: The Ultimate Win-Win (http://www.feedkindness.com). It is a gold mine of ideas, examples, evidence, and resources for adding kindness to the world.

For Organizations

- Systematically assess the quality of interpersonal relations within the organization. If conflict is common, initiate a program to help members adopt more nurturing and less conflictual ways of communicating. An example of such an approach is the Glasers' BreakThrough Conflict program (http://www.theglasers.com/breakthrough-conflict.html).

- Just increasing fun in the workplace can be beneficial. A recent meta-analysis of studies showed that in workplaces with greater humor, employees have higher levels of job satisfaction, better work performance, and less burnout and turnover (Mesmer-Magnus, Glew, and Viswesvaran 2012).

For Policy Makers

- Fund research on how coercive interpersonal relationships can be reduced in families, schools, workplaces, and communities. How can dispute resolution become more effective? What kinds of interventions can reduce conflict in key relationships, and how can those interventions be made widely available?

- Through Surgeon General and Institute of Medicine reports, organize and effectively communicate strategies for reducing coercion and conflict, as well as the evidence about the importance of doing so.

- Increase the availability of effective dispute resolution, including for divorce. Develop legal procedures that provide incentives for parties to enter dispute resolution. Psychologist Irwin Sandler's work on divorce adjustment provides an excellent model of how to proceed (Sandler, Tein, and West 1994; Tein et al. 2004).

For the Entertainment Industry

- Just as the entertainment industry has changed our culture with respect to race relations, smoking, and alcohol use, it could influence all of us to embrace and build values of empathy, compassion, and forgiveness. Compelling movies, television shows, and songs can serve as models for how to respond to people's aversive behavior with forbearance and skill.

CHAPTER 11

Evolving the Society We Want

It is 2042. My grandson Grayson is thirty-one. He sits with his wife, Fatima, and their sleeping newborn, listening to the president's State of the Union address. President Maria Barrera says that she is happy to report that the state of the union is strong. The human well-being index shows that virtually every indicator of psychological, social, and physical health has continued the steady improvement that began around 2020. The index, which has become as closely watched as the unemployment rate and the gross domestic product, shows that the percentage of children living in poverty—a leading indicator of problems in years to come—has reached its lowest level ever. She attributes this to a combination of factors: a steady increase in minimum wage, greater use of the earned income tax credit, programs that help the diminishing number of at-risk mothers get education and employment, and the generally robust economy. Crime, drug abuse, and academic failure have continued their historic decline.

On the downside, she reports that obesity continues to be a stubborn problem, with research over the past three decades indicating that epigenetic processes can pass on metabolic stinginess that is difficult to reverse. However, the food marketing practices that were a major contributor to the explosion of obesity in the 1990s have ended, thanks to policies and regulations outlawing the marketing of unhealthful foods and providing incentives for marketing healthier ones.

President Barrera credits much of the nation's progress to strong bipartisan support for policies that have funded effective family and school programs. She mentions that the well-being index includes a measure of citizens' participation in civic affairs, added because of evidence that participation is a leading indicator of community well-being and people's life satisfaction—more powerful than winning the lottery. After the dark days of the first twenty years of the century, partisan warfare subsided when a new generation of Americans banded together via the Internet to advocate for positive political action and policies. Rather than attacking the media conglomerates and politicians who were using divisive methods to keep their constituency angry at the "other side," this new breed of civic advocates uses humor and warmth to show that public discourse can be more civil, respectful, and focused on everyone's well-being.

It is hard to make contact with dry statistics, but these statistics mean that a little girl in Louisville, Kentucky, whose mother died in a tragic accident, has a network of family, friends, and organizations making sure that she is cared for and gets what she needs to blossom into a successful young woman. It means that across the nation, fewer children are teased, abused, or neglected. The heartening statistics President Barrera shares wouldn't exist without the many warm and generous people who made the well-being of others a higher priority than their own financial success: a grandfather who chose to build a play structure for his grandchildren rather than sit at home watching golf on TV, a stranger who intervened in a thoughtful way to help a single mother find a job when she was laid off, a high school football star who made it a point to be friends with one of the school's most rejected kids, a multimillionaire who lobbied to have his taxes raised to ensure that teachers wouldn't be laid off.

Is such a scenario possible? I think something of this sort is not only possible, but inevitable. I cannot look at the progress made in public health in the past five hundred years and in behavioral science in the past fifty years without feeling optimistic that all nations will focus increasingly on improving the well-being of their citizens. They will be guided by the knowledge that the most meaningful measure of well-being is not wealth, but life satisfaction. They will use and promote the growing number of programs, policies, and practices that clearly achieve better outcomes.

But optimism is not a substitute for action. So in this chapter, I'll discuss how we might evolve toward the world described above—the world I want my grandson to live in.

A Compelling Vision

We need a simple, unifying, and emotionally evocative vision of the kind of world we can create. The best description I've been able to come up with for this world is "nurturing environments." The quality of human life, perhaps even the survival of life as we know it, depends on finding ways to make everyone's environment more nurturing—less coercive and more caring, supportive of human development, and focused on doing what works.

I am acutely aware of my limitations as a creative persuasion artist. And after spending hundreds of hours studying cigarette marketing campaigns on which tobacco companies spent hundreds of millions of dollars, I know how important money is in developing an effective, persuasive campaign and reaching millions of people. Yet even with millions of dollars and highly skilled marketers, the folks at R. J. Reynolds spent two decades tearing their hair out while trying to come up with a campaign that could wrest market share from the Marlboro Man.

When Reynolds came up with the Joe Camel campaign, they finally began to capture some of the youth market away from Marlboro. In fact, Joe Camel had such a tremendous impact that Philip Morris was alarmed. They commissioned focus groups to see if they could pinpoint what was working for Camel. The report on this study, titled "The Viability of the Marlboro Man Among the 18–24 Segment," concluded, "Marlboro should act to minimize the effectiveness of Camel's appeal to the values of the 18–24 segment... Belonging is important to the 18–24 segment." It recommended that they "broaden the advertising to make [the Marlboro man]... less aloof, less severe and tough, more accessible" (Biglan 2004, Demonstrative 11, 7). Philip Morris responded by creating an ad that proved effective in focus groups. It showed two cowboys petting two puppies. So when it comes to persuasion, remember the puppies!

One of the other expert witnesses in *United States v. Philip Morris et al.* was Paul Slovic, a psychologist who studies human decision making. He described the basic principle that explains why puppies work. He calls it the "affect heuristic." A *heuristic* is anything that aids efficient decision making. Slovic's research (2000) shows that people are much more likely to make choices based on how something makes them feel than on any sort of rationale or reasoning process. Kids start smoking Camel because Joe is having fun. Camel equals fun! Got 'em!

In the end, the compelling vision we need to build must have all the emotional appeal of the best marketing. I've mentioned the goal of the Institute of Medicine report on prevention: "a society in which young people arrive at adulthood with the skills, interests, assets, and health habits needed to live healthy, happy, and productive lives in caring relationships with others" (IOM and NRC 2009, 387). I've described how such a society can be achieved by creating nurturing environments. In advertising terms, "nurturing environments" is the brand. Its value for target audience members is built by getting them to associate it with all the things they already value and with preventing things they fear or dislike.

Thus, we need emotionally evocative messages that associate nurturing environments with kindness, innovation, academic success, health, and prosperity, along with messages underscoring that nurturing environments are the key to preventing crime, academic failure, alcohol abuse and alcohol-related problems, tobacco use, drug abuse, teenage pregnancy, marital discord, child abuse, poverty, depression, anxiety, and schizophrenia. We also need to tailor these messages to specific target audiences. Everyone will benefit from hearing about how promoting nurturing environments can help them and those around them, especially when the details of these messages are targeted to specific groups, such as parents, youth, policy makers, law enforcement personnel, health care providers, and educators.

If I had a budget of several million dollars and one year of uninterrupted time, I could hire a top-notch advertising agency to come up with a better term than "nurturing environments." I could create media communications that motivate people to really want nurturing environments. Give me a hundred million dollars, and I could reach millions of people with effective messages. That isn't a lot of money, especially in comparison to statistics indicating that the cigarette industry spent $12.49 billion on advertising in 2006 (T. T. Clark et al. 2011).

The vision we create must also be compelling to the scientific community, so it must be empirically sound. I submit that this book presents the evidence supporting the value of creating nurturing environments, along with a great deal of information on how to achieve such environments.

Creative Epidemiology

In chapter 6, I described how creative the tobacco control movement has been in reducing tobacco use. It dramatically illustrated the magnitude of the problem by comparing the epidemic of smoking-related deaths to two Boeing 747s crashing every day of the year. This movement led to the production of Surgeon General and Institute of Medicine reports and National Cancer Institute monographs that marshaled the evidence in support of specific policy changes, such as clean indoor air laws.

A similar effort can convince millions of Americans that their well-being and the well-being of the nation depend on making families, schools, workplaces, neighborhoods, and communities more nurturing. Imagine a Surgeon General report titled *The Importance of Nurturing Environments for Mental, Behavioral, and Physical Health*. Such a report would bring together all of the evidence regarding the wide range of problems that stem from conflict and coercion in families, schools, workplaces, and neighborhoods. It would document how all of these environments could be guided to become more nurturing, and how such a transformation would vastly enhance human well-being.

Imagine news stories with headlines like "Study Finds Children Do Better in Nurturing Families and Schools." Over time, people would begin to ask themselves whether the environments around them were nurturing. Parents might begin to spend more time just playing with their children. Teachers might increase their efforts to help students become more psychologically flexible. Midlevel managers who read about the importance of nurturing environments and their key features might ask whether their workplace could become more nurturing. A community might determine whether it is preventing family conflict by providing evidence-based family support programs. Prison wardens might join the fledgling effort to replace extreme isolation with effective rehabilitation practices.

Current advocacy for public health focuses mostly on single problems: driving under the influence, drug abuse, obesity, cigarette smoking, academic failure, child abuse, depression, lack of exercise, and so on. Yet the same basic environmental conditions affect every one of these problems. As suggested in chapter 6, rather than focusing on preventing individual problems, we need to cut to the chase and attend to how nonreinforcing, neglectful, and conflict-filled environments contribute to all of these problems—and how interventions that make these environments more nurturing can alleviate all of these problems.

Disseminating Evidence-Based Programs, Policies, and Practices

The spread of good interventions, including several described in chapter 2, is well underway. I mentioned how Marion Forgatch has helped the nation of Norway implement the behavioral parenting skills program she helped develop throughout the country. She is also implementing it in Michigan, Kansas, Denmark, and the Netherlands. Likewise, Patti Chamberlain, who developed Multidimensional Treatment Foster Care for adolescents and young children, has created a center that is working with states around the nation to implement her approach to foster care in child protective services agencies. And Tom Dishion and Beth Stormshak are training people in the implementation of their Family Check-Up in middle schools and preschools. In addition, Matt Sanders's Triple P program, the system described in chapter 6 for getting parenting skills information to parents throughout a community, is in place in more than twenty countries.

In chapter 6, I also talked about how Dennis Embry created a version of the Good Behavior Game designed to make it easier to train large numbers of teachers. He is currently supporting implementation of the Good Behavior Game in classrooms in thirty-eight US states as well as throughout the Canadian province of Manitoba, with more than 8,000 teachers using it and at least 105,000 students impacted. In addition, he is helping people all around North America implement kernels—those simple techniques for influencing behavior described in chapter 6. These approaches help parents, teachers, and other behavior change agents nurture prosocial behavior and prevent problems from developing.

Programs are not the only evidence-based approaches to increasing nurturance. In chapter 6, I mentioned the work of Alex Wagenaar and Kelli Komro at the University of Florida. They have identified more than fifty evidence-based policies that can contribute to human well-being (Komro et al. 2013). As just one example, here are details on some alcohol-related policies with proven benefit: Increasing the tax on alcoholic beverages leads to reductions in alcohol consumption, alcohol-related morbidity and mortality, motor vehicle deaths, sexually transmitted disease, and violent crime (Chaloupka, Grossman, and Saffer 2002). Likewise, limiting the density of alcohol outlets leads to large and significant reductions in alcohol consumption and interpersonal violence (Campbell et al. 2009).

And reducing the hours in which alcohol may be sold leads to reductions in alcohol consumption and related harm, such as violence (Popova et al. 2009). Clearly, all of these reductions in problematic outcomes would greatly contribute to our environments becoming more nurturing.

The Need for More Research

The cliché "More research is needed" has adorned many a master's thesis. One year it was the slogan on our Oregon Research Institute T-shirt. So even if I've convinced you that behavioral science research has made enormous progress in understanding human behavior and taking practical action to improve it, think of how much more progress we can make if we continue to expand this research. We will undoubtedly produce more numerous and effective interventions for families, schools, and communities. And increasingly, research is turning to the problem of how to ensure that interventions are widely and effectively implemented.

Research that strengthens the case for nurturing environments will also be important. Studies that document the common pathway from family conflict and other forms of threat to multiple psychological, behavioral, and health problems will bring policy makers and citizens together around the goal of making our families, schools, communities, and workplaces more nurturing. Such research will create a context for more effective, creative epidemiology and advocacy and generate support for the adoption of evidence-based programs and policies.

Most of the funding for the prevention research I've described has come from the National Institutes of Health (NIH), the bulk of it from the National Institute on Drug Abuse (NIDA). The prevention research branch at NIDA has funded many family and school interventions that have proven effective in preventing not just drug abuse, but all of the most common and costly psychological and behavioral problems. NIDA could have insisted on funding only research narrowly focused on drug abuse, but to their credit, they acted on evidence that drug abuse results from stressful life conditions that can precede the start of drug use by many years. As a result, NIDA has funded research on all risk factors that lead to drug abuse.

Unfortunately, funding for the NIH is dwindling. Despite the fact that, for many years, the NIH has been the most important source of funding for health research worldwide, during the last three years its budget has declined. And thanks to sequestration in fiscal year 2013, its budget decreased by two billion dollars, resulting in a failure to fund 640 projects, many of which involved prevention research. Given the history of the NIH in funding projects that lead to improved health and well-being, this is a tragic development.

Obviously, I am a biased reporter on this; my income for the past thirty years has come almost entirely from NIH funding. But hopefully I've demonstrated how much our society has gained by spending on behavioral science research—which, by the way, has been just a tiny fraction of NIH expenditures.

The Importance of Promoting Psychological Flexibility

Research on psychological flexibility can contribute to making American society more nurturing. If you aren't immersed in this research, that may seem unlikely to you. But I've seen profound changes in the way we deal with so-called mental illness. Already, more than seventy randomized controlled trials have shown the benefit of ACT for virtually every type of psychological or behavioral problem, and for many physical illnesses and health-related behaviors. This research shows that the fundamentals of acting effectively in the world involve being willing to have whatever thoughts and feelings arise without trying to avoid them, and being able to look *at* our private experience instead of letting it be a lens that colors whatever is there to be seen. This approach to life involves taking whatever actions can further our goals and values in a particular situation. I believe ACT has illuminated a way of being in the world that can serve not simply as a way for troubled people to overcome specific problems but also as a cultural innovation that contributes to everyone's well-being.

This assertion is admittedly speculative, and I am acutely aware of the risk that you may dismiss my assertions as the ramblings of a cultist. After all, I am suggesting that incremental behavioral science has produced a qualitatively different view of human functioning. My view grows out of the empirical evidence for ACT and my own observations of what happens to people (myself included) when they become more psychologically flexible. I am convinced that learning to accept our thoughts and feelings in a nonjudgmental way is an act of self-compassion and the first step toward reducing conflict and coercion among people.

Let me give you an example of how this orientation has reduced conflict in my life. One day I was supposed to give our cat Ginger a shot of insulin in the morning. I forgot to do it. My wife, Georgia, who is in charge of cat care, was not pleased. She is as nurturing to cats as to humans, and she does whatever they need. She did not seem angry, however. After all, she is nurturing toward me too. That evening she prepared Ginger's food and syringe of insulin, then handed them to me. She was "making" me do it. I felt humiliated and angry at being told what to do—and because I felt guilty for not having done what I was supposed to. Fuming, I went upstairs to give Ginger her shot.

In the past, this event might have led to a couple of days of not speaking to each other—not saying anything about it, but being sour and noncommunicative, both of us knowing what it was about, and each punishing the other. But on my way upstairs, I found myself accepting that I felt angry and humiliated and that I had made a mistake. What do I mean by "accepted"? I mean my emotions were just there. They could be there, and I didn't need to do anything about them. Rather than being within the humiliation and anger, I sort of stepped back and looked at them. As I did, my emotional experience got smaller. I wasn't struggling to get rid of it or to justify my mistake, so I didn't need to be angry at Georgia or blame her for my humiliation. Through this process, I realized that I wanted to have the kind of warm, cuddly evening that we so often have these days. So I went downstairs and had such an evening. (Georgia has also gotten good at letting thoughts and feelings be there without having to do something about them, so she too could let it go and move on.)

I see this process at work in all of the examples I gave in chapter 10 of people choosing to act in loving ways. The Amish families that forgave the family of Charles Roberts, who killed five Amish girls, were able to do this not because they had no anger, but because they were willing to have the anger and still act on their value of forgiveness. Gandhi must have felt great frustration that the Hindu man beseeching him had killed a Muslim child while Gandhi was in the process of starving himself to death to stop the killing. But he forgave the man and offered him a way out of his pain. When Christ counseled that we should turn the other cheek, he did not suggest we wouldn't feel anger. The civil rights workers who were willing to risk their lives and in some cases die for their cause certainly felt fear. However, they chose to accept their fear and take actions that they believed would arouse the conscience of the majority of Americans. We view these acts as heroic precisely because people were willing to have thoughts and feelings that conflicted with the actions they took.

ACT-based interventions ask people to think deeply about their most important values and envision what they want their life to be about. Sometimes practitioners ask their clients to imagine what might be on their tombstones if they lived up to their own highest ideals. In ACT workshops with Oregon teachers (Hinds et al. 2011), no one suggests what values the teachers should have. Yet all across the state, in both rural and urban settings, teachers usually list the same values: respect, integrity, caring, honesty, family, acceptance, forgiveness, tolerance, faith, fun, trust, kindness, friendship, exercise, and laughter. After teachers have identified their values, we help them take steps to make these values a bigger part of their lives. For example, they might set a specific goal for increasing the respect they get and the respect they give. One teacher decided she would try to listen more attentively to students when they talked to her. She decided that at least once a week for each class, she would take time between periods to talk to the students she had challenging relationships with, asking them about what was happening in their lives. She found that these students became softer and less confrontational.

What would happen if values became a much bigger part of our private lives and our public discourse? Suppose that creative epidemiology could encourage people to focus on valued living and become more psychologically flexible. A movement to nurture psychological flexibility could influence society at every level, including entertainment and the media, the same way that messages about not smoking helped shrink the culture of smoking. If this movement joined with religions that teach turning the other cheek, it might ignite an effort to bring public discussion of our most important problems back to a pragmatic focus on improving everyone's well-being. This kind of social evolution won't come from attacking the "other side"; instead, we need to take actions that model a third way: pragmatic problem solving.

Creating a New Breed of Advocacy Organizations

Social movements depend on advocacy organizations that can mobilize millions of people to take the actions needed for meaningful change. To create the kind of society I envision, we need two significant developments. The first is the creation of organizations that advocate for nurturing families, schools, workplaces, and communities. As mentioned earlier in this chapter, numerous advocacy organizations are already working on specific problems, such as driving under the influence, tobacco control, crime reduction, prevention of child abuse, poverty reduction, getting people to exercise more or eat better, preventing racial discrimination, reducing academic failure, and so on. Name a problem, and there is an organization working on it.

Yet all of these problems are rooted in a failure to ensure that families, schools, workplaces, and communities are nurturing and promote kind, caring, productive, enthusiastic, and conscientious behavior. If we can get all of these advocacy organizations to cooperate in promoting this central message and advocating for policies, programs, and practices that increase nurturance, we can significantly reduce all of the problems they target.

The second thing we need is to strengthen foundations, nonprofits, and advocacy organizations that are working for the common good. Current law places considerable restrictions on what these organizations can do to advocate for policies and practices that would promote nurturing environments. At the same time, the power of for-profit corporations to advocate for policies that benefit business—but may not benefit the common good—has become virtually unlimited, thanks to recent Supreme Court decisions such as *Citizens United v. Federal Election Commission*, which held that the First Amendment prohibits the government from restricting political independent expenditures by corporations, associations, or labor unions, and *McCutcheon v. Federal Election Commission*, which struck down political donor limits. The Alliance for Justice, an association of more than one hundred organizations working on progressive causes, is looking into ways to increase the ability of nonprofit organizations to work for the common good. We need more organizations like the Alliance for Justice.

Evolving a More Beneficial Form of Capitalism

I've already described the marketing, lobbying, and advocacy practices of corporations that harm human well-being. Failing to limit these practices will impair our ability to improve well-being. To address these harmful practices, we need to change the contingencies that select and maintain them. To some extent, increased regulation and increased penalties for harmful actions can help achieve this (perhaps through litigation, as in the case of *United States v. Philip Morris et al.*). Actions of this sort will become more common if we achieve policies that strengthen nonprofit advocacy organizations. However, fundamental changes in the culture of the for-profit world will also be necessary.

One encouraging development is the creation of benefit corporations. Under existing law, a corporation risks a lawsuit by shareholders if it does anything that diminishes profits—even if that action may be beneficial to the community at large. However, a benefit corporation can pursue a general public benefit (Hanson Bridgett LLP 2012). A nonprofit organization (B Lab) is tracking the spread of this innovation. Twenty-six states have adopted laws allowing the creation of such corporations, and there are now more than one thousand of these corporations operating worldwide.

From an evolutionary perspective, we can influence corporate behavior by increasing the negative consequences for harmful corporate actions and the positive consequences for beneficial actions. The straightforward application of this kind of contingency management has been far too long in coming, but it is likely to grow.

The problem, however, is that many corporate leaders who make the pursuit of profit their highest value will work assiduously to prevent passage of any laws that might impinge on profitability. A two-pronged approach can address this problem. One aspect is to advocate for specific contingencies that will curtail harmful actions. The other is to try to change the values of the for-profit corporate world.

Georgia and I once dined at the Four Seasons Restaurant in New York. I noticed that Domaine Drouhin, an Oregon Pinot Noir, was on the menu for $200 per bottle. (We didn't buy one.) I find it hard to believe that anyone can detect a difference in quality between a $100 bottle of wine and a $200 bottle. Perhaps I am just unsophisticated. It seems more likely, however, that being able to go into an upscale restaurant and order a $200 bottle of wine is about status. People living in the moneyed culture of Wall Street are motivated to go for bigger bonuses, and to create investment instruments that net their companies a great deal of money but produce a bubble that eventually results in a recession. Do their actions improve the quality of Americans' lives? Obviously not—even though they pay millions to media pundits to convince Americans otherwise.

We might also consider whether their actions improve even their own lives. Tim Kasser's research on materialistic goals (Kasser and Ryan 1993, 1996; Kasser et al. 2007) suggests that the pursuit of more pay and bigger bonuses doesn't make people happier. After all, seated at the table next to you at the Four Seasons is someone richer than you who just bought a $300 bottle of wine.

If we can create a cultural movement to promote nurturing environments and prosocial values, we may be able to influence many corporate leaders to abandon practices that are harmful to the greater good. I recently got encouraging words in this regard from Dennis Tirch, an ACT therapist who emphasizes the cultivation of self-compassion for clients who are having stress-related problems (see Tirch 2012). He told me that he has treated a number of hedge fund managers in his practice, and that as they become more self-compassionate, they also become more motivated to contribute to the well-being of others.

Changing Popular Culture

Changing popular culture may be the biggest challenge we face. We need entertainment that promotes nurturing environments: movies, TV shows, social media, and so on that model, reward, and recognize the things people do to protect, teach, care for, and forgive others. Violence and conflict currently dominate entertainment, and media corporations deny that this affects behavior, despite solid evidence to the contrary. For example, one study measured the TV viewing habits of children when they were six to ten years old and then assessed their aggressive behavior fifteen years later (Huesmann, Lagerspetz, and Eron 1984). Young people who had watched more violence on TV as children were more likely to be aggressive as adults. These relationships were true even when the researchers controlled statistically for children's socioeconomic status and intellectual ability and the behavior of their parents.

As the diversity of media expands, it becomes ever more difficult to prevent young people from being exposed to images and entertainment that promote conflict, distrust, and aggression. It will be a tall order to change this aspect of our culture. The First Amendment makes legal restrictions on what can be shown difficult to achieve in the United States. But substantial changes in media depictions of cigarette smoking have emerged, thanks to relentless advocacy by tobacco prevention advocates, including Jim Sargent and Stan Glantz. Sargent's research showed an association between kids watching movies that depict heroes smoking and subsequently taking up smoking themselves (Sargent et al. 2002). Stan Glantz (2003) successfully advocated for putting R ratings on movies that depict smoking, and this policy has been beneficial. Creative epidemiological approaches to the media's promotion of nonnurturing behavior could have a similar impact.

Empowering Dramatic Cultural Change

In the mid-nineteenth century, London was the largest and richest city in the world. Yet sewage flowed freely in the streets and into the Thames, fouling the drinking water and causing hundreds of deaths due to cholera. Thanks to scientific research, we now know that contaminated water causes cholera, and we would be shocked to hear of anyone allowing sewage to flow into the street. Our culture has changed.

Scientific evidence regarding the harm that coercive, nonnurturing environments do to human beings is just as strong as that for the harm of contaminated water. We have the capability to help families, schools, workplaces, and communities become more nurturing. At the same time, efforts like the tobacco control movement are teaching us how we can change harmful practices throughout a culture. Making our environments more nurturing is a bigger challenge than reducing tobacco use, but we can do it.

Creating and communicating a compelling vision of the society we could have if we promote nurturing environments can organize everything that must be done. Using creative epidemiology, we can educate citizens about the critical importance of reducing conflict and increasing nurturance. Continued research can expand our understanding of the harm caused by nonnurturing environments and strengthen interventions to support increased nurturance. Continued dissemination of evidence-based programs, policies, and practices will increase the prevalence of nurturing environments. Increased promotion of psychological flexibility through clinical interventions, workshops, and the media will accelerate these trends. Creating and strengthening advocacy organizations will generate support for this movement and empower all of the other approaches. Influencing the corporate world to embrace values that promote nurturing environments will moderate their harmful practices and align corporations with other efforts to promote nurturance. If we can influence popular culture, at least in part, to promote prosocial, nurturing values, we very well may be able to make nurturance an explicit norm for most members of society.

The work that remains is to apply the vast body of knowledge and research methods that has accumulated—to not just disseminate the programs, policies, and practices that are currently available, but to innovate and strengthen them and improve our ability to affect entire populations. We must also use the same principles of selection by consequences that have proved so fruitful in helping people lead more productive and caring lives. We can change the consequences for business, government entities, and nonprofit organizations so that their values and actions will better serve the well-being of everyone.

Taken together, all of these approaches will promote the greater good, creating the world that we and our children deserve. I hope you'll join me in working toward realizing this vision.

Afterword

Evolving the Future

A number of years ago, I received an e-mail from someone named Tony Biglan, who introduced himself as president of the Society for Prevention Research. He invited me to attend a symposium on prevention research from an evolutionary perspective that he was organizing for the society's next annual meeting.

I had never heard of Tony or the Society for Prevention Research, but I was happy to accept his invitation because I had just started to use my evolutionary expertise in a practical way to improve the quality of life in my city of Binghamton, New York. I outlined my new project, which I called the Binghamton Neighborhood Project, to Tony in my reply to his e-mail. Within seconds I had a return reply:

"Oh boy. You need me. This is what I do."

Indeed it was. Over the ensuing weeks and months, I was amazed and delighted to discover that Tony and his colleagues were already doing what I aspired to do: accomplish positive change in real-world settings. Some of their change methods worked at the individual level. If your view of psychotherapy is to spend years on a couch talking about your childhood, think again. I discovered that there are therapeutic methods that can be taught on the basis of reading a single book or attending a single three-hour session. Some of the change methods worked at the level of small groups. One of these was the Good Behavior Game, which provides lifelong benefits when played in the first and second grades. Perhaps most amazingly, some of the change methods worked at the level of large populations, such as a program that reduced cigarette sales to minors in the states of Wyoming and Wisconsin and another program implemented at a countywide scale in South Carolina that reduced the rate of child maltreatment. In a world of problems that seem to defy solutions, I felt that I had stumbled across a secret society of benign wizards.

Many practical change methods are poorly validated, which makes it difficult to know whether, how, or why they work. But Tony and his colleagues were also wizards at assessment. The gold standard of assessment is the randomized controlled trial, in which the individuals or groups that undergo the change method are randomly drawn from a larger pool, creating a comparison group that is similar in every other way. For example, in the South Carolina study (headed by Ron Prinz), eighteen counties were selected that were roughly comparable in size and demographics. Of these, nine were randomly selected to receive the treatment, and their child maltreatment statistics were compared to the other nine counties. Why weren't the results of such a high-quality study front page news?

I was so impressed by what I discovered that I began to wonder what I had to contribute with my own nascent efforts. I needn't have worried. Tony and his colleagues—especially Steven C. Hayes and Dennis Embry—were as eager to "discover" me as I was to "discover" them. The very fact that their work was largely unknown was a problem that I was in a position to help solve.

In my book *Evolution for Everyone*, I write that the Ivory Tower would be more aptly named the Ivory Archipelago—many islands of thought with little communication among islands. The world of public policy and practical change efforts suffers from the same problem. A change method that works arises and spreads within a given island but goes no further unless "discovered" by some brave wayfarer from another island. Evolutionary theory can transform the Ivory Archipelago into the *United* Ivory Archipelago by providing a unifying theoretical framework. This unification took place in the biological sciences during the twentieth century (and continues), and it is in the process of taking place for the human-related academic disciplines. It can also work its magic for the world of public policy and practical change efforts. Tony, Steve, and Dennis sensed this possibility, which made them as excited to work with me as I was to work with them.

I tell the story of teaming up with Tony, Steve, and Dennis for a general audience in my book *The Neighborhood Project*. We outline our vision for a professional audience in an article titled "Evolving the Future: Toward a Science of Intentional Change," which is published with peer commentaries and our reply in the journal *Behavioral and Brain Sciences*. Now Tony has outlined the vision in his own words in *The Nurture Effect* with great wisdom, experience, and humanity.

I think of what Tony and the rest of us are trying to accomplish in historic terms. Historians will look back upon the twenty-first century as a period of synthesis for human-related knowledge, similar to the synthesis of biological knowledge that took place during the twentieth century. With understanding comes the capacity to improve. There is no doubt that the synthesis is taking place, but *how fast* is less certain—and speed is of the essence, because the need to solve our most pressing problems won't wait. The more people who read *The Nurture Effect* and absorb its meaning, the faster the world will become a better place.

—David Sloan Wilson
    President, Evolution Institute
    SUNY Distinguished Professor of Biology and Anthropology
    Binghamton University

References

Adams, G. L., and S. Engelmann. 1996. *Research on Direct Instruction: 25 Years Beyond DISTAR.* Seattle: Educational Achievement Systems.

Alfieri, L., P. J. Brooks, N. J. Aldrich, and H. R. Tenenbaum. 2011. Does discovery-based instruction enhance learning? *Journal of Educational Psychology* 103: 1–18.

Allen, N. B., and P. B. T. Badcock. 2006. Darwinian models of depression: A review of evolutionary accounts of mood and mood disorders. *Progress in Neuro-Psychopharmacology and Biological Psychiatry* 30: 815–826.

American Academy of Child and Adolescent Psychiatry. 2011. Drinking alcohol in pregnancy. *Facts for Families*, number 93. Available at http://www.aacap .org/App_Themes/AACAP/docs/facts_for_families/93_drinking_alcohol_ in_pregnancy_fetal_alcohol_effects.pdf. Accessed May 14, 2014.

Aos, S., S. Lee, E. Drake, A. Pennucci, M. Miller, L. Anderson, and M. Burley. 2012. *Return on Investment: Evidence-Based Options to Improve Statewide Outcomes.* Olympia: Washington State Institute for Public Policy.

Aos, S., S. Lee, E. Drake, A. Pennucci, T. Klima, M. Miller, L. Anderson, J. Mayfield, and M. Burley. 2011. *Return on Investment: Evidence-Based Options to Improve Statewide Outcomes.* Olympia: Washington State Institute for Public Policy.

Arcus, D. 2002. School shooting fatalities and school corporal punishment: A look at the states. *Aggressive Behavior* 28: 173–183.

Astin, A. W. 2002. *The American Freshman: Thirty-Five Year Trends, 1966–2001.* Los Angeles: Higher Education Research Institute.

Atkins, P. W. B. 2014. Empathy, self-other differentiation, and mindfulness. In *Organizing Through Empathy*, edited by K. Pavlovich and K. Krahnke. New York: Routledge.

Azrin, N. H., R. R. Hutchinson, and R. McLaughlin, R. 1972. The opportunity for aggression as an operant reinforcer during aversive stimulation. In *The Experimental Analysis of Social Behavior*, edited by R. E. Ulrich and P. T. Mountjoy. New York: Appleton-Century-Crofts.

Bach, P., and S. C. Hayes. 2002. The use of acceptance and commitment therapy to prevent the rehospitalization of psychotic patients: A randomized controlled trial. *Journal of Consulting and Clinical Psychology* 70: 1129–1139.

Ballard, K. D. 1983. Teaching children to do what they say they will do: A review of research with suggested applications for exceptional children. *Exceptional Child* 30: 119–125.

Bandura, A. 1974. Behavior theory and models of man. *American Psychologist* 29, 859–869.

Bardo, M. T., D. H. Fishbein, and R. Milich. 2011. *Inhibitory Control and Drug Abuse Prevention*. New York: Springer.

Barrera, M., Jr., A. Biglan, T. K. Taylor, B. K. Gunn, K. Smolkowski, C. Black, D. F. Ary, and R. C. Fowler. 2002. Early elementary school intervention to reduce conduct problems: A randomized trial with Hispanic and non-Hispanic children. *Prevention Science* 3: 83–94.

Barrish, H. H., M. Saunders, and M. M. Wolf. 1969. Good behavior game: Effects of individual contingencies for group consequences on disruptive behavior in a classroom. *Journal of Applied Behavior Analysis* 2: 119–124. Available at http://www.ncbi.nlm.nih.gov/pmc/articles/PMC1311049/?tool=pubmed . Accessed May 14, 2014.

Bavarian, N., K. M. Lewis, D. L. DuBois, A. Acock, S. Vuchinich, N. Silverthorn, et al. 2013. Using social-emotional and character development to improve academic outcomes: A matched-pair, cluster-randomized controlled trial in low-income, urban schools. *Journal of School Health* 83: 771–779.

Beach, S. R. H., F. D. Fincham, and J. Katz. 1998. Marital therapy in the treatment of depression: Toward a third generation of therapy and research. *Clinical Psychology Review* 18: 635–661.

Beach, S., R. H. Jones, D. J. Franklin, and J. Kameron. 2009. Marital, family, and interpersonal therapies for depression in adults. In *Handbook of Depression*, 2nd ed., edited by I. H. Gotlib and C. L. Hammen. New York: Guilford.

Beets, M. W., B. R. Flay, S. Vuchinich, F. J. Snyder, A. Acock, K.-K. Li, K. Burns, I. J. Washburn, and J. Durlak. (2009). Using a social and character development program to prevent substance use, violent behaviors, and sexual activity among elementary-school students in Hawaii. *American Journal of Public Health*, 99: 1438–1445.

Biglan, A. 1991. Distressed behavior and its context. *Behavior Analyst* 14: 157–169.

———. 1995. *Changing Cultural Practices: A Contextualist Framework for Intervention Research*. Reno, NV: Context Press.

———. 2003. Selection by consequences: One unifying principle for a transdisciplinary science of prevention. *Prevention Science* 4: 213–232.

———. 2004. *United States v. Philip Morris et al. Direct Written Examination of Anthony Biglan, Ph.D. Submitted by the United States Pursuant to Order #471. Civil No. 99-CV-02496 (GK).* Available at http://www.justice.gov/civil/cases/tobacco2/20050103%20Biglan_Written_Direct_and_%20Demonstratives. pdf. Accessed June 12, 2014.

———. 2009. The role of advocacy organizations in reducing negative externalities. *Journal of Organizational Behavioral Management* 29: 1–16.

———. 2011. Corporate externalities: A challenge to the further success of prevention science. *Prevention Science* 12: 1–11.

Biglan, A., D. V. Ary, K. Smolkowski, T. E. Duncan, and C. Black. 2000. A randomized control trial of a community intervention to prevent adolescent tobacco use. *Tobacco Control* 9: 24–32.

Biglan, A., P. A. Brennan, S. L. Foster, and H. D. Holder. 2004. *Helping Adolescents at Risk: Prevention of Multiple Problem Behaviors.* New York: Guilford.

Biglan, A., and C. Cody. 2013. Integrating the human sciences to evolve effective policies. *Journal of Economic Behavior and Organization* 90(Suppl): S152–S162.

Biglan, A., B. R. Flay, D. D. Embry, and I. Sandler. 2012. Nurturing environments and the next generation of prevention research and practice. *American Psychologist* 67: 257–271.

Biglan, A., and E. Hinds. 2009. Evolving prosocial and sustainable neighborhoods and communities. *Annual Review of Clinical Psychology* 5: 169–196.

Biglan, A., H. Hops, and L. Sherman. 1988. Coercive family processes and maternal depression. In *Social Learning and Systems Approaches to Marriage and the Family.* New York: Brunner/Mazel.

Binns, H. J., C. Campbell, and M. J. Brown. 2006. Interpreting and managing blood lead levels of less than 10 microg/dL in children and reducing childhood exposure to lead: Recommendations of the Centers for Disease Control and Prevention Advisory Committee on Childhood Lead Poisoning Prevention. *Pediatrics* 120: e1285–e1298.

Blakemore, S. J., and S. Choudhury. 2006. Development of the adolescent brain: Implications for executive function and social cognition. *Journal of Child Psychology and Psychiatry* 47: 296–312.

Boles, S., A. Biglan, and K. Smolkowski. 2006. Relationships among negative and positive behaviors in adolescence. *Journal of Adolescence* 29: 33–52.

Borzekowski, D. L. G., and T. N. Robinson. 2001. The 30-second effect: An experiment revealing the impact of television commercials on food preferences of preschoolers. *Journal of the American Dietetic Association* 101: 42–46.

Bradshaw, C. P., C. W. Koth, L. A. Thornton, and P. J. Leaf. 2009. Altering school climate through school-wide Positive Behavioral Interventions and Supports: Findings from a group-randomized effectiveness trial. *Prevention Science* 10: 100–115.

Bricker, J. B., S. L. Mann, P. M. Marek, J. Liu, and A. V. Peterson. 2010. Telephone-delivered acceptance and commitment therapy for adult smoking cessation: A feasibility study. *Nicotine and Tobacco Research* 12: 454–458.

Brown, A. 2012. With poverty comes depression, more than other illnesses. Available at http://www.gallup.com/poll/158417/poverty-comes-depression-illness.aspx. Accessed June 30, 2014.

Brown, C. H., R. G. Adams, and S. G. Kellam. 1981. A longitudinal study of teenage motherhood and symptoms of distress: The Woodlawn Community Epidemiological Project. *Research in Community and Mental Health* 2: 183–213.

Bullard, L., M. Wachlarowicz, J. DeLeeuw, J. Snyder, S. Low, M. Forgatch, and D. DeGarmo. 2010. Effects of the Oregon model of Parent Management Training (PMTO) on marital adjustment in new stepfamilies: A randomized trial. *Journal of Family Psychology* 24: 485–496.

Campbell, C. A., R. A. Hahn, R. Elder, R. Brewer, S. Chattopadhyay, J. Fielding, T. S. Naimi, T. Toomey, B. Lawrence, and J. C. Middleton. 2009. The effectiveness of limiting alcohol outlet density as a means of reducing excessive alcohol consumption and alcohol-related harms. *American Journal of Preventive Medicine* 37: 556–569.

Capaldi, D. M., T. J. Dishion, M. Stoolmiller, and K. Yoerger. 2001. Aggression toward female partners by at-risk young men: The contribution of male adolescent friendships. *Developmental Psychology* 37: 61–73.

Capaldi, D. M., K. C. Pears, and D. C. R. Kerr. 2012. The Oregon Youth Study Three-Generational Study: Theory, design, and findings. *Bulletin of the International Society of the Study of Behavioural Development* 2: 29–33.

Caprara, G. V., C. Barbaranelli, C. Pastorelli, A. Bandura, and P. G. Zimbardo. 2000. Prosocial foundations of children's academic achievement. *Psychological Science* 11: 302–306.

Carr, J. 2002. With RFK in the delta. *American Heritage* 53: 93. Available at http://www.americanheritage.com/content/rfk-delta. Accessed May 28, 2014.

Carter, S. C. 2000. *No Excuses: Lessons from 21 High-Performing, High-Poverty Schools.* Washington, DC: Heritage Foundation.

CDC (Centers for Disease Control and Prevention). 2008. Smoking-attributable mortality, years of potential life lost, and productivity losses—United States, 2000–2004. *Morbidity and Mortality Weekly Report* 57: 1226–1228.

———. 2011. Quitting smoking among adults: United States, 2001–2010. *Morbidity and Mortality Weekly Report* 60: 1513–1519.

———. 2012. Teen drivers: Fact sheet. Available at http://www.cdc.gov/motor vehiclesafety/teen_drivers/teendrivers_factsheet.html. Accessed May 14, 2014.

————. 2013. Fact sheets: Alcohol use and health. Available at http://www.cdc .gov/alcohol/fact-sheets/alcohol-use.htm. Accessed May 14, 2014.

————. 2014. Overweight and obesity: Adult obesity facts. Available at http:// www.cdc.gov/obesity/data/adult.html. Accessed May 27, 2014.

————. n.d. Preventing Teen Pregnancy, 2010–2015. Available at http://www .cdc.gov/TeenPregnancy/PDF/TeenPregnancy_AAG.pdf. Accessed May 14, 2014.

Chaloupka, F. J., M. Grossman, and H. Saffer. 2002. The effects of price on alcohol consumption and alcohol-related problems. *Alcohol Research and Health* 26: 22–34.

Chamberlain, P. 2003. *Treating Chronic Juvenile Offenders: Advances Made Through the Oregon Multidimensional Treatment Foster Care Model.* Washington, DC: American Psychological Association.

Choi, J., B. Jeong, M. L. Rohan, A. M. Polcari, and M. H. Teicher. 2009. Preliminary evidence for white matter tract abnormalities in young adults exposed to parental verbal abuse. *Biological Psychiatry* 65: 227–234.

Clark, K. E., and G. W. Ladd. 2000. Connectedness and autonomy support in parent-child relationships: Links to children's socioemotional orientation and peer relationships. *Developmental Psychology* 36: 485–498.

Clark, T. T., M. J. Sparks, T. M. McDonald, and J. D. Dickerson. 2011. Post-tobacco master settlement agreement: Policy and practice implications for social workers. *Health and Social Work* 36: 217–224.

Conger, R. D., and K. J. Conger. 2008. Understanding the processes through which economic hardship influences families and children. In *Handbook of Families and Poverty*, edited by D. R. Crane and T. B. Heaton. Thousand Oaks, CA: Sage.

Congressional Budget Office. 2011. *Trends in the Distribution of Household Income Between 1979 and 2007.* Washington, DC: Congressional Budget Office.

Connell, A. M., and T. J. Dishion. 2006. The contribution of peers to monthly variation in adolescent depressed mood: A short-term longitudinal study with time-varying predictors. *Development and Psychopathology* 18: 139–154.

Connell, A. M., T. J. Dishion, M. Yasui, and K. Kavanagh. 2007. An adaptive approach to family intervention: Linking engagement in family-centered intervention to reductions in adolescent problem behavior. *Journal of Consulting and Clinical Psychology* 75: 568–579.

Copeland, L. 2013. School cheating scandal shakes up Atlanta. *USA Today*, April 14.

Costello, E. J., S. N. Compton, G. Keeler, and A. Angold. 2003. Relationships between poverty and psychopathology: A natural experiment. *Journal of the American Medical Association* 290: 2023–2029.

Dahl, G., and L. Lochner. 2012. The impact of family income on child achievement: Evidence from the earned income tax credit. *American Economic Review* 102: 1927–1956.

DeBaryshe, B. D., G. R. Patterson, and D. M. Capaldi. 1993. A performance model for academic achievement in early adolescent boys. *Developmental Psychology* 29: 795–804.

Deci, E. L., R. Koestner, and R. M. Ryan. 1999. A meta-analytic review of experiments examining the effects of extrinsic rewards on intrinsic motivation. *Psychological Bulletin* 125: 627–668.

DeNavas-Walt, C., B. D. Proctor, and J. C. Smith. 2010. *Income, Poverty, and Health Insurance Coverage in the United States: 2009.* Washington, DC: US Government Printing Office.

Dennison, B. A., T. A. Erb, and P. L. Jenkins. 2002. Television viewing and television in bedroom associated with overweight risk among low-income preschool children. *Pediatrics* 109: 1028–1035.

De Vries, M. W. 1987. Cry babies, culture, and catastrophe: Infant temperament among the Masai. In *Child Survival.* Dordrecht, Holland: D. Reidel Publishing Company.

Dill, K. 2014. Report: CEOs earn 331 times as much as average workers, 774 times as much as minimum wage workers. Available at http://www.forbes.com/sites/kathryndill/2014/04/15/report-ceos-earn-331-times-as-much-as-average-workers-774-times-as-much-as-minimum-wage-earners. Accessed June 23, 2014.

Dishion, T. J., and D. W. Andrews. 1995. Preventing escalation in problem behaviors with high-risk young adolescents: Immediate and 1-year outcomes. *Journal of Consulting and Clinical Psychology* 63: 538–548.

Dishion, T. J., T. Ha, and M. H. Véronneau. 2012. An ecological analysis of the effects of deviant peer clustering on sexual promiscuity, problem behavior, and childbearing from early adolescence to adulthood: An enhancement of the life history framework. *Developmental Psychology* 48: 703–717.

Dishion, T. J., and K. Kavanagh. 2003. *Intervening in Adolescent Problem Behavior: A Family-Centered Approach.* New York: Guilford.

Dishion, T. J., K. Kavanagh, A. Schneiger, S. Nelson, and N. K. Kaufman. 2002. Preventing early adolescent substance use: A family-centered strategy for the public middle school. *Prevention Science* 3: 191–201.

Dishion, T. J., S. E. Nelson, and B. M. Bullock. 2004. Premature adolescent autonomy: Parent disengagement and deviant peer process in the amplification of problem behavior. *Journal of Adolescence* 27: 515–530.

Dishion, T. J., S. E. Nelson, and K. Kavanagh. 2003. The Family Check-Up with high-risk young adolescents: Preventing early-onset substance use by parent monitoring. *Behavior Therapy* 34: 553–571.

Dishion, T. J., K. M. Spracklen, D. W. Andrews, and G. R. Patterson. 1996. Deviancy training in male adolescent friendships. *Behavior Therapy* 27: 373–390.

Dixon, H. G., M. L. Scully, M. A. Wakefield, V. M. White, and D. A. Crawford. 2007. The effects of television advertisements for junk food versus nutritious food on children's food attitudes and preferences. *Social Science and Medicine* 65: 1311–1323.

Dodge, K. A., T. J. Dishion, and J. E. Lansford. 2006. *Deviant Peer Influences in Programs for Youth: Problems and Solutions*. New York: Guilford.

Domitrovich, C. E., R. C. Cortes, and M. T. Greenberg. 2007. Improving young children's social and emotional competence: A randomized trial of the preschool "PATHS" curriculum. *Journal of Primary Prevention* 28: 67–91.

Douglas Mental Health University Institute. 2014. Prenatal maternal stress. Available at http://www.douglas.qc.ca/info/prenatal-stress. Accessed May 16, 2014.

Eaker, E. D., L. M. Sullivan, M. Kelly-Hayes, R. B. S. D'Agostino, and E. J. Benjamin. 2007. Marital status, marital strain, and risk of coronary heart disease or total mortality: The Framingham Offspring Study. *Psychosomatic Medicine* 69: 509–513.

Eaton, D. K., L. Kann, S. Kinchen, S. Shanklin, K. H. Flint, J. Hawkins, et al. 2012. Youth Risk Behavior Surveillance—United States, 2011. *Morbidity and Mortality Weekly Report* 61: 1–162.

Eifert, G. H., and J. P. Forsyth. 2005. *Acceptance and Commitment Therapy for Anxiety Disorders: A Practitioner's Treatment Guide to Using Mindfulness, Acceptance, and Values-Based Behavior Change Strategies*. Oakland, CA: New Harbinger.

Embry, D. D., and A. Biglan. 2008. Evidence-based kernels: Fundamental units of behavioral influence. *Clinical Child and Family Psychology Review* 11: 75–113.

Engelmann, S., P. Haddox, and E. Bruner. 1983. *Teach Your Child to Read in 100 Easy Lessons*. New York: Simon and Schuster.

Escuriex, B. F., and E. E. Labbé. 2011. Health care providers' mindfulness and treatment outcomes: A critical review of the research literature. *Mindfulness* 2: 242–253.

Fisher, P. A., and P. Chamberlain. 2000. Multidimensional treatment foster care: A program for intensive parenting, family support, and skill building. *Journal of Emotional and Behavioral Disorders* 8: 155–164.

Flay, B. R., C. G. Allred, and N. Ordway. 2001. Effects of the Positive Action program on achievement and discipline: Two matched-control comparisons. *Prevention Science* 2: 71–89.

Forgatch, M. S., G. R. Patterson, D. S. DeGarmo, and Z. G. Beldavs. 2009. Testing the Oregon delinquency model with nine-year follow-up of the Oregon Divorce Study. *Development and Psychopathology* 21: 637–660.

Forrester, K., A. Biglan, H. H. Severson, and K. Smolkowski. 2007. Predictors of smoking onset over two years. *Nicotine and Tobacco Research* 9: 1259–1267.

Fothergill, K. E., M. E. Ensminger, K. M. Green, R. M. Crum, J. Robertson, and H. S. Juon. 2008. The impact of early school behavior and educational achievement on adult drug use disorders: A prospective study. *Drug and Alcohol Dependence* 92: 191–199.

Fryar, C. D., T. C. Chen, and X. Li. 2012. *Prevalence of Uncontrolled Risk Factors for Cardiovascular Disease: United States, 1999–2010.* Hyattsville, MD: National Center for Health Statistics.

Fuchs, L. S., D. Fuchs, S. R. Powell, P. M. Seethaler, P. T. Cirino, and J. M. Fletcher. 2008. Intensive intervention for students with mathematics disabilities: Seven principles of effective practice. *Learning Disability Quarterly* 31: 79–92.

Galobardes, B., J. W. Lynch, and G. D. Smith. 2004. Childhood socioeconomic circumstances and cause-specific mortality in adulthood: Systematic review and interpretation. *Epidemiologic Reviews* 26: 7–21.

Galobardes, B., J. W. Lynch, and G. D. Smith. 2008. Is the association between childhood socioeconomic circumstances and cause-specific mortality established? Update of a systematic review. *Journal of Epidemiology and Community Health* 62: 387–390.

Gandhi, A. 1998. Overcoming hatred and revenge through love. *Fellowship Magazine*, July–August.

Gaudiano, B. A., and J. D. Herbert. 2006. Acute treatment of inpatients with psychotic symptoms using acceptance and commitment therapy: Pilot results. *Behaviour Research and Therapy* 44: 415–437.

Gilpin, E. A., W. S. Choi, C. C. Berry, and J. P. Pierce. 1999. How many adolescents start smoking each day in the United States? *Journal of Adolescent Health* 25: 248–255.

Glantz, S. A. 2003. Smoking in movies: A major problem and a real solution. *Lancet* 362: 258–259.

Glaser, S. R., P. A. Glaser, and A. Matthews. 2006. *Be Quiet, Be Heard: The Paradox of Persuasion.* Eugene, OR: Communications Solutions.

Gonzales, P., T. Williams, L. Jocelyn, S. Roey, D. Kastberg, and S. Brenwald. 2008. *Highlights from TIMSS 2007: Mathematics and Science Achievement of US Fourth- and Eighth-Grade Students in an International Context.* Washington, DC: National Center for Education Statistics, Institute of Education Sciences.

Goodman, L. A., M. Pugach, A. Skolnik, and L. Smith. 2013. Poverty and mental health practice: Within and beyond the 50-minute hour. *Journal of Clinical Psychology* 69: 182–190.

Gordon, J., A. Biglan, and K. Smolkowski. 2008. The impact on tobacco use of branded youth anti-tobacco activities and family communications about tobacco. *Prevention Science* 9: 73–87.

Gottman, J. M., with J. Declaire. 1997. *Raising an Emotionally Intelligent Child.* New York: Simon and Schuster.

Gray, P. 2013. *Free to Learn: Why Unleashing the Instinct to Play Will Make Our Children Happier, More Self-Reliant, and Better Students for Life.* New York: Basic Books.

Greenfeld, L. A. 1998. *Alcohol and crime: An analysis of national data on the prevalence of alcohol involvement in crime.* Washington, DC: US Department of Justice.

Grouzet, F. M. E., T. Kasser, A. Ahuvia, J. M. Fernandez-Dols, Y. Kim, S. Lau, R. M. Ryan, S. Saunders, P. Schmuck, and K. M. Sheldon. 2005. The structure of goal contents across 15 cultures. *Journal of Personality and Social Psychology* 89: 800–816.

Grube, J. W. 1995. Television alcohol portrayals, alcohol advertising, and alcohol expectancies among children and adolescents. In *The Effects of the Mass Media on the Use and Abuse of Alcohol,* edited by S. E. Martin and P. D. Mail. Rockville, MD: National Institute on Alcohol Abuse and Alcoholism.

Grube, J. W., P. A. Madden, and B. Friese 1996. Television alcohol advertising increases adolescent drinking. Poster presented at the annual meeting of the Research Society on Alcoholism, Washington, DC, June 22–27, 1996.

Grube, J. W., and P. Nygaard. 2005. Alcohol policy and youth drinking: Overview of effective interventions for young people. In *Preventing Harmful Substance Use: The Evidence Base for Policy and Practice,* edited by T. Stockwell, P. J. Gruenewald, J. W. Toumbourou, and W. Loxley. New York: Wiley.

Gunn, B., A. Biglan, K. Smolkowski, and D. Ary. 2000. The efficacy of supplemental instruction in decoding skills for Hispanic and non-Hispanic students in early elementary school. *Journal of Special Education* 34: 90–103.

Hacker, J. S., and P. Pierson. 2010a. Winner-take-all politics: Public policy, political organization, and the precipitous rise of top incomes in the United States. *Politics and Society* 38: 152–204.

Hacker, J. S., and P. Pierson. 2010b. *Winner-Take-All Politics: How Washington Made the Rich Richer—and Turned Its Back on the Middle Class.* New York: Simon and Schuster.

Hamlin, J. K., K. Wynn, P. Bloom, and N. Mahajan. 2011. How infants and toddlers react to antisocial others. *Proceedings of the National Academy of Sciences* 108: 19931–19936.

Hanson Bridgett LLP. 2012. Flexible purpose corporation vs. benefit corporation. Available at http://www.hansonbridgett.com/Publications/articles/2012-09-flexible-purpose.aspx. Accessed June 11, 2014.

Harris, R. 2007. *The Happiness Trap: Stop Struggling, Start Living.* Wollombi, New South Wales, Australia: Exisle Publishing.

———. 2009a. *ACT Made Simple: An Easy-to-Read Primer on Acceptance and Commitment Therapy.* Oakland, CA: New Harbinger.

———. 2009b. *ACT with Love: Stop Struggling, Reconcile Differences, and Strengthen Your Relationship with Acceptance and Commitment Therapy.* Oakland, CA: New Harbinger.

Hart, B., and T. R. Risley. 1995. *Meaningful Differences in the Everyday Experience of Young American Children.* Baltimore, MD: Brookes Publishing.

Hawkins, J., S. Oesterle, E. C. Brown, R. D. Abbott, and R. F. Catalano. 2014. Youth problem behaviors 8 years after implementing the Communities That Care Prevention System: A community-randomized trial. *JAMA Pediatrics* 168: 122–129.

Hayes, S. C. 1987. A contextual approach to therapeutic change. In *Psychotherapists in Clinical Practice: Cognitive and Behavioral Perspectives,* edited by N. S. Jacobson. New York: Guilford.

———. 1993. *Analytic Goals and the Varieties of Scientific Contextualism.* Reno, NV: Context.

Hayes, S. C., with S. Smith. 2005. *Get Out of Your Mind and Into Your Life: The New Acceptance and Commitment Therapy.* Oakland, CA: New Harbinger.

Hayes, S. C., L. J. Hayes, H. W. Reese, and T. R. Sarbin, eds. 1993. *Varieties of Scientific Contextualism.* Reno, NV: Context.

Hayes, S. C., K. D. Strosahl, and K. G. Wilson. 1999. *Acceptance and Commitment Therapy: An Experiential Approach to Behavior Change.* New York: Guilford.

Henggeler, S. W., S. K. Schoenwald, C. M. Borduin, M. D. Rowland, and P. B. Cunningham. 2009. *Multisystemic Therapy for Antisocial Behavior in Children and Adolescents.* New York: Guilford.

Henshaw, S. K. 1998. Unintended pregnancy in the United States. *Family Planning Perspectives* 30: 24–29, 46.

Hibbeln, J. R., L. R. Nieminen, T. L. Blasbalg, J. A. Riggs, and W. E. Lands. 2006. Healthy intakes of n-3 and n-6 fatty acids: Estimations considering worldwide diversity. *American Journal of Clinical Nutrition* 83: 1483S–1493S.

Himmelstein, D. U., D. Thorne, E. Warren, and S. Woolhandler. 2009. Medical bankruptcy in the United States, 2007: Results of a national study. *American Journal of Medicine* 122: 741–746.

Hinds, E., C. Cody, A. Kraft, A. Biglan, L. B. Jones, and F. M. Hankins. 2011. Using acceptance and commitment therapy to improve the wellbeing of teachers. In *Evidence-Based Education*, edited by J. S. Twyman and R. Wing. Oakland, CA: Association for Behavior Analysis International and Wing Institute.

Horner, R. H., G. Sugai, K. Smolkowski, L. Eber, J. Nakasato, A. W. Todd, and J. Esperanza. 2009. A randomized, wait-list controlled effectiveness trial assessing school-wide positive behavior support in elementary schools. *Journal of Positive Behavior Interventions* 11: 133–144.

Huesmann, L. R., K. Lagerspetz, and L. D. Eron. 1984. Intervening variables in the TV violence–coaggression relation: Evidence from two countries. *Developmental Psychology* 20: 746–775.

Huxley, A. 1932. *Brave New World*. London: Chatto and Windus.

Ialongo, N. S., L. Werthamer, S. G. Kellam, C. H. Brown, S. Wang, and Y. Lin. 1999. Proximal impact of two first-grade preventive interventions on the early risk behaviors for later substance abuse, depression, and antisocial behavior. *American Journal of Community Psychology* 27: 599–641.

IOM and NRC (Institute of Medicine and National Research Council). 2009. *Preventing Mental, Emotional, and Behavioral Disorders Among Young People: Progress and Possibilities*. Washington, DC: National Academies Press.

IOM (Institute of Medicine) Committee on Food Marketing and the Diets of Children and Youth. 2006. *Food Marketing to Children and Youth: Threat or Opportunity?* Edited by J. M. McGinnis, J. A. Gootman, and V. I. Kraak. Washington, DC: National Academies Press.

Irvine, A. B., A. Biglan, K. Smolkowski, C. W. Metzler, and D. V. Ary. 1999. The effectiveness of a parenting skills program for parents of middle school students in small communities. *Journal of Consulting and Clinical Psychology* 67: 811–825.

Isaacson, W. 2007. "Einstein & Faith." *TIME*. April 5. http://content.time.com/time/magazine/article/0,9171,1607298,00.html

Jablonka, E., and M. J. Lamb. 2014. *Evolution in Four Dimensions, Revised Edition: Genetic, Epigenetic, Behavioral, and Symbolic Variation in the History of Life*. Boston: MIT Press.

Jablonka, E., and G. Raz. 2009. Transgenerational epigenetic inheritance: Prevalence, mechanisms, and implications for the study of heredity and evolution. *Quarterly Review of Biology* 84: 131–176.

Jacobson, E. 1938. *Progressive Relaxation*. Chicago: University of Chicago Press.

Jacobson, N. S., K. S. Dobson, P. A. Truax, M. E. Addis, K. Koerner, J. K. Gollan, E. Gortner, and S. E. Prince. 1996. A component analysis of cognitive-behavioral treatment for depression. *Journal of Consulting and Clinical Psychology* 64: 295–304.

Johnson, S. 2006. *The Ghost Map: The Story of London's Most Terrifying Epidemic—and How It Changed Science, Cities, and the Modern World*. New York: Riverhead Books.

Johnston, L. D., P. M. O'Malley, J. G. Bachman, and J. E. Schulenberg. 2013. *Monitoring the Future National Results on Drug Use: 2012 Overview, Key Findings on Adolescent Drug Use*. Ann Arbor: Institute for Social Research, University of Michigan.

Jones, L. B., K. Whittingham, and L. Coyne. Forthcoming. Cultural evolution in families. In *The Wiley-Blackwell Handbook of Contextual Behavioral Science*, edited by R. D. Zettle, S. C. Hayes, A. Biglan, and D. Barnes-Holmes. Chichester, West Sussex, UK: Wiley and Sons.

Kam, C. M., M. T. Greenberg, and C. A. Kusché. 2004. Sustained effects of the PATHS curriculum on the social and psychological adjustment of children in special education. *Journal of Emotional and Behavioral Disorders* 12: 66–78.

Kasser, T. 2004. The good life or the goods life? Positive psychology and personal well-being in the culture of consumption. In *Positive Psychology in Practice*, edited by P. A. Linley, and S. Joseph. Hoboken, NJ: Wiley.

Kasser, T. 2011. Cultural values and the well-being of future generations: A cross-national study. *Journal of Cross-Cultural Psychology* 42: 206–215.

Kasser, T., S. Cohn, A. D. Kanner, and R. M. Ryan. 2007. Some costs of American corporate capitalism: A psychological exploration of value and goal conflicts. *Psychological Inquiry* 18: 1–22.

Kasser, T., and R. M. Ryan. 1993. A dark side of the American dream: Correlates of financial success as a central life aspiration. *Journal of Personality and Social Psychology* 65: 410–422.

Kasser, T., and R. M. Ryan. 1996. Further examining the American dream: Differential correlates of intrinsic and extrinsic goals. *Personality and Social Psychology Bulletin* 22: 280–287.

Kellam, S. G., C. H. Brown, J. M. Poduska, N. S. Ialongo, W. Wang, P. Toyinbo, et al. 2008. Effects of a universal classroom behavior management program in first and second grades on young adult behavioral, psychiatric, and social outcomes. *Drug and Alcohol Dependence* 95: S5–S28.

Kellam, S. G., C. H. Brown, B. R. Rubin, and M. E. Ensminger. 1983. Paths leading to teenage psychiatric symptoms and substance use: Developmental epidemiological studies in Woodlawn. In *Childhood Psychopathology and Development*, edited by S. B. Guze, F. J. Earls, and J. E. Barrett. New York: Raven.

Kellam, S. G., L. S. Mayer, G. W. Rebok, and W. E. Hawkins. 1998. Effects of improving achievement on aggressive behavior and of improving aggressive behavior on achievement through two preventive interventions: An investigation of causal paths. In *Adversity, Stress, and Psychopathology*, edited by B. P. Dohrenwend. New York: Oxford University Press.

Koh, H. K. 2002. Accomplishments of the Massachusetts Tobacco Control Program. *Tobacco Control* 11: ii1–ii3.

Kohn, A. 1993. *Punished by Rewards: The Trouble with Gold Stars, Incentive Plans, A's, Praise, and Other Bribes*. Boston: Houghton, Mifflin.

Komro, K. A., B. R. Flay, A. Biglan, and the Promise Neighborhoods Research Consortium 2011. Creating nurturing environments: A science-based framework for promoting child health and development within high-poverty neighborhoods. *Clinical Child and Family Psychology Review* 14: 111–134.

Komro, K. A., A. Tobler, A. Delisle, R. O'Mara, and A. Wagenaar. 2013. Beyond the clinic: Improving child health through evidence-based community development. *BMC Pediatrics* 13: 172–180.

Kuhn, T. S. 1970. The structure of scientific revolutions. *International Encyclopedia of Unified Science* 2: 1–210.

Lakein, A. 1973. *How to Get Control of Your Time and Your Life*. New York: Signet.

Landry, S. H., K. E. Smith, P. R. Swank, and C. Guttentag. 2008. A responsive parenting intervention: The optimal timing across early childhood for impacting maternal behaviors and child outcomes. *Developmental Psychology* 44: 1335–1353.

Landry, S. H., K. E. Smith, P. R. Swank, T. Zucker, A. D. Crawford, and E. F. Solari. 2012. The effects of a responsive parenting intervention on parent-child interactions during shared book reading. *Developmental Psychology* 48: 969–986.

Lapham, L. 2004. Tentacles of rage. *Harper's*, September, 31–41.

Leflot, G., P. A. C. van Lier, P. Onghena, and H. Colpin. 2013. The role of children's on-task behavior in the prevention of aggressive behavior development and peer rejection: A randomized controlled study of the Good Behavior Game in Belgian elementary classrooms. *Journal of School Psychology* 5: 187–199.

Leigh, A. 2009. Top incomes. In *The Oxford Handbook of Economic Inequality*, edited by W. Salverda, B. Nolan, and T. Smeeding. London: Oxford University Press.

Lewis, K. M., N. Bavarian, F. J. Snyder, A. Acock, J. Day, D. L. DuBois, P. Ji, M. B. Schure, N. Silverthorn, S. Vuchinich, and B. R. Flay. (2012). Direct and mediated effects of a social-emotional and character development program on adolescent substance use. *International Journal of Emotional Education*, 4: 56–78.

Lewis, K. M., D. L. DuBois, N. Bavarian, A. Acock, N. Silverthorn, J. Day, P. Ji, S. Vuchinich, and B. R. Flay. (2013). Effects of Positive Action on the emotional health of urban youth: A cluster-randomized trial. *Journal of Adolescent Health*, 53: 706–711.

Lewis, K. M., M. B. Schure, N. Bavarian, D. L. Dubois, J. Day, P. Ji, N. Silverthorn, A. Acock, S. Vuchinich, and B. R. Flay. (2013). Problem behavior and urban, low-income youth: A randomized controlled trial of Positive Action in Chicago. *American Journal of Preventive Medicine*, 44: 622–630.

Lewinsohn, P. M. 1975. The behavioral study and treatment of depression. In *Progress in Behavioral Modification*, vol. 1, edited by M. Hersen, R. M. Eisler, and P. M. Miller. New York: Academic Press.

Li, C., L. S. Balluz, C. A. Okoro, C. W. Strine, J. M. Lin, M. Town, et al. 2011. Surveillance of certain health behaviors and conditions among states and selected local areas: Behavioral Risk Factor Surveillance System, United States, 2009. *Morbidity and Mortality Weekly Report Surveillance Summaries* 60, no. 9.

Liebal, K., T. Behne, M. Carpenter, and M. Tomasello. 2009. Infants use shared experience to interpret pointing gestures. *Developmental Science* 12: 264–271.

Lundgren, T., J. Dahl, N. Yardi, and L. Melin. 2008. Acceptance and commitment therapy and yoga for drug-refractory epilepsy: A randomized controlled trial. *Epilepsy and Behavior* 13: 102–108.

Manning, J. 2008. The Midwest farm crisis of the 1980s. Available at http://eightiesclub.tripod.com/id395.htm. Accessed October 28, 2012.

Mayer, G. R. 1995. Preventing antisocial behavior in the schools. *Journal of Applied Behavior Analysis* 28: 467–478.

McLean, B., and J. Nocera. 2010. *All the Devils Are Here: The Hidden History of the Financial Crisis.* New York: Penguin.

McLoyd, V. C. 1998. Socioeconomic disadvantage and child development. *American Psychologist* 53: 185–204.

Menand, L. 2001. *The Metaphysical Club.* New York: Farrar, Straus and Giroux.

Mesmer-Magnus, J., D. J. Glew, and C. Viswesvaran. 2012. A meta-analysis of positive humor in the workplace. *Journal of Managerial Psychology* 27: 155–190.

Metzler, C. W., A. Biglan, J. C. Rusby, and J. R. Sprague. 2001. Evaluation of a comprehensive behavior management program to improve school-wide positive behavior support. *Education and Treatment of Children* 24: 448–479.

Miller, G. E., E. Chen, A. K. Fok, H. Walker, A. Lim, E. F. Nicholls, S. Cole, and M. S. Kobor. 2009. Low early-life social class leaves a biological residue manifested by decreased glucocorticoid and increased proinflammatory signaling. *Proceedings of the National Academy of Sciences* 106: 14716–14721.

Miller, G. E., M. E. Lachman, E. Chen, T. L. Gruenewald, A. S. Karlamangla, and T. E. Seeman. 2011. Pathways to resilience: Maternal nurturance as a buffer against the effects of childhood poverty on metabolic syndrome at midlife. *Psychological Science* 22: 1591–1599.

Miller, T. 2004. The social costs of adolescent problem behavior. In *Helping Adolescents at Risk: Prevention of Multiple Problem Behaviors*, edited by A. Biglan, P. Brennan, S. Foster, and H. Holder. New York: Guilford.

Mrazek, P., A. Biglan, and J. D. Hawkins. 2005. *Community-Monitoring Systems: Tracking and Improving the Well-Being of America's Children and Adolescents.* Falls Church, VA: Society for Prevention Research.

National Cancer Institute. 2008. *The Role of the Media in Promoting and Reducing Tobacco Use.* Bethesda, MD: US Department of Health and Human Services, National Institutes of Health, National Cancer Institute.

National Center for Education Statistics. 2014. The condition of education: Mathematics performance. Available at http://www.nces.ed.gov/programs/coe/indicator_cnc.asp. Accessed June 14, 2014.

National Highway Traffic Safety Administration. 2008. *Traffic Safety Facts 2006.* Washington, DC: US Department of Transportation, National Highway Traffic Safety Administration. Available at http://www-nrd.nhtsa.dot.gov/Pubs/810818.pdf. Accessed May 14, 2014.

National Institute on Alcohol Abuse and Alcoholism. 2013. Underage drinking. Available at http://www.niaaa.nih.gov/alcohol-health/special-populations-co-occurring-disorders/underage-drinking. Accessed May 14, 2014.

National Transportation Safety Board. 2013. *Reaching Zero: Actions to Eliminate Alcohol-Impaired Driving.* Washington, DC: NTSB.

Nestle, M. 2002. *Food Politics: How the Food Industry Influences Nutrition and Health.* Berkeley: University of California Press.

Nyhlén, A., M. Fridell, M. Bäckström, M. Hesse, and P. Krantz. 2011. Substance abuse and psychiatric co-morbidity as predictors of premature mortality in Swedish drug abusers a prospective longitudinal study 1970–2006. *BMC Psychiatry* 11: 122.

Olds, D. L. 2007. Preventing crime with prenatal and infancy support of parents: The Nurse-Family Partnership. *Victims and Offenders* 2: 205–225.

Olds, D. L., P. L. Hill, R. O'Brien, D. Racine, and P. Moritz, P. 2003. Taking preventive intervention to scale: The Nurse-Family Partnership. *Cognitive and Behavioral Practice* 10: 278–290.

Olds, D. L., L. Sadler, and H. Kitzman. 2007. Programs for parents of infants and toddlers: Recent evidence from randomized trials. *Journal of Child Psychology and Psychiatry* 48: 355–391.

Patricelli, L. 2012. *Yummy, Yucky.* Somerville, MA: Candlewick Press.

Patterson, G. R. 1982. *Coercive Family Process. Volume 3.* Eugene, OR: Castalia.

Patterson, G. R., M. S. Forgatch, and D. S. DeGarmo. 2010. Cascading effects following intervention. *Development and Psychopathology* 22: 949–970.

Patterson, G. R., and E. Gullion. 1968. *Living with Children: New Methods for Parents and Teachers.* Champaign, IL: Research Press.

Patterson, G. R., and H. Hops. 1972. Coercion, a game for two: Intervention techniques for marital conflict. In *The Experimental Analysis of Social Behavior*, edited by R. E. Ulrich and P. T. Mountjoy. New York: Appleton-Century-Crofts.

Patterson, G., J. Reid, and T. Dishion. 1992. *Antisocial Boys. Volume 4: A Social Interactional Approach.* Eugene, OR: Castalia.

Paul, G. L. 1966. *Insight vs. Desensitization in Psychotherapy: An Experiment in Anxiety Reduction.* Stanford, CA: Stanford University Press.

Pechmann, C., A. Biglan, J. Grube, and C. Cody. 2011. Transformative consumer research for addressing tobacco and alcohol consumption. In *Transformative Consumer Research for Personal and Collective Well-Being*, edited by D. G. Mick, S. Pettigrew, C. Pechmann, and J. L. Ozanne. New York: Routledge.

Pechmann, C., and S. J. Knight. 2002. An experimental investigation of the joint effects of advertising and peers on adolescents' beliefs and intentions about cigarette consumption. *Journal of Consumer Research* 29: 5–19.

Perie, M., R. Moran, and A. D. Lutkus. 2005. *NAEP 2004 Trends in Academic Progress: Three Decades of Student Performance in Reading and Mathematics.* National Center for Education Statistics, U. S. Department of Education, Institute of Education Sciences.

Pierce, J. P., J. M. Distefan, C. Jackson, M. M. White, and E. A. Gilpin. 2002. Does tobacco marketing undermine the influence of recommended parenting in discouraging adolescents from smoking? *American Journal of Preventive Medicine* 23: 73–81.

Pierce, J. P., E. A. Gilpin, and W. S. Choi. 1999. Sharing the blame: Smoking experimentation and future smoking-attributable mortality due to Joe Camel and Marlboro advertising and promotions. *Tobacco Control* 8: 37–44.

Popova, S., N. Giesbrecht, D. Bekmuradov, and J. Patra. 2009. Hours and days of sale and density of alcohol outlets: Impacts on alcohol consumption and damage: A systematic review. *Alcohol and Alcoholism* 44: 500–516.

Powell, L. F., Jr. 1971. Confidential memorandum: Attack on American free enterprise system. Available at http://scalar.usc.edu/works/growing-apart-a-political-history-of-american-inequality/the-powell-memorandum. Accessed May 28, 2014.

Powell, L. M., G. Szczypka, F. J. Chaloupka, and C. L. Braunschweig. 2007. Nutritional content of television food advertisements seen by children and adolescents in the United States. *Pediatrics* 120: 576–583.

Prinz, R. J., M. R. Sanders, C. J. Shapiro, D. J. Whitaker, and J. R. Lutzker. 2009. Population-based prevention of child maltreatment: The US Triple P System Population Trial. *Prevention Science* 10: 1–12.

Rangel, J. M., P. H. Sparling, C. Crowe, P. M. Griffin, and D. L. Swerdlow. 2005. Epidemiology of *Escherichia coli* O157:H7 outbreaks, United States, 1982–2002. *Emerging Infectious Diseases* 11: 603–609.

Reeves, A., D. Stuckler, M. McKee, D. Gunnell, S. S. Chang, and S. Basu. 2012. Increase in state suicide rates in the USA during economic recession. *Lancet* 380: 1813–1814.

Richardson, J. L., B. Radziszewska, C. W. Dent, and B. R. Flay. 1993. Relationship between after-school care of adolescents and substance use, risk taking, depressed mood, and academic achievement. *Pediatrics* 92: 32–38.

Roberts, D. M., M. Ostapchuk, and J. G. O'Brien. 2004. Infantile colic. *American Family Physician* 70: 735–740.

Robinson, P., and K. Strosahl. 2008. *The Mindfulness and Acceptance Workbook for Depression: Using Acceptance and Commitment Therapy to Move Through Depression and Create a Life Worth Living.* Oakland, CA: New Harbinger.

Roeser, R. W., and J. S. Eccles. 1998. Adolescents' perceptions of middle school: Relation to longitudinal changes in academic and psychological adjustment. *Journal of Research on Adolescence* 8: 123–158.

Rogers, C. R. 1951. *Client-Centered Therapy: Its Current Practice, Implications, and Theory.* Boston: Houghton Mifflin.

Ross, N. A., M. C. Wolfson, J. R. Dunn, J. M. Berthelot, G. A. Kaplan, and J. W. Lynch. 2000. Relation between income inequality and mortality in Canada and in the United States: Cross-sectional assessment using census data and vital statistics. *British Medical Journal* 320: 898–902.

Rozanski, A., J. A. Blumenthal, and J. Kaplan. 1999. Impact of psychological factors on the pathogenesis of cardiovascular disease and implications for therapy. *Circulation* 99: 2192–2217.

Rusby, J. C., K. K. Forrester, A. Biglan, and C. W. Metzler. 2005. Relationships between peer harassment and adolescent problem behaviors. *Journal of Early Adolescence* 25: 453–477.

Sandler, I. N., J. Y. Tein, and S. G. West. 1994. Coping, stress, and the psychological symptoms of children of divorce: A cross-sectional and longitudinal study. *Child Development* 65: 1744–1763.

Sapolsky, R. M. 1994. *Why Zebras Don't Get Ulcers.* New York: Freeman.

Sargent, J. D., M. A. Dalton, M. L. Beach, L. A. Mott, J. J. Tickle, M. B. Ahrens, et al. 2002. Viewing tobacco use in movies: Does it shape attitudes that mediate adolescent smoking? *American Journal of Preventive Medicine* 22: 137–145.

Schmuck, P., T. Kasser, and R. M. Ryan. 2000. Intrinsic and extrinsic goals: Their structure and relationship to well-being in German and US college students. *Social Indicators Research* 50: 225–241.

Seligman, M. E. 1970. On the generality of the laws of learning. *Psychological Review* 77: 406–418.

Shadish, W. R., and S. A. Baldwin. 2005. Effects of behavioral marital therapy: A meta-analysis of randomized controlled trials. *Journal of Consulting and Clinical Psychology* 73: 6–14.

Sheldon, K. M., and T. Kasser. 2008. Psychological threat and extrinsic goal striving. *Motivation and Emotion* 32: 37–45.

Skinner, B. F. 1953. *Science and Human Behavior*. New York: Macmillan Company.

———. 1972. *Beyond Freedom and Dignity*. New York: Bantam Books.

Slovic, P. E. 2000. *The Perception of Risk*. London: Earthscan Publications.

Smith, G. D., and C. Hart. 2002. Life-course socioeconomic and behavioral influences on cardiovascular disease mortality: The collaborative study. *American Journal of Public Health* 92: 1295–1298.

Snyder, F., B. R. Flay, S. Vuchinich, A. Acock, I. Washburn, M. W. Beets, and K.-K. Li. (2010). Impact of the Positive Action program on school-level indicators of academic achievement, absenteeism, and disciplinary outcomes: A matched-pair, cluster randomized, controlled trial. *Journal of Research on Educational Effectiveness*, 3: 26–55.

Snyder, F.J., A. Acock, S. Vuchinich, M. W. Beets, I. Washburn, and B. R. Flay. (2013). Preventing negative behaviors among elementary-school students through enhancing students' social-emotional and character development. *American Journal of Health Promotion*, 28: 50–58.

Snyder, F. J., S. Vuchinich, A. Acock, I. J. Washburn, and B. R. Flay. (2012). Improving elementary-school quality through the use of a social-emotional and character development program: A matched-pair, cluster-randomized, controlled trial in Hawaii. *Journal of School Health*, 82: 11–20.

Soby, J. M. 2006. *Prenatal Exposure to Drugs/Alcohol: Characteristics and Educational Implications of Fetal Alcohol Syndrome and Cocaine/Polydrug Effects*. Springfield, IL: Charles C. Thomas.

Spoth, R., C. Redmond, C. Shin, M. Greenberg, M. Feinberg, and L. Schainker. 2013. Longitudinal effects of universal PROSPER community-university partnership delivery system effects on substance misuse through 6 1/2 years past baseline from a cluster randomized controlled intervention trial. *Preventive Medicine* 56: 190–196.

Stebbins, L. B., R. G. St. Pierre, E. C. Proper, R. B. Anderson, and T. R. Cerva. 1977. *Education as Experimentation: A Planned Variation Model. Volume IV-A: An Evaluation of Follow Through*. Cambridge, MA: Abt Associates.

Strom, S. 2011. Local laws fighting fat under siege. *New York Times*, June 30. Available at http://www.nytimes.com/2011/07/01/business/01obese.html?pagewanted=all&_r=0. Assessed July 1, 2014.

Sugai, G., R. Horner, and B. Algozzine, eds. 2011. *Reducing the Effectiveness of Bullying Behavior in Schools*. Available at http://www.pbis.org/common/cms/files/pbisresources/PBIS_Bullying_Behavior_Apr19_2011.pdf. Accessed May 14, 2014.

Tein, J. Y., I. N. Sandler, D. P. MacKinnon, and S. A. Wolchik. 2004. How did it work? Who did it work for? Mediation in the context of a moderated prevention effect for children of divorce. *Journal of Consulting and Clinical Psychology* 72: 617–624.

Tirch, D. 2012. *The Compassionate-Mind Guide to Overcoming Anxiety: Using Compassion-Focused Therapy to Calm Worry, Panic, and Fear.* Oakland, CA: New Harbinger.

Törneke, N. 2010. *Learning RFT: An Introduction to Relational Frame Theory and Its Clinical Application.* Oakland, CA: New Harbinger.

Truax, C. B., and R. T. Carkuff. 1967. *Toward Effective Counseling and Psychotherapy.* Chicago: Aldine.

Twenge, J. M. 2009. Status and gender: The paradox of progress in an age of narcissism. *Sex Roles* 61: 338–340.

Twenge, J. M., and W. K. Campbell. 2008. Increases in positive self-views among high school students: Birth-cohort changes in anticipated performance, self-satisfaction, self-liking, and self-competence. *Psychological Science* 19: 1082–1086.

Twenge, J. M., and W. K. Campbell. 2009. *The Narcissism Epidemic: Living in the Age of Enlightenment.* New York: Free Press.

Twenge, J. M., and J. D. Foster. 2010. Birth cohort increases in narcissistic personality traits among American college students, 1982–2009. *Social Psychological and Personality Science* 1: 99–106.

Twenge, J. M., S. Konrath, J. D. Foster, W. K. Campbell, and B. J. Bushman. 2008. Further evidence of an increase in narcissism among college students. *Journal of Personality* 76: 919–928.

US Department of Health and Human Services. 1980. *The Health Consequences of Smoking for Women: A Report of the Surgeon General.* Washington, DC: US Department of Health and Human Services, Public Health Service, Office of the Assistant Secretary for Health, Office on Smoking and Health.

———. 1981. *The Health Consequences of Smoking: The Changing Cigarette. A Report of the Surgeon General.* Washington, DC: US Department of Health and Human Services, Public Health Service, Office of the Assistant Secretary for Health, Office on Smoking and Health.

———. 1982. *The Health Consequences of Smoking: Cancer. A Report of the Surgeon General.* Washington, DC: US Department of Health and Human Services, Public Health Service, Office of the Assistant Secretary for Health, Office on Smoking and Health.

———. 1983. *The Health Consequences of Smoking: Cardiovascular Disease. A Report of the Surgeon General.* Washington, DC: US Department of Health and Human Services, Public Health Service, Office of the Assistant Secretary for Health, Office on Smoking and Health.

————. 1984. *The Health Consequences of Smoking: Chronic Obstructive Lung Disease. A Report of the Surgeon General*. Washington, DC: US Department of Health and Human Services, Public Health Service, Office of the Assistant Secretary for Health, Office on Smoking and Health.

————. 1986. *The Health Consequences of Involuntary Smoking. A Report of the Surgeon General*. Washington, DC: US Department of Health and Human Services, Public Health Service, Office of the Assistant Secretary for Health, Office on Smoking and Health.

————. 1988. *The Health Consequences of Smoking: Nicotine Addiction. A Report of the Surgeon General*. Washington, DC: US Department of Health and Human Services, Public Health Service, Office of the Assistant Secretary for Health, Office on Smoking and Health.

————. 1989. *Reducing the Health Consequences of Smoking: 25 Years of Progress. A Report of the Surgeon General*. Washington, DC: US Department of Health and Human Services, Public Health Service, Office of the Assistant Secretary for Health, Office on Smoking and Health.

————. 2014. *The Health Consequences of Smoking—50 Years of Progress: A Report of the Surgeon General*. Atlanta, GA: US Department of Health and Human Services, Centers for Disease Control and Prevention, National Center for Chronic Disease Prevention and Health Promotion, Office on Smoking and Health.

Van Meurs, K. 1999. Cigarette smoking, pregnancy, and the developing fetus. Available at http://med.stanford.edu/medicalreview/smrp14-16.pdf. Accessed May 14, 2014.

Van Ryzin, M. J., and T. J. Dishion. 2013. From antisocial behavior to violence: A model for the amplifying role of coercive joining in adolescent friendships. *Journal of Child Psychology and Psychiatry* 54: 661–669.

Wachlarowicz, M., J. Snyder, S. Low, M. Forgatch, and D. DeGarmo. 2012. The moderating effects of parent antisocial characteristics on the effects of Parent Management Training-Oregon (PMTO). *Prevention Science* 13: 229–240.

Wagenaar, A. C., and S. C. Burris, eds. 2013. *Public Health Law Research: Theory and Methods*. New York: Wiley and Sons.

Wagenaar, A. C., and T. L. Toomey. 2002. Effects of minimum drinking age laws: Review and analyses of the literature from 1960 to 2000. *Journal of Studies on Alcohol Supplement* 14: 206–225.

Walker, O. L., and H. A. Henderson. 2012. Temperament and social problem solving competence in preschool: Influences on academic skills in early elementary school. *Social Development* 21: 761–779.

Washburn, I. J., A. Acock, S. Vuchinich, F. J. Snyder, K.-K. Li, P. Ji, J. Day, D. L. DuBois, and B. R. Flay. (2011). Effects of a social-emotional and character development program on the trajectory of behaviors associated with character development: Findings from three randomized trials. *Prevention Science*, 12: 314–323.

Washington State Institute for Public Policy [WSIPP]. (2014). Per-pupil expenditures: 10% increase for one student cohort from kindergarten through grade 12. Available at http://www.wsipp.wa.gov/BenefitCost/ProgramPdf/182/Per-pupil-expenditures-10-increase-for-one-student-cohort-from-kindergarten-through-grade-12. Accessed August 19, 2014.

WebMD. 2013. Eating right when pregnant. Available online at http://www.webmd.com/baby/guide/eating-right-when-pregnant. Accessed May 14, 2014.

Webster-Stratton, C. 1992. *The Incredible Years: A Trouble-Shooting Guide for Parents of Children Aged 3–8*. Toronto, Ontario, Canada: Umbrella Press.

Webster-Stratton, C., and K. C. Herman. 2008. The impact of parent behavior-management training on child depressive symptoms. *Journal of Counseling Psychology* 55: 473–484.

Webster-Stratton, C., M. J. Reid, and M. Stoolmiller. 2008. Preventing conduct problems and improving school readiness: Evaluation of the Incredible Years Teacher and Child Training Programs in high-risk schools. *Journal of Child Psychology and Psychiatry* 49: 471–488.

Wechsler, H., and T. F. Nelson. 2008. What we have learned from the Harvard School of Public Health College Alcohol Study: Focusing attention on college student alcohol consumption and the environmental conditions that promote it. *Journal of Studies on Alcohol and Drugs* 69: 481–490.

Wegman, H. L., and C. Stetler. 2009. A meta-analytic review of the effects of childhood abuse on medical outcomes in adulthood. *Psychosomatic Medicine* 71: 805–812.

Weiss, R. L., and B. A. Perry. 2002. Behavioral couples therapy. In *Comprehensive Handbook of Psychotherapy. Volume 2: Cognitive-Behavioral Approaches*, edited by F. W. Kaslow and T. Patterson. New York: Wiley and Sons.

Whiting, C. 2004. Income inequality, the income cost of housing, and the myth of market efficiency. *American Journal of Economics and Sociology* 63: 851–879.

Wilkinson, R. 1992. Income distribution and life expectancy. *British Medical Journal* 304: 165–168.

Wilkinson, R., and K. Pickett. 2009. *The Spirit Level: Why Greater Equality Makes Societies Stronger*. New York: Bloomsbury.

Wilson, D. S. 1998. Adaptive individual differences within single populations. *Philosophical Transactions of the Royal Society of London. Series B: Biological Sciences* 353, 199–205.

————. 2003. *Darwin's Cathedral: Evolution, Religion, and the Nature of Science.* Chicago: University of Chicago Press.

————. 2007. *Evolution for Everyone: How Darwin's Theory Can Change the Way We Think About Our Lives.* New York: Delacorte Press.

Wilson, D. S., and M. Csikszentmihalyi. 2008. Health and the ecology of altruism. In *Altruism and Health: Perspectives from Empirical Research*, edited by S. G. Post. New York: Oxford University Press.

Wilson, D. S., S. C. Hayes, A. Biglan, and D. D. Embry. 2014. Evolving the future: Toward a science of intentional change. *Behavioral and Brain Sciences*, 37: 395–416.

Wilson, D. S., D. T. O'Brien, and A. Sesma. 2009. Human prosociality from an evolutionary perspective: Variation and correlations at a city-wide scale. *Evolution and Human Behavior* 30: 190–200.

Wilson, E. O. 1998. *Consilience: The Unity of Knowledge.* New York: Alfred A. Knopf.

Wolpe, J. 1958. *Psychotherapy by Reciprocal Inhibition.* Stanford, CA: Stanford University Press.

Working Group on Extreme Inequality. 2007. *Presenting the findings of the Working Group on Extreme American Inequality.* Available at http://www.zerohedge .com/article/presenting-findings-working-group-extreme-american-inequality. Accessed on July 1, 2014.

Wray-Lake, L., C. A. Flanagan, and D. W. Osgood. 2010. Examining trends in adolescent environmental attitudes, beliefs, and behaviors across three decades. *Environmental Behavior* 42: 61–85.

Zeilberger, J., S. E. Sampen, and H. N. Sloane Jr. 1968. Modification of a child's problem behaviors in the home with the mother as therapist. *Journal of Applied Behavior Analysis* 1: 47–53.

Anthony Biglan, PhD, is a senior scientist at Oregon Research Institute, and a leading figure in the development of prevention science. His research over the past thirty years has helped to identify effective family, school, and community interventions to prevent the most common and costly problems of childhood and adolescence. He is a leader in efforts to use prevention science to build more nurturing families, schools, and communities throughout the world. Biglan lives in Eugene, OR.

Foreword writer **Steven C. Hayes, PhD,** is Nevada Foundation Professor in the department of psychology at the University of Nevada. An author of thirty-four books and more than 470 scientific articles, he has shown in his research how language and thought leads to human suffering. He cofounded acceptance and commitment therapy (ACT)—a powerful therapy method that is useful in a wide variety of areas. Hayes has been president of several scientific societies and has received several national awards, including the Lifetime Achievement Award from the Association for Behavioral and Cognitive Therapies.

Afterword writer **David Sloan Wilson, PhD**, is president of the Evolution Institute and SUNY distinguished professor of biology and anthropology at Binghamton University. He applies evolutionary theory to all aspects of humanity, in addition to the biological world. His books include *Darwin's Cathedral, Evolution for Everyone: How Darwin's Theory Can Change the Way We Think About Our Lives, The Neighborhood Project*, and *Does Altruism Exist?*

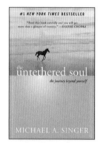
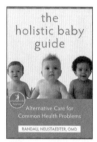
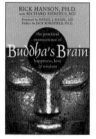